Constructi

Property and Construction Economics

Timothy Eccles, Sarah Sayce
and **Judy Smith**

INTERNATIONAL THOMSON BUSINESS PRESS
I(T)P® An International Thomson Publishing Company

London • Bonn • Johannesburg • Madrid • Melbourne • Mexico City • New York • Paris
Singapore • Tokyo • Toronto • Albany, NY • Belmont, CA • Cincinnati, OH • Detroit, MI

Property and Construction Economics

First published by International Thomson Business Press

 I T P® A division of International Thomson Publishing Inc.
The ITP logo is a trademark under licence

British Library Cataloguing-in-Publication Data
A catalogue record for this book is available from the British Library

First edition 1999

Typeset by J&L Composition Ltd, Filey, North Yorkshire
Printed in the UK by Clays Ltd., St Ives plc

ISBN 1–86152–158–8
International Thomson Business Press
Berkshire House
168–173 High Holborn
London WCIV 7AA
UK

http://www.itbp.com

Contents

Preface

PROPERTY, CONSTRUCTION AND ECONOMICS

All students of the built environment, in addition to learning their technical disciplines, generally study economics. Often this is as a discrete subject. The reasoning behind this on university courses was often because the Royal Institution of Chartered Surveyors (RICS) (which exempts 'surveying' courses) and the Chartered Institute of Building (CIOB) (which exempts 'building' courses), *inter alia*, have traditionally demanded economics on their syllabuses. Often it used to be taught by economists with little practical experience of the property or construction industries and professions, and has been perceived by students as a necessary first-year syllabus filler.

However, construction and property cannot exist without economics. It provides the framework that allows for both their actual and philosophical existence. An understanding of the fundamentals is therefore a bedrock of other studies.

Indeed, construction and property economics are dynamic and interesting specializations in the body of 'pure' economics. This book seeks to renew and invigorate the depth of that division. It is *not* an economic textbook; it *is* a construction economics *and* property economics textbook. It is an exciting time to write such a text, as the accepted wisdoms of economic theory are increasingly placed under pressure with the search to find new 'values' to life, and as society faces huge and potentially difficult choices about how to use both natural and manmade resources.

AIM

The aim is to introduce the study of this branch of industrial (or possibly *post-industrial*) economics thoroughly and show both its vibrancy and integration within the other subject areas of built environment studies. It is intended that students who have grasped the concepts contained in this book will have a sound basis from which to develop their studies in construction economics, development or property.

APPROACH

In writing the book, the authors have taken an essentially qualitative approach without resorting to the need for high levels of mathematical understanding. The book seeks to explain economics for future built environment professionals in a meaningful, not technical, manner. Hence attention will be paid to the practical aspects of the subject and the application of theory, rather than presenting the world of property and construction economics as compliant with perfect models of theory.

However, the book does seek to use models in order to help students to understand the principles involved. It is important to understand the context in which property and construction economics operate, hence the devotion of a whole chapter to the history of economics, which is a subject usually overlooked completely in introductory texts.

Yet unless we grasp that our understanding of economics at any time is dependent on the wider social context, and that economics is striving to find solutions to changing problems in relation to the way in which resources of all types are distributed and valued, the result will be that the student will develop close-ended views of economic realities.

Thus, as we are writing at a time in which the rate of change within society is rapid, when whole economic systems have crumbled in a decade, as in the case of Eastern Europe, we considered it important to introduce students to the view that what is 'right', 'normal' or even 'theoretically sound' has both time and space dimensions.

The book also uses a number of models created from research, which to the modern reader, bred on instant news, may now seem antiquated. However, the models themselves are not any less useful because their statistics are out of date. Although economic theories change and certainly their acceptance, in both business and political terms, alters rapidly, they may still provide useful perspectives on property and construction economics. In so doing they offer means to understand how the mechanics of the subject work.

As in any discipline, a simple textbook cannot on its own hope to teach a subject, but only to act as a foundation for good-quality teaching. This book is not an alternative to undertaking a complete lecture programme; it is a companion to such a programme.

Level of readership

This book is intended as an introductory first-year text, and as such will present a complicated academic subject in, hopefully, an interesting and straightforward manner. This will lead to some simplification and the presentation of certain possible events as definite facts.

There is also a problem in discussing economics as an industry specialism, in this case construction and property. Pre-university economic education covers only a very narrow band of economic thought. GCSE and GCE 'A'-level economics syllabuses regard, for all practical purposes, only neoclassical theories as important. This preference is continued in the majority of specialist textbooks, where neoclassical ideas are first explained, and then applied to the construction and property industries. Surveying course syllabuses have also traditionally recognized neoclassical economics as the sole forum for property and construction operations. This series of assumptions has an obvious bias towards the needs of the existing industrial economy, and particularly towards such vocational subjects as surveying. Intellectually, however, for the reasons expressed above, this is unacceptable. Neoclassical economics is merely one branch of academic thought that has less than 200 years of history behind it. To ignore other concepts of economics is not only to be incomplete, but also results in students missing a number of dynamic and interesting concepts, at least one of which is of particular interest to property professionals.

Of course, it is important to cover neoclassical economic thought and to ensure that traditional syllabus subjects are covered thoroughly. This book does that. It will, however, also try within the restricted space available to provide students with a more complete picture of economics by use of other theories. Further, property and construction are completely integrated within the text; this book is effectively an industrial study. Both this integration and the width of economic theories are aimed at producing the most complete textbook available at a competitive price. A starting point for the practical application of this textbook was, in fact, to keep the price as low as possible while ensuring this completeness of subject matter.

With the increasing importance of the globalization of economics, it becomes important that students develop a grasp of the economic cultures of other countries, particularly the emergent Central European and Far Eastern systems. However, in writing the book we have not professed an international completeness. Although it makes reference to other systems, it is primarily a British textbook concerned with Western (European) economic thought, and a peculiarly British construction and property profession and industry. These ideas may have been imposed internationally originally through British imperialism, but latterly they have been spread through the influence of British businesses. The book looks at the ideas as they have evolved within a British context and been applied to British construction and property.

The generics of the book lay in a dissatisfaction with standard economics texts as an adjunct to the teaching programmes of Timothy Eccles and Judy Smith, and the resultant desire to produce something of more relevance. So, encouraged and assisted by Sarah Sayce and supported by the editorial team at Thomson, the work has emerged. As with all texts, this has been at the expense of many leisure hours and as a result of numerous discussions and debates, both amongst ourselves and our colleagues.

Any errors lie entirely with the authors; but any contribution we have given to the debate on the role of economics in property and construction must lie as much with our students and our colleagues at Kingston as with ourselves.

Timothy Eccles
Sarah Sayce
Judy Smith
Kingston University

Acknowledgements

The writing of any textbook inevitably requires the help, cooperation and patience of many people. This book is no different. Our thanks and acknowledgements have been well earned by all those whose contributions – both intellectual and practical – have enabled this book to reach print. First our thanks must go to Kingston University for providing us with the 'back-up' to enable the project to go ahead. We would also like to thank our students who have provided fruitful opportunities for debate to stimulate and challenge us! On a more practical note, our colleagues Fiona Smith and Henry Cirkel have been a major source of help as they have so good naturedly, efficiently and quietly got on with the task of deciphering our writing and annotations, typed and retyped numerous copies of the draft and generally 'held the fort' for us on so many occasions. Special mention also must go to Richard Cooper and John Harris for their cheerfulness, skill, expertise and amazing speed in producing the diagrams and tables; also to Richard for obtaining and analysing the data. Much of the data was supplied by DTZ Debenham Thorpe to whom thanks are also extended.

Many manuscripts do not reach the publishers *quite* on the date they should. Our thanks are due to the editorial team at International Thomson Business Press who have both encouraged us and exercised forbearance when time and again we have been tardy or wished to alter material! Lastly, although the University has provided support, the writing has absorbed much personal time on all our parts. So, a big thank you to all our families and friends for your support and tolerance of our neglect of you.

Property economic concepts | 1

OBJECTIVES

The objectives of this chapter are to:

- define what is meant by economics, and explain why its definition has given rise to difficulties;
- explain why economics as a subject of study is so important to the property and construction world;
- define what we mean by the construction and property industries, and link them to economics;
- introduce some basic neo-classical economic principles;
- lay the foundations for the reader to understand the remainder of the book, and develop within the reader an appreciation of both the depth and breadth of the subject material.

1.1 WHAT IS ECONOMICS?

Economics is very difficult to define, but it is important to define it because many differences in opinion between economists are due to differences in definition. The word is derived from Greek, as is shown below:

oikos, a house
nomos, to manage
oikonomos, a steward

The word literally means the wise and legitimate government of the household. In practice, the term meant the management of the household by the family head for the common good of the whole family, a hierarchal and paternalistic arrangement, but one with nobility and trust. If one widens the concept of the 'family' to the tribe, the business organization or the country, it is apparent that the importance of the root of the word is still felt today. Economics is seen as a study to enable this sound management to be carried out by heads of family, heads of business and heads of state. The history of economics has progressed through a variety of stages, as will be shown in Chapter 3, but it is important that the origin of the word is not forgotten. It is still often said today that it is useful to see the nation-state as a family and that the economic good sense of the family can be simply applied to the economic planning of the state.

Economics has been defined in many ways and Table 1.1 provides some famous examples. Economics consists of the creation of theories, which are models of causes and effects based upon a series of assumptions. The veracity and reasonableness of these models lead to much debate, but this debate itself can prove useful in judging the desirability of given outcomes. In order to be informed about this process, it is necessary to study economics. Table 1.2 reproduces these arguments. This book will attempt to highlight these arguments and show how assumptions about these meanings affect the entire economic debate.

The apparent inability of economics to reach guaranteed conclusions has led many to question the precise nature of the subject: is it scientific fact or philosophical fiction?

Economics as a social science

The ancient Greeks philosophized on many issues. Today, there is an increasing belief in 'specialization', since there is too much knowledge for one 'expert' to know. Consequently, information is divided into increasingly specialist classifications. This process also affects economics, which is now a series of specialist fields, as highlighted in Table 1.3. This textbook itself belongs to a specialist field, that of construction and property economics.

Some economists argue that economics is the study of a wide variety of subject areas that are more conventionally regarded in fields such as geography, history,

Table 1.1 What is economics?

Author	Definition
Alfred Marshall	'Political Economy or Economics is a study of mankind in the ordinary business of life.'
J.K. Galbraith	'To have a working understanding of economics is to understand the largest part of life.'
W.S. Jevons, quoted by J.K. Galbraith	'"Economics … must be a mathematical science." From a mathematical science moral values are obviously extruded.'
E.F. Schumacher	'something is uneconomic when it fails to earn an adequate profit in terms of money.'
Thomas Carlyle	'Economists are Respectable Professors of the Dismal Science.'
Anon.	'If you want three opinions ask two economists.'
Karl Marx	'Economic ideas are "the ideas of its ruling class".'

Table 1.2 Why study economics?

1   **To learn a way of thinking** – they suggest in terms of opportunity cost, marginalism and efficient markets (or 'there's no such thing as a free lunch')

2   **To understand society** – via its economy and economic history

3   **To understand world affairs** – i.e. the tensions caused by socialist/capitalist animosities and the gap between rich developed and underdeveloped countries

4   **To be an informed voter** – as economic issues are central to elections

Source: Case and Fair (1989).

Table 1.3 Special fields in economics

- Comparative economic systems
- Industrial organization
- Urban and regional economics
- Econometrics
- Economic development
- Labour economics
- International trade/international monetary economics
- Public finance
- Economic history
- Law and economics
- The history of economic thought

Source: Case and Fair (1989)

politics, sociology, philosophy, management and psychology. In other words, it balances social studies with scientific reason; it is a science through its disinterested search after truth, which involves the systematic formulation and arrangement of knowledge, and a social science as it is concerned with the study of human beings living within a society. But can it be classed as an exact science, capable of accurate laws and future predictions?

Economics as an exact science

It is impossible for economists to match the scientist in the laboratory, who is able to manipulate conditions perfectly and to arrange test cases. Economists live in the real world, and must contend with human vagaries and a chaotic environment. They cannot experiment and the world is dynamic. Historical data will always be at best an approximation of the current state. The world moves on and what has happened in the past may or may not provide good evidence as to what will hold in the future – and it is generally what will happen that interests people, especially economists. So the past is used as a tool of analysis from which to create models to use for both an understanding of the present and a guide to the future.

This inability to examine perfect exhibits leads economists to talk of tendencies (generalizations and mass aggregations) and work within non-real-world assumptions to enable them to build models. These models are useful, provided they are used within their qualifying assumptions, and enable economists to study real events and offer advice. At the moment the specialism of economic forecasting is a growing area as people seek to make optimal decisions regarding their surplus monies or carry out investment projects – such as building new shops or offices.

Textbook economics

Most economic theorists recognize two major branches of the subject: macro-economics and micro-economics. Over time, the relative attention of both writers and course material shifts.

Currently the majority of standard texts in the field of introductory applied economics look at **micro-economics**. This is involved with economic issues as they affect the individual person or the individual organization (the economics of the firm). Micro-economics examines a number of tools for explaining and predicting their behaviour with a view to ensuring that scarce resources are allocated to their best use. It does not look at collective behaviour patterns and their impact on resource allocation.

Macro-economics, on the other hand, does. Currently the less well-provided for area in terms of texts, macro-economics looks at the question of resource allocation in respect of the aggregation of a mass of individuals and hence has much closer involvement with issues such as political intervention; if any government can reach an understanding of the aggregate picture it is likely to become more able to manage the country in a way which makes best use of increasingly scarce resources. Macro-economics was, in fact, the first area of economics to be explored, but lapsed in importance until revived by John Maynard Keynes in his *General Theory of Employment, Interest and Money* in 1936. Over recent years it has in practice been very important as the British government has sought to use macro-economic theories, such as monetarist theory, to regulate the economy. The development of the European Union (EU) and global economic systems also demands an understanding of macro-economic issues. Indeed, it could be argued that as a process of convergence of economies takes place, what was previously regarded as a macro-economic system (i.e. a national economy) becomes almost a micro-economic one as the ability of one country to operate in isolation from others is reduced.

1.2 THE METHOD OF ECONOMICS

It is generally accepted that there are two broad economic methodologies: positive economics and normative economics. **Positive economics** seeks to understand behaviour and the operation of systems without making judgements. The economist in positive economics takes essentially a commentator's stance, seeking to observe and explain. **Normative economics**, on the other hand, analyses outcomes of economic behaviour, evaluates them as good or bad, and may suggest improvements.

In normative economics, for example, one would say that inflation is too high; in positive economics one would say that inflation is at 5 per cent. Positive economics seeks to be scientifically neutral. Personal bias is considered not only irrelevant, but dangerous. The alternative normative view is to argue that, by their very humanity, economists and their models are bound to be biased in some way. Problems of method are thus central to conflict in economics, since these two attitudes are diametrically opposed. Even where agreement on facts is possible – and subjective opinions may make even this impossible – it is still necessary to reach agreement on desired outcomes before any discussion can take place about the best method of transforming the facts into the required outcome. For this reason economists are renowned for their inability to arrive at agreed forecasts or diagnoses of current conditions.

1.3 ECONOMIC CONCEPTS

In addition to its methodology, economics has a number of concepts which economists use in developing their theories. These are outlined below.

Rationality

Economics claims to be rational. It assumes a rational world occupied by rationally behaving individuals. By rationality, economic theory means that it assumes that individuals act in a reasonable, logical and sensible manner. When individual behaviour is aggregated into models, behaviour is thus predictable and plannable. Some economists recognize the concept of 'bounded rationality', which suggests that individuals act only on the information which they possess, and that this may be incomplete or incorrect information. Thus, to someone who has complete information an individual who possesses only partial information may appear to be acting irrationally, while she is in actual fact following perfectly rational thought processes, but with incomplete data. Most economists, as will be shown later, assume perfect knowledge and thus consider only complete rationality. Rationality is also assumed to imply financial rationality. The difficulty with a rational approach is that, as we have already seen above, what constitutes 'complete' information is often highly debatable. Even with the increased use and availability of information technology, complete information is not the norm. This is particularly true with property, for which data is often very deficient, and construction, in which the large number of small firms militate against the collection of complete information.

Efficiency

When applied to economics, efficiency is the condition in which the economic system is producing what people want at the least cost. More formally, it is a condition in which no one can be made better off without making someone else worse off. In short, it represents a time at which resources are being used optimally.

Scarcity

Neoclassical economic theories, in particular, are concerned with scarcity. There is an assumption that all resources are scarce and that there is thus competition to obtain them. Economics has been defined as the process of ensuring the optimal distribution of scarce resources. In recent years increasing concern for the finite nature of resources has led to an expansion of the scarcity debate to consider the sustainability of resources. Sustainable use of resources is that which guarantees their existence for future generations. This debate is very prevalent among economists working in the field of construction and property: the issues concern what materials should be used in the building process to balance the need to reduce construction costs, increase building life and minimize the necessity of expending money on maintenance and general running costs (notably energy) during the life of a building. The wider sustainability arguments which affect property, concern issues of where to locate developments and of the total stock of buildings that society should allow to be developed. Now, more than ever before, there is a recognition that long-term scarcity must have an impact on short-term decisions.

Resources

Resources are anything provided by nature or previous generations that can be used directly or indirectly to satisfy human wants. These scarce resources are commonly classed as follows:

- land;
- labour;
- materials/capital;
- time.

Entrepreneurship may also be added to the list as a specific resource to enable the other resources to be utilized to their optimum. The common view is that land is a finite and fixed resource: as the old adage goes, 'they don't make land any more'. In reality, land, while almost fixed in totality – the creation of 'new lands' or 'polders' in the Netherlands and land reclamation in Hong Kong are rarities – is capable of flexibility between uses. This theme we return to later in the book.

Labour as a resource is, in economic terms, scarce – whatever the unemployment statistics might say. People in any capitalist system generally demand money in return for their efforts as a 'reward'. At certain levels of reward or wages they are not prepared to offer their services; if more people of a particular skill are needed, then a shortage of appropriate labour will result. This, under neoclassical theory, will bid up the wages or 'reward' that such people can negotiate until such time as the market ensures more people train and acquire the requisite skill. The balancing of skills is crucial in the construction industry, in which the demand for particular types of labour can vary radically over a short space of time.

Materials and capital are needed for production: production of consumer items (such as food or clothing) or of the built stock, which concerns us in this book. For example, difficulties in obtaining finance for certain projects can be a major impediment to property development, and this we refer to again later.

'Time is money' is an expression often quoted. Time is important economically not only in the sense that developments are often funded through borrowed money on which interest is charged. The trading of time for free time will be an issue in determining labour demands.

Supply, demand and the market

Neoclassical economics is based on the theory of supply and demand. Supply is the measure of the amount of goods that producers will be prepared to bring forward at any given price. If prices rise for any reason, then, under pure theory, the supply will increase. On the other hand, if prices fall producers will decrease their activity. Demand, in economic terms, must not be equated with need or desire; it relates to the aggregate level of goods which will be purchased of any product at any given price. Thus, while many people may have a *need* for a scarce resource, the economic *demand* for the product will be restricted to those who can pay the price. If demand increases, the reaction in a free-market economy will be twofold.

First, and in the short term, the price will rise. This will allow suppliers to make 'supernormal' profits; hence more suppliers will move into the marketplace to produce the product in the hope of obtaining similar returns. However, as the supply increases, demand will be satisfied and the price will be decreased until supply and demand are once more in 'equilibrium'. Conversely, if demand decreases, oversupply occurs and in the short term prices fall until supply contracts. Thus price forms the mechanism by which supply and demand are reflected in the marketplace.

In a 'free' market there are no restraints on the operation of the supply-and-demand model. However, it has long been recognized by governments that to allow the market alone to allocate resources will mean that those unable to exercise economic demand will suffer. For example, the sick and elderly and young have health *needs* which in a free market they could not *afford* to demand. Thus, for example, the National Health Service (NHS) works primarily on the allocation of resources on the basis of *need*. This presents the practical difficulty that with no effective limit on the *required* supply, the cost to the nation of satisfying need (as opposed to demand) is in danger of becoming unacceptably high. This has lead to much debate and dispute about the standard of care which any individual has the right to expect, given that resources are not being allocated according to the pricing model. As technology and scientific knowledge improve so the position becomes more acute as more *needs* can be satisfied, and this costs the state more and more.

In relation to property a commonly quoted example of government interference with the operation of supply and demand has been in relation to housing. The aim of the government is to ensure that everyone is decently housed; however, many people are at times economically unable to pay the 'market price' for rented or purchased accommodation. Thus over the last century, with the growth of notions of welfare provision, governments have intervened in several ways:

● by controlling the levels of rent that landlords can charge;
● by undertaking direct provision on a needs basis through local authorities;
● through the provision of tax allowances against house purchase.

The results of such interventions have not always been to increase availability of stock as intended; in particular, rent-control measures tended to reduce the number of houses brought forward for rent, thus exacerbating the housing shortage for certain categories of people. The theory of supply and demand related to property and construction is developed further in Chapter 4.

Marginality

Economics is particularly concerned with the 'marginal case', be this marginal production, marginal cost or marginal value. The concept of marginality is based on the 'law of diminishing returns'. This law is in turn founded on the observation that, when additional units of a variable input are added to fixed inputs, after a certain point the additional production of a unit of the added variable input declines. Thus economics is interested in studying the results of producing this additional unit. In short, there comes a time at which the production of one extra unit becomes uneconomic. An example of marginality quoted is in relation to the necessities of life, such as food. While at an individual level, the principle states, I would give up anything for a loaf of bread if I was hungry and without other food, the amount of satisfaction or – to use economic language – the 'utility' I would obtain from a second loaf would be less than from the first, as my hunger would be decreased; after, say, five or six loaves no extra benefit would be derived and the marginal utility would thus have diminished to zero. Thus marginality is connected with the principle of a 'tendency' to decline, and is equally true of all products, including houses, roads and hospitals.

Marginal cost and environmental tragedy

The marginal-cost principle is also used by environmentalists to explain why apparently irrational environmental degradation is in fact economically rational. A commonly quoted example of this is the so-called 'tragedy of the commons'. Under this, there is an area of common land on which herders graze cattle. Each will graze as many as possible, until the optimum carrying capacity is reached. No more should be added, but individuals continue to increase their herd size to maximize their returns. Since the income from an additional animal goes to its owner, whereas the negative costs are felt by all herders, the result is a net gain to the individual who increases herd size, and so herd sizes continue to grow until eventually the land is exhausted.

Take, for example, a case where when the land is at its sustainable capacity each animal produces a return of 100. An additional animal reduces the average return to only 99, because the quality of the grazing land declines slightly. If one herder adds an animal above the carrying capacity, therefore, increasing the herd size from 20 to 21, the extra income is 99. The herder also loses 20 (i.e. one each) because of the reduced value of the other 20, but the net outcome is that income grows from 2,000 to 2,079: it is clearly in the herder's interest to add that twenty-first animal. If the other herders do not increase their herd size also, they will lose one for every animal owned. They will therefore respond by adding further animals too, accelerating the rate of deterioration of the commons.

This same principle can be applied to many areas which touch on the built environment, in particular to developments which produce a high pollution or contaminating effect borne not by the owner or developer, but by the community at large. Similarly with traffic flows, the effect of each and every car added to the number travelling on a motorway at any given time is that congestion increases, but to any individual the impact of that single decision – to travel by car or not – has little impact, yet the alternative may be a significantly increased journey time. Thus at an individual level people make decisions which are rational but which add up to a situation in which all suffer.

Capitalism

The dominant economic system of the modern world is termed a capitalist economy, or capitalism. This is derived from the term capital. Capital is money that is invested with the aim of seeking a return (profit) on that investment. Capitalists are those who invest capital and gain financial reward from their investment. Capitalists are also referred to in many advanced texts as the bourgeoisie, which is derived from the French, meaning the 'middle class' or mercantile people. Capitalists may be individuals; however, increasingly those who control capital are not individuals but corporate bodies: the banks, the industrial companies and the financial intermediaries whose role is concerned with capital flows. The impact of these organizations on the construction and property markets is considered in Chapters 8 and 9.

Capitalism operates in a *laissez-faire* economy (literally French for 'allow to do'). At its most extreme, this is an economy in which individual people and firms pursue their own self-interest without any interference or direction by government. The free market operates entirely without restraint. In reality, no market is without *any* restraint, and most economies in Western civilisation are heavily regulated at both macro and micro levels. The complexity in the study of economics arises from the impact of restraints, normally in the form of government intervention, on part of the workings of the economy. Just as with 'the tragedy of the commons', this will have various – often unforeseen – impacts.

Investment

Investment is concerned with capital – money invested in order to gain a return (profit). Investment is purchase by firms of the new buildings, equipment and inventories that add to their capital stock. Investment may be by individuals or organizations, such as banks and financial institutions, to provide the capital required by the corporate sector for business development. It implies the use of *time* and the foregoing of consumption. The role of capital is central to investment, and those who are in possession of capital have an impact on the nature of the new building stock in the country. If those who control capital are not prepared to invest in any sector of the economy, be it manufacturing, property or tourism, then those entrepreneurs wishing to create new investments will be thwarted in their ambitions.

Consumption (spending)

Households spend part of their income on purchasing 'consumer' goods. Goods purchased are of three categories: durable goods, non-durable goods and services. Durable goods are those that last a relatively long time, such as buildings. Non-durable goods are those that are used up fairly quickly, such as food and clothing. Services do not involve the production of physical things, for example professional services. In the context of this text we consider consumption of construction-industry products, which are durables, and of property, which are normally services. Consumption spending is thus distinct from investment spending, in which money is given up for the purchase of goods and services, not now, but at some date, either specified or not, in the future. So the decision to spend money on an insurance endowment policy which will give back money with accumulated interest in, say, twenty years' time, so that a world cruise can be enjoyed, is an *investment* decision to enable future *consumption* spending. The money invested can be used by the insurance company to invest in companies, adding to production. This idea is explored further in Chapter 7.

Saving

Saving is that part of household income that a household does not consume during a given period. Surplus money not required for consumption now can be used for investment, in which case it can provide a bedrock for increased production. But surplus money may not be invested; it might just be saved in which case it is money which is removed from circulation and the money supply (see Chapter 8), and it does not help to create new goods or services – or, in the case of property and construction, new buildings or infrastructure.

Profit

Profit is the financial return on an investment. Normal profit is that which is earned by firms manufacturing or selling goods in perfect competition with each other (see Chapter 5). Supernormal profit is that which is made by monopolies and monopsonies (see Chapter 5), and which cannot occur in markets of perfect competition. To an individual making surplus money available for investment through, for example, the financial intermediaries or the banks, interest payments may be equated to profit. Profit is often regarded as an emotive term, but in a capitalist system without the prospect of profit no entrepreneurs would come forward with products and services; it is the question of the level of profit, rather than the actual concept, which gives rise to political debate.

Cost

Economic cost is the full cost of production, including a normal rate of return on investment and the opportunity cost of each factor of production. Costs can be regarded in a number of different ways by economists and professionals, three of which are:

- **Fixed costs** are any costs that a firm bears in the short run that do not depend on its level of output. These costs are incurred even if the firm is producing nothing. There are no fixed costs in the long run, because nothing *is* fixed in the long run. Buildings and machinery all age, wear out and are eventually removed, replaced or improved. The exception to this, many argue, is land, which has a totally fixed supply. But even land may be increased (reclamation) and, more importantly, the use of land may be released or improved via physical (e.g. decontamination) or non-physical (through exercise of planning powers) measures. Typical short-term fixed costs relate to the costs of maintaining assets (buildings) and labour costs.
- **Variable costs** are a cost which a firm bears as a result of production and which depends on the level of production chosen. There are no variable costs if there is no production. So for the shopkeeper, for example, the costs of buying the stock that will be sold are variable costs; the costs of employing the staff and paying the rates are fixed.
- **Opportunity cost** is that which has been given up, or foregone, when one item is chosen over another. In a world of scarcity, the satisfaction of one want can be achieved only by ignoring other wants. For example, the cost of a hospital

can be expressed as so many miles of motorway, because the resources used to build a hospital cannot be used on other projects such as a motorway.

A more qualitative view of cost could portray it as a priority ranking (or excuse). This is particularly useful for governments and businesses who do not wish to embark upon certain actions. Unpopular policies are deemed too costly; favoured options are affordable on the basis of 'public good' rather than actual monetary or opportunity cost. For 'public good' schemes, cost–benefit analysis can be used, which attempts to measure qualitative factors by balancing their costs with their social benefits and to place this into an overall financial calculation. The validity of such methods has been seriously questioned over recent years.

Price

Price is defined, most simply, as being the sum of cost and profit. Price is determined by the market, hence the term 'market price'. It is the result of many individual decisions concerning the ability and willingness to supply and to demand the good involved. If the supply of and demand for a particular good at a particular time are equally matched at a particular price, this price is said to be an 'equilibrium price'. If any supplier seeks to increase the price over this level it will – if all else remains static – adversely affect demand, so that the price is forced down to the original level.

Value

The issue of a good's value was highlighted by Adam Smith's water-and-diamonds paradox. (Adam Smith, the founder of modern economics, is discussed in 3.6.) While water was of infinite value, because life could not exist without it, it was of little market value, because at the time that Smith was writing water was not a scarce commodity. The reverse was true for useless, yet expensive, diamonds. The abundance of water and the scarcity of diamonds were deemed to be the cause of this. This gives rise to the concept of marginal utility, which recognizes that a good's or a service's value reduces with each extra unit consumed: the first glass of water is most welcome, the second is worth less, and the third even less.

The water-and-diamonds paradox introduced the following ideas on value:

● marginal utility;
● differences between market value and personal value (or worth as it is now called within the surveying world);
● exchange value and use value.

The question of value is important to the surveying profession, particularly those who specialize in valuation. Valuers are experts at determining rational values of property and land. Such values sometimes equate to price, and sometimes are based instead upon notions of cost or worth to the individual (RICS 1995). It has been suggested that surveyors know the price of everything, but the value of nothing. The problem lies in the inability of traditional economic concepts of cost and price to recognize qualitative concepts of value, such as moral, aesthetic, personal and historical. It cannot understand the concept of (say) a public park, *as a public park*, but merely sees it as a land value or an opportunity cost. Valuation techniques see land and buildings as simple objects that can be compared in the absolute terminology of their market value. In the past, land and property in the public sector were not generally valued in terms of market value as, by definition, they did not exist in such terms. A council house is not a house, but a *home*, a park not a parcel of land, but a place for private (individual) existence – a public space. They are personal values. Thus they cannot be valued in simple economic measurements of price and cost. However, in recent years, with a move towards economic efficiency in the public sector, attempts to introduce the concept of market value or opportunity cost have been introduced for many public-sector assets.

In economics value is traditionally classified as use value and exchange value. Use value is concerned with the individual usefulness (or utility) which purchasers will gain by purchasing the good or service. Exchange value is concerned with the barter value (or market price) of the good or service. Modern production of goods and services is generally for their exchange value, as mass production seeks to predict (and create through advertising) likely demand and does not produce to individual order. However, in property it is possible to recognize a bespoke market where individual buildings are designed and built to the orders of a single client. This is not universal, however, and the housing market in particular will produce goods on a 'speculative' basis.

The issue of value is so important to the work of the surveying profession that the Royal Institution of Chartered Surveyors (RICS 1995) imposes various definitions of value for use in different situations.

Inflation

Inflation refers to a general increase in both prices and wages, often associated with a spiral effect in which as either wages or prices start to move the other factor is pushed up – or, according to other theorists, the former pulls up the latter. Inflation has been generally regarded as endemic to capitalist societies and, in political terms at least, as a bad thing as it introduces uncertainty. However, traditionally it has also been seen as useful for preventing excessive saving and encouraging spending, consumption and investment. More recently some economists have challenged the inevitability of inflation and anticipate a zero-inflation economy.

National Wealth

There are two means of measuring national wealth. **Gross domestic product** (GDP) is the total market value of all final goods and services produced within a given period of time by factors of production located within the country regardless of who owns them. **Gross national product** (GNP) is the total market value of all finite goods and services produced within a given period by factors of production owned by the country's citizens. With an increase in the growth of multinational companies, it becomes difficult at times to distinguish between what is domestic and what is non-domestic.

Units of action

There are two types of units operating in the economy. They are 'the firm' and 'the household'. The **firm** is an organization that comes into being when someone or some group decides to transform resources (inputs) into products (outputs) for sale in the market. Firms are the primary producing units in a market economy. The product may be tangible (manufactured goods) or intangible (services and/or advice). Over the last fifty years the UK has experienced a major shift, from an economy primarily based on manufacturing to one based on service industries. The **household** is the consuming unit in the economy and, over time, as real incomes have grown, the amount consumed has become ever more discretionary. By this we mean that as real incomes rise so the proportion of money spent on necessities decreases, thus releasing a greater percentage of money to spend according to personal choice.

Cycles

It is generally, although not universally, recognized that modern (capitalist) economies operate in cycles, termed 'economic cycles' or 'business cycles'. These cycles are endemic and consist of a series of booms and slumps where demand and supply are not in equilibrium. Too many goods are produced and too many services are offered in slumps; in booms demand for goods and services outstrips short-term supply. In addition, more specific cycles have also been recognized, particularly the building cycle and the property cycle. Chapter 6 examines the economic cycle, and how governments react, plan and attempt to manipulate it.

1.4 VOCATIONAL DEFINITIONS

When considering the subject area in terms of the English language, two words will be encountered that are sometimes, misleadingly or interchangeably applied to the industries which are being studied. These are 'construction' and 'property'.

Property

Property as a concept has two interrelated facets to its meaning.

1. Philosophical–legal concept.
2. Physical concept.

Philosophically and legally, the concept of property is associated with **private property** and the idea of **ownership**. Society and economic theories assume this tenet. By it, rights are claimed, and recognized, over certain things or tangibles. These things, in this study, will include buildings, land, roads, bridges, tunnels and the like. For these items ownership consists of rights over the land and buildings, not the objects themselves. Property over which rights are owned is called 'real estate' or 'realty'. Absolute ownership resides with 'personal items' or 'personalty'. Such things may be intangible such as intellectual property (copyright and patents, information) or physical (pens, clothes, cars, books and furniture, for example). In addition, not only does ownership award rights, it also imposes duties and obligations to act and use that property in a socially reasonable and legally responsible manner. The role of the government, in part, is to ensure, by either compulsion or encouragement, that this occurs.

The physical concept of property is the actual thing that people own. In the surveying field, property is the buildings and land which buyers and sellers are buying, selling, developing or letting. We talk about 'a property'. Chapter 3 will show how property has been regarded over time, and in what ways economics used property in developing theories.

The property profession

The people who buy, sell, develop and let property are regarded as property professionals. The profession is controlled by professional institutions (the most widely recognized are the Royal Institution of Chartered Surveyors (RICS), the Chartered Institute of Building (CIOB) and the Incorporated Society of Valuers and Auctioneers (ISVA)), which have regulations and rules of conduct, minimum entry requirements and a recognized career progression in order to obtain professional qualifications. The RICS, in fact, terms itself 'the property profession'. Surveyors, as professionals and thus members of a professional body, obey its strictures and should act professionally at all times. Surveying firms also act in a professional manner, being both professional firms and employers of professionals. Property professionals are involved with all aspects of the development of land and buildings, construction, management, together with its valuation and sale processes. All these require a deep understanding of economic principles, not just from a theoretical stance, but as they apply to professional duties.

The built environment

The importance of the built environment as a focus for the study of economics by property and construction professionals cannot be overemphasized. Apart from the obvious fact that it is the area in which the majority of citizens will live and work, the built environment has both economic and social importance.

Economically, approximately half the United Kingdom's assets are now houses and the housing stock forms the single most important component of national wealth. The value of residential property is over three times greater than the stock of plant and machinery, and the value of owner-occupied housing has increased five times faster than GDP. Remembering that the built environment also includes offices and factories in addition to housing can only increase its importance to macro-economic theory. The value of the commercial property stock balance has been estimated to equate to between 30 and 40 per cent of all corporate assets. Hence any movement in the market value of the built stock affects the ability of corporate owners to raise capital through borrowing, and this in turn has an impact on investment levels.

Socially, the built environment is linked with civilization both as a product of the city and as the location in which human beings exist, work, play and develop. Indeed, in 1842 Robert Vaughan claimed the city as the bringer of the great rewards of modern society: science, art and literature, popular intelligence, morals and religion. Modern thought also tends to hold urban areas as central to civilization. Recently the depopulation of city centres and the perceived need to revitalize and regenerate urban areas have been key areas of work concerning property and construction professionals.

Construction

Construction is the process of building. It is the means by which property is usefully created in the built environment (villages, towns and cities). It includes not just 'new' buildings but the conservation, maintenance and redevelopment of buildings in accordance with economic and social requirements.

The construction industry

An industry is a branch of manufacture or trade. The construction industry is thus a branch of manufacture whose purpose is to build – by fitting parts together and by managing this process – some output to be incorporated into the built environment.

The United Nations (UN) constructed an International Standard Industrial Classification (ISIC) to serve as a framework for collecting, collating and disseminating industrial statistics. The ISIC originally categorized industrial activities at three levels: division, major group and group (one-, two- and three-digit categories, respectively). The divisions were:

- agriculture;
- mining and quarrying;
- manufacturing;
- electricity, gas and water;
- construction;
- wholesale and retail trade, restaurants and hotels;
- transport, storage and communication;
- financing, insurance, real estate and business services;
- community, social and personal services, and other activities not adequately defined.

Thus the construction industry is a recognized division of industry. However, there is debate on whether property can properly be considered in the scope of the industry, as shown in Table 1.4. It should also be noted that property is not technically an industry separate from or included within construction. Some activities of property professionals fall within the ambit of construction, but many others are more concerned with finance, insurance, real estate and business services or with agriculture.

Revision in 1992 arose out of problems with the earlier system. The UK Standard Industrial Classification 1992 is much more prescriptive, but was due for revision in late 1997 (it was not revised). These continual revisions highlight the problems of defining modern industries in general, and not just construction and property.

The current United Nations ISIC of all economic activities recognizes construction, architecture and engineering activities (as 'other business activities') and real-estate activities. The actual classifications are:

Table 1.4 Definitions of the construction industry

Indeed, there is no clear definition as to just what the construction industry is. Certainly it must include the hundreds of thousands of general and speciality construction contractors. But to understand the industry really, one must extend its scope to include designers of facilities, materials suppliers, and equipment manufacturers. Labour organizations add still another dimension, as do public and private consumers of construction services, many of whom have considerable construction expertise of their own. Government regulatory agencies in such areas as safety, health, employment practices, and fair trade also play an increasingly important role.

(Barrie and Paulson 1992: 6)

The product area covered in this book is that of the Standard Industrial Classification 1968 for construction as follows:

● Erecting and repairing buildings of all types; constructing and repairing roads and bridges; erecting steel and reinforced concrete structures; other civil engineering work such as laying sewers, gas or water mains, and electricity cables, erecting overhead lines and line supports and aerial masts, extracting coal from opencast workings, etc. The building and civil engineering establishments of government departments, local authorities and New Town Corporations and Commissions are included. On-site industrialised building is also included.
● Establishments specialising in demolition work or in sections of construction civil engineering to materials manufacturing, property development, trade specialisation, and even opencast coal-mining. In addition, there are the design consultants – architects, engineers, quantity surveyors, etc. – many of whom now practice in multidisciplinary firms. Peripheral services such as materials supply and plant hire, and the newly emerging project management firms, contribute to a complex industrial structure.

(Hillebrandt 1988: 1)

The projects undertaken by the industry are very wide ranging, but can be classified by work type under two main headings:

(a) Building
(b) Civil Engineering.

The construction industry is perhaps one of the few industries that encompass such widely differing sizes of job, such as the replacing of a roof slate, to the building of a multi-storey office block or motorway. In size of firm again there is a great variation between, at the one extreme, many sole traders who concentrate mainly on local maintenance work, to the other extreme of national organizations whose turnover is measured in millions of pounds.

(Shutt 1988: 97)

Division 45   Construction

451	Site preparation
452	Building of complete construction or parts thereof; civil engineering
453	Building installations
454	Building completion
455	Renting of construction or demolition equipment with an operator

● Other business activities:

742	Architectural, engineering and other technical activities

7421	Architectural and engineering activities and related technical consultancy
7422	Technical testing and analysis
Division 70	Real-estate activities
701	Real-estate activities with own or leased property
702	Real-estate activities on a fee or contract basis

It should be noted that these classes exclude, *inter alia*, the manufacture of plastics, metals and mineral products, all of which are used to make building products, the renting of machinery (including plant hire), research, and pensions and other investment activities.

Thus, although the classification goes some way to providing measures whereby the economic contribution of the construction and property industries to the UK economy can be measured, the resultant figures of activity actually underestimate the contribution made by land and buildings and those who work within the sectors.

1.5 CONCLUSION

This chapter has introduced the concept of economics and sought to demonstrate that it has a wide-reaching impact on many human activities: it does, however, present difficulties in respect of its definition and the scope of what is legitimately claimed to be 'economics'. It is concluded that economics touches every branch of human activity; as such it is hard to define what is 'economics' and what is, for example, 'management'. Thus, although economics has developed as a 'pure' discipline, it is in its relationship with the broader sphere of activities that it finds its reason for development. One of the aspects of activity to which economics relates is that of property and construction.

Within the context of the UK, the neoclassical interpretation of economics prevails and the basic tenets on which the theory, as applied to property and construction, is based have been introduced. These work on the overriding principle of the market, a concept which is developed further in subsequent chapters.

These issues lead to a discussion in more detail of the nature of the construction industry and the characteristics which distinguish it from other sections of the economy.

1.6 SUMMARY
- Economics has many possible definitions, and this leads to some of the problems economists face.
- The same is true of the construction industry and the property profession.
- The predominant theories of economics found in the UK are based on neoclassicism.
- There are two main branches of economics: macro-economics, concerned with matters to do with the wide economy; and micro-economics, concerned with the theory of individuals and individual organizations.
- Under accepted economic theory within a capitalist economy the market principles of supply and demand are the prime drivers of pricing structures if no government intervention takes place.
- A totally free-market economy is not normally acceptable in political and social terms as there is a recognition that some resources need to be allocated on grounds of need as well as demand.
- Construction and property economics is concerned with the efficient design, production, sale, operation and renewal of the built environment.

FURTHER READING

Galbraith, J.K. and Salinger, N. (1981) *Almost Everyone's Guide to Economics*, London: Penguin.
Pen, J. (1965) *Modern Economics,* London: Pelican.
Robinson, J. (1964) *Economic Philosophy*, London: Pelican.
Williams, G. (1972) *The Economics of Everyday Life*, 3rd edn, London: Pelican.

EXAMPLE QUESTIONS

Below are questions relating to this chapter. For each chapter model answers have been prepared for some of the questions set; these are found in the Appendix.

1.1   Economics can be defined as the science which studies human behaviour as a relationship between ends and scarce means which have alternative uses.
  (a)   In what sense is economics a science?
  (b)   Why do economists use theories?

1.2   What are the problems posed in economics by the fact that we cannot undertake laboratory experiments?

1.3   (a)   Explain what is meant by the term 'positive economics'.
  (b)   Why is it that disagreements over 'normative' statements cannot be settled merely by an appeal to the facts?
  (c)   To what extent do you believe that economists can make policy recommendations without at the same time making value judgements?
  (d)   Explain why the statement that 'the level of unemployment in Britain is too high' is a normative one. Suggest a reformulation to turn it into a positive statement and consider how it might then be tested.

1.4   Many economic models rest on a fundamental assumption: namely, that the decision-maker behaves 'rationally'. What do we mean by *rational* behaviour?

(a) Is it a term of approval?

(b) Is it concerned with means or ends?

1.5 Given that resources are finite and wants infinite, how do societies determine the allocation of resources? How infinite are wants?

1.6 Giving examples, explain the term 'opportunity cost'.

1.7 Can you think of a reason why it would be useful for construction and property professionals to have an accurate forecast of inflation?

1.8 What is the opportunity cost of training to be a surveyor?

1.9 Give examples of free-market, centrally controlled and mixed economies.

1.10 What factors do you expect to influence the demand for surveyors in the industry?

1.11 Define the terms 'cost', 'value' and 'price'. How do they arise within the construction industry, and how would you calculate them?

2 The peculiar nature of the construction industry

OBJECTIVES

The objectives of this chapter are to:

● describe what is meant by the terms 'the construction industry' and 'property';
● consider the characteristics of the constuction industry in the light of major survey work;
● examine the construction industry in comparison with 'general manufacturing' industries;
● examine how modern the construction and property industry is by measuring its flexibility and capacity to produce.

2.1 INTRODUCTION

The definition and scope of the construction industry, as discussed in Chapter 1, is open to differing interpretations. Its meaning is in part formed by the theoretical bounds of property economics, but in part it depends on the data that is available (for example government statistics on construction). As with other branches of economics, definitions of property and construction economics are constantly changing both as the industry changes and as the wider economy changes. The construction industry is regarded as being distinctively different from most other industries and this is what renders it suitable for study as a specialist area of economics; it does not in fact adhere to the behaviour observed in other industries, from observation of which general theories have been drawn.

There are three aspects in particular which help to provide an understanding of the nature of the British construction industry, as distinct from any other industry. These are its:

● flexibility;
● capacity;
● characteristics compared to other industries.

Two major studies of the construction industry by the National Economic Development Office (NEDO) (1978) and Hillebrandt (1975) were carried out and these are now used as a basis for analysis of the industry using the headings set out above. Although they were carried out in the 1970s, they have not been superseded in terms of their economic thinking for the construction industry, although some issues have been addressed by Latham (1994).

2.2 THE CONSTRUCTION INDUSTRY: FLEXIBLE OR NOT?

It is recognized that any industry which contains no element of flexibility in its operation will have major difficulty in adapting to changes both within and outside itself. If flexibility is not present, then any change in, say, demand for the product will not quickly result in change in supply, and the consequence is likely to be oversupply, falling prices and, in due course, bankruptcy for the supplier. Similarly, if demand for the product rises and the supply is not flexible in response, the opportunity to adjust quickly will not take place and, while short-term gain to the supplier may result, in the longer term little will be gained as the demand will fall away because of price rises. Indeed, it will be even more problematic if supply does adjust, but only at a rate so slow that by the time the increased number of products are made demand has switched to another, more accessible, product.

Although the talk currently has become very vociferous in terms of the 'flexible economy' and the need to be able to respond, such notions are not new. The issue of flexibility within the construction industry was first investigated by NEDO (1978) for the government of the day as part of its general interest in the constituent industries of the economy. The aim of the research was to understand the mechanisms of change within the construction industry and so to provide government with the information it deemed necessary to manage it and the economy as a whole. The resultant report divided the industry into six parts:

- clients and developers;
- professions;
- contractors and subcontractors;
- operatives;
- materials;
- contractors' plant.

The analysis, albeit dated, provides a still-valid framework to commence a description of the characteristics of the construction industry and, in particular, to compare its characteristics against those required of a modern, flexible, responsive industry.

Clients and developers

The 1978 NEDO paper pointed to an ongoing change in the traditional demand for construction products; a change even more marked today. At that time, it noted that the traditional public-sector client demand for new building work was declining amid a rapidly fluctuating rise and fall in demand for work in the private sector. Since then the move within the client base has become increasingly focused on the private sector, partly as a consequence of privatization, which meant the sale of publicly owned assets, and partly because of the way contracts are now handled (described below).

The NEDO report highlighted repair and maintenance as major areas of work necessary to conserve the nation's built resources. They still account for 40–50 per cent of all work. Within this context, the role of the client generally was seen as both important for a successful project and extremely vague in delineating boundaries of responsibility. The client was responsible for employing professionals to design and build the project, and for strategically planning the project and designing the brief. Planning procedures were perceived by clients and developers as a major source of delay, while the process was admittedly necessary to protect community interests.

The trends of 1978 have proven consistent. Modern demand is increasingly from private-sector clients, who are exhibiting greater expertise in controlling the construction process and its participants. The planning process has faced a great deal of criticism and become much more focused on the needs of developers. Debate continues on the role of planners in protecting greenfield sites, historic buildings and maintaining the quality of the urban environment.

Although the client base was recognized as being composed of a disparate group of public- and private-sector institutions, all clients were seen as fundamentally interested in the financial repercussions of building, most particularly the initial raising of finance. Finance (investment, in economic terms) was seen as a key determinant in defining the organization of the construction industry. NEDO (1978) identified the following major sources of client finance:

- **mortgage**, either on a simple repayment basis or with some degree of equity participation with the lender;
- **sale and leaseback**, whereby the lending institution buys land, pays for construction and then leases the development back to the developer;
- **forward purchase**, where the developer sells before, or on, building completion.

Since this report the influence of public-sector clients has changed. Successive moves to privatize property and industry have resulted in few public schemes other than those associated with road infrastructure. Even where ownership is vested in the public sector the investment schemes are increasingly financed by the private sector. For example, the Private Finance Initiative (PFI) is a mechanism now being introduced whereby private funding is used to procure major public schemes such as hospitals. Within local authority ownership, compulsory competitive tendering (CCT) has been seen as another way of introducing private funding and investment in social provision, although government changes in 1997 are leading to less emphasis on the element of compulsion. Instead CCT is gradually shifting towards voluntary competitive tendering (VCT) or schemes of best practice. The importance of the client, and the mechanism by which the client's finances work within the construction industry impacts on the supply of goods (e.g. new building, refurbishment schemes, roads and infrastructure) and hence affects the pricing mechanism (as seen in Chapter 1). When funding is problematic, the effective 'supply' of clients is reduced and this produces ramifications for employment, quality and type of product, and, indeed, prices.

Not only the world of public finance has become more complex since the NEDO report was published, but also that of private finance, with clients seeking ever more flexible deals to create developments. Thus, in summary, the NEDO report pointed to the need for the construction industry to be flexible to meet the changing client base; twenty years on, the requirement is accentuated.

Professions

The 'main building professionals' identified in the report were:

- civil engineers;
- architects;
- building-services engineers;
- quantity surveyors;
- structural engineers.

The number of professionals available was regarded as inflexible, because of the long training period from being a student to obtaining final qualifications. The number and type of professional required was seen as fluctuating with regard to the volume of construction work, the type and complexity of work, and the definition and relationship of professional roles on projects.

However, just as the nature of 'clients' has changed over twenty years, so too has the scope of professionals. While all those previously described continue to operate, increasing numbers of building surveyors with specialist skills, and, more recently, new professionals such as the facilities manager are having an impact on the operation of the construction industry.

The problem of the numbers required by the volatile industry still remains. With professional qualifications taking, on average, six years and demand changing rapidly, this problem appears insoluble. The deep recession in the property and construction industries in the early 1990s was bound to be associated with over-supply of professionals. However, coincidental moves by the government to encourage greater numbers to study to degree level and beyond exacerbated the problem, and for the first time produced significant levels of unemployment among property and construction professionals.

Contractors and subcontractors

In 1978 the construction industry contained over 90,000 firms, the majority of which were small. Figures from 1975 showed that 92.5 per cent of firms employed fewer than twenty-five staff, while 22.5 per cent of work was carried out by 0.1 per cent of contractors. Specialist trade contractors made up over half of firms. Even in 1978 public-sector contracting departments were of only marginal importance, and government policy since then has been to remove them completely. Thus the industry was dominated by a large number of small operators, but with a few 'big players' commanding an abnormally large section of the work.

Firms were generally optimistic at that time, particulary as they were experiencing a growth in overseas work which was helping to maintain workload levels. Finance was not seen as a problem. Payments were received regularly for work as it was carried out. The need for flexibility was not considered a problem. Annual growth rates of 10 per cent were regarded as achievable, while recession would remove less efficient firms, leaving the rest in good shape for the future.

Since 1978 construction firms have become a lot less optimistic. Not only did recession in the 1990s caused the failure of less efficient firms, as noted in the NEDO report, but it also caused a massive shift in resources out of the industry. Profit levels have been so low that few firms have sought to operate within construction, and finance has remained persistently difficult and expensive to raise. This will no doubt change as workloads increase and profit levels rise, but it has left a different industry than that recognized by NEDO in 1978.

There were over twice as many firms operating in 1996 as in 1978, although many pre-existing firms have reduced in size considerably. In 1993, 94 per cent of firms employed fewer than eight staff and 98 per cent employed fewer than twenty-five. Less than 0.1 per cent of firms employed 300 or more people, and yet they carried out 28 per cent of all work. It appears in this case that NEDO's prediction was inaccurate; there seems to be a polarization of the industry into large (multinational) firms and a multitude of small firms operating at the industry's margins.

Operatives

Operatives were defined by NEDO (1978) as being classified as shown below:

- carpenters and joiners;
- painters;
- bricklayers;
- mechanical plant operators;
- electricians;
- plumbers and gas fitters;
- heating and ventilating engineers;
- plasterers;
- paviours;
- scaffolders;
- roof slaters and tilers;
- masons;
- steel erectors and sheeters;
- bar benders and fixers;
- glaziers;
- other building and civil engineering crafts;
- general labourers.

Probably the largest category of employee in 1978 was 'general labourers' and these were seen as the most flexible, having no skill and being easy to obtain and dismiss. Skilled tradesmen were facing a serious employment shortage since the days of full employment in the early 1970s. Traditional trade delineations had been eroded in the desire for efficiency and flexibility, which made job titles less clear than in previous decades. These trends have continued. NEDO (1978) calculated the exact demand for work different types of construction would demand. Their findings are reproduced in Table 2.1. The key issues facing the flexibility of building labour at that time are still relevant today:

- **labour mobility**. Workers were seen to be geographically mobile and thus able to travel distances to gain work.
- **labour loss**. A major source of concern was the large number of skilled workers who saw themselves as building workers but were employed in other industries. On leaving construction many did not return, as the persistent insecurity

Table 2.1 Employment of site operatives for various market sectors of new work (site man-days* per £1000 contract value at 1970 prices)

Trade groups	Housing		General building					Civil engineering			
Trades	Private	Public	Education	Hospitals	Other Public	Industrial	Commercial	Roads	Harbours	Water	Sewerage
Structure											
Bricklayer	9.1	9.0	5.4	4.9	5.1	5.0	3.3	0.3	0.2	0.7	0.6
Roofer	1.1	0.9	0.9	0.6	0.7	3.2	0.6	–	–	–	–
Steel erector	–	0.3	0.5	0.2	0.4	1.5	0.1	–	–	–	–
Erector	–	0.3	0.1	0.6	0.3	0.8	0.5	–	–	–	–
Glazier	0.2	0.2	0.5	0.2	0.3	0.8	0.2	–	–	–	–
Others	0.2	–	0.4	0.2	0.7	0.1	0.8	0.1	–	–	–
Total	10.6	10.4	7.8	6.8	7.5	11.4	5.5	0.4	0.2	0.7	0.6
Carpenter	8.3	7.9	11.3	8.7	9.3	6.3	6.3	1.1	3.1	3.2	3.5
Services											
Plumber	2.8	2.5	1.8	1.8	1.4	1.3	1.0	0.1	–	–	–
Heating	0.2	0.8	3.8	6.4	3.2	2.9	2.9	–	–	–	–
Electrician	1.8	2.5	3.5	4.4	3.5	3.1	3.0	0.1	0.2	–	–
Others	0.2	0.4	0.9	0.8	0.5	–	0.7	–	–	–	–
Total	5.0	6.2	10.0	13.4	8.6	7.3	7.6	0.2	0.2	–	–
Finishes											
Plasterer	4.2	3.7	1.8	2.6	1.6	0.5	1.2	–	–	–	–
Painter	4.5	4.6	3.0	2.4	2.4	3.4	0.9	0.1	–	–	0.2
Floorlayer	0.5	0.5	1.0	1.2	0.3	0.7	0.2	–	–	–	–
Others	0.8	0.4	1.4	0.6	0.5	0.6	1.7	0.2	–	0.1	0.1
Total	10.0	9.2	7.2	6.8	4.8	5.2	4.0	0.3	0.2	–	0.3
Other											
General labourer	14.5	16.8	15.5	12.6	16.3	15.5	9.7	13.2	7.7	8.1	14.3
Plant operator	2.0	1.1	1.0	0.8	1.9	0.6	0.7	6.0	3.7	6.1	6.1
Scaffolder	0.8	0.3	0.4	0.3	0.6	0.3	1.0	0.2	–	–	–
Steelfixer	–	0.3	0.3	0.6	0.8	0.2	0.8	0.4	3.2	0.6	0.8
Welder	–	0.3	0.3	0.6	0.8	0.2	0.8	0.4	3.2	0.6	0.8
Pipelayer	0.2	0.8	0.3	0.2	0.3	0.1	0.1	0.6	0.5	2.2	1.9
Drainlayer	0.2	0.8	0.3	0.2	0.3	0.1	0.1	0.6	0.5	2.2	1.9
Tarmac/asphalt	0.2	0.2	0.8	0.3	0.3	0.2	0.1	1.4	–	–	–
Others	0.8	0.4	0.6	0.2	0.8	0.4	0.5	2.1	5.0	2.8	0.7
Total	18.5	19.9	18.9	15.0	21.0	17.3	12.9	23.9	20.1	19.8	23.8
General foreman	3.3	3.0	3.1	2.2	3.4	2.8	2.2	1.6	0.3	0.4	0.3
All trades	55.7	56.6	58.3	52.9	54.6	50.3	38.5	27.5	23.9	24.1	28.5

Source: NEDO (1978: 29).
Note: *8½ hours per day (5½ days per week) for building; 9 hours per day (6 days per week) for civil engineering.

of employment was a major cause of disincentive. This resulted in the loss of skill and experience to the industry.

● **labour entry**. Apprenticeships were the major source of industry entry. There was also a high degree of late entry, from both related and unrelated trades in other industries. However, since NEDO (1978) published its report the general move to higher qualifications at the expense of apprentice entry has been a signal that there may be a possible labour shortage at the entry point of apprenticeship.

The situation in the late 1990s is a complex one. The recession and general financial situation faced by the majority of contractors described above had led to falling wages and poor employment prospects. Entry into the workforce has been low, due to the oversupply of workers. However, with the end of recession, labour shortages are occurring. Those factors highlighted by NEDO encourage a certain flexibility, but skilled workers need a training and remuneration commitment that cannot be met by such flexible methods. It seems that the industry is destined to have a pool of unskilled labour, while the supply of skilled workers is likely to lag behind demand, thus ensuring an ongoing lack of equilibrium in the marketplace.

Materials

Materials were seen by NEDO (1978) as counting for 40 per cent of the value of work carried out, ranging from 15 per cent in repair and maintenance work to 60 per cent in services installation intensive work. NEDO had great difficulty assessing the relative significance of individual materials because of their usage in other industries and their variety in production statistics. Figure 2.1 provides the results of their attempts to relate material usage to individual trades as indicated in Table 2.2.

Obviously, the amount of materials required depends not only on the type of trade and on the construction being built, as the two tables suggest, but also on the total amount of construction work being undertaken. NEDO examined the shifts in demand caused by shifts in both type and amount of construction, but without definitive conclusion beyond the obvious. Increasingly, Europe is today becoming dominated by a few large suppliers, which restricts flexibility by restricting product ranges. However, the producers argue that they are able to invest in new and better ranges through research and development, and to plan a European materials strategy in the global market which will prevent foreign imports.

Material imports and exports were seen by NEDO as increasingly important. Exports accounted for 17 per cent and imports 27 per cent of total construction material usage in Great Britain in 1976. Forest products were the major import. Importation did affect flexibility, but the most important factors affecting supply were changes in the size of stocks held, the utilization rate of manufacturing capacity and changes (either reduction or increase) in that capacity. Transport facilities, to deliver the mass of material and to a specific time, were also important. The degree of substitution was also important. The degree of substitution for a given material is the ease with which material can be replaced by an alternative material capable of providing the same function.

NEDO has been proved correct: imports and exports are important. Trade deficit in building materials has continued to be a factor, although exports have also been

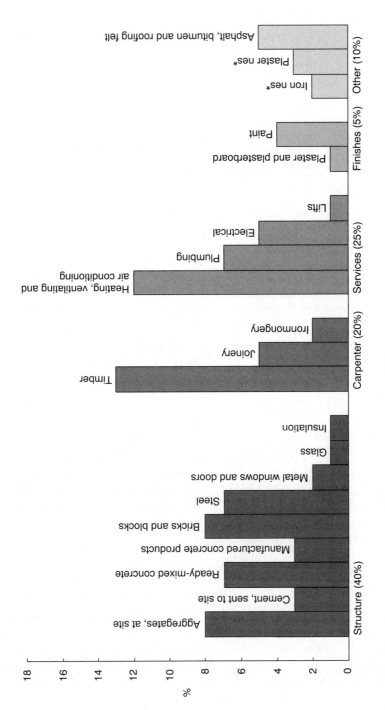

Figure 2.1 Estimated relative significance by value of construction materials
Note: * not elsewhere specified
Source: NEDO (1978: 48).

Table 2.2 Materials: use by trade

Structure	Aggregates, at site
	Cement, sent to site
	Ready-mixed concrete
	Manufactured concrete products
	Bricks and blocks
	Steel
	Metal windows and doors
	Glass
	Insulation
Carpenter	Timber
	Joinery
	Ironmongery
Services	Heating, ventilating and air conditioning
	Plumbing
	Electrical
	Lifts
Finishes	Plaster and plasterboard
	Paint
Other	Iron not elsewhere specified
	Plastics not elsewhere specified
	Asphalt, bitumen and roofing felt

substantial. For example, in 1995 materials exports were worth approximately £3.5 billion, a £0.5 billion increase on the previous year, and led to a reduction in the deficit, from £1.74 billion at the start of 1995 to £1.46 billion at the end of the year.

Contractors' plant

NEDO (1978) estimated that 5 per cent of the cost of a new construction project was spent on contractors' plant, but was unsure as to whether this would increase. Availability and operational flexibility were not seen as a problem, but inefficient use of the machinery was. Hiring was seen as a flexible method of machine ownership which helped reduce poor usage rates. In 1978 30–60 per cent of all machinery was hired. Little has changed.

2.3 CAPACITY

A more specific but equally important analysis of the British construction industry was carried out by Hillebrandt in 1975 for publication in a paper called 'The capacity of the construction industry'. Her interest was in creating a method for determining the capacity of the British construction industry, and in doing so she offered a useful economic description. There are three types of capacity according to Hillebrandt and they are outlined below.

Sustainable output

Sustainable output defines as a technological output the maximum output per unit of time that it is possible to obtain from a given factory or industry. The techno-logical definition often specifies that it is maximum **sustainable** output which is relevant, so that allowance is made for repair and maintenance to the fixed factors. It is a relatively simple concept, but difficult to apply in practice.

Economic output

An economic definition is that output at which average costs are at a minimum. The relationship between costs (including normal profit) and output as represented by a supply-and-demand graph explains this concept. In Figure 2.2 AB is the total cost curve of a representative firm in the industry at a point in time. It is made up of fixed costs (0A) shown by the line AC, which consist of plant, equipment and buildings, and variable costs (0D), which are costs for materials, manpower and fuel. Variable costs may increase in direct proportion to output or may increase more than in proportion to output. This is usually due to the higher costs of over-time working. Figure 2.3 shows the corresponding average costs. Average fixed costs (DA) decrease per unit of output because the larger the output, the smaller the fraction of the fixed costs attributable to the unit of output. Average variable costs (FB) increase with output. Average total costs (EC) combine the two curves and first decrease, influenced largely by average fixed costs, and then increase as the increasing variable costs become more important.

According to this economic definition, the capacity of an industry is that level of output at which all the firms in the industry are producing at lowest average costs. A perfectly competitive situation is assumed, allowing free entry to the industry, and all firms are assumed to be homogeneous. Therefore, if it happens that sales are made at greater than average total cost, more firms will enter the

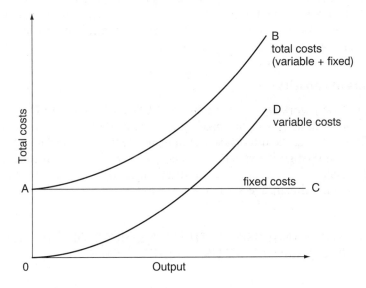

Figure 2.2 Total cost curves of a firm

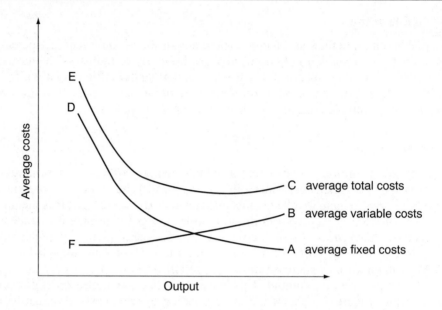

Figure 2.3 Average cost curves of a firm

industry and produce at their lowest average cost until the output of all other firms is reduced to lowest average costs.

National industrial planning

National industrial planning represents the maximum output which is attainable by the industry within the limits considered acceptable by the government of the day. This is now generally considered to be an outdated concept, as the prevalent assumption is that government will seek to intervene in the economy only because it is waging a war or because it believes in centralized control and planning, which has not been the case in the UK for many years.

Determinants of capacity

Hillebrandt's (1975) work was a forerunner of NEDO's 1978 report *How Flexible Is Construction?*, and her views on capacity were expanded there. She stressed the necessity of recognizing the importance of time and capacity, in particular the time period over which change is expected to occur. Within this general time context, the four determinants of capacity change highlighted were operatives, materials, management and administrative staff, and fixed assets.

2.4 COMPARATIVE ANALYSIS OF THE CONSTRUCTION INDUSTRY AND GENERAL MANUFACTURING INDUSTRIES

The construction industry can be described by comparing it with 'general manufacturing industries'. These manufacturing industries are a mythical construct, a series of assumptions about how traditional manufacturing industries operate, which provides a contrast to the purportedly individualistic characteristics of construction. It should be stressed that this analysis is purely a broad description of construction industry trends and, as will be seen, not necessarily a completely accurate picture of every detail of the industry. Table 2.3 summarizes the following description.

The construction industry is an extremely important industry to the entire British economy as a major employer, a major contributor to national wealth and national output (GNP and GDP), and the producer of the infrastructure and buildings necessary for others to operate. Traditionally regarded as a labour-intensive and domestic industry, it has been seen as a major user of British materials, workers, finance, and technical and management skills. Much of this has been because of the large size of projects and their physical immobility, but this is increasingly untrue. While the land and property, once built, are quite clearly unmovable, the components (used to construct the property) are transportable, the money which finances construction is extremely portable, labour is flexible and, in the increasingly single world and European markets serviced by highly advanced technology, the choice of location can be an extremely varied decision. Therefore the British construction industry faces competition from countries throughout the world for its building components and materials, for the right to borrow limited finances, to design, build and manage the construction process, and to be able to offer the correct location for prospective businesses. It also, of course, competes in the world market to win orders for construction work. For example, in 1995 £5.5 billion and in 1994 £3.8 billion in new work contracts was won by British firms.

The production of the built environment is unique from both a product and a business perspective. Not only is it large, bulky and immoveable, but it is relatively

Table 2.3 The construction industry: general characteristics compared with general manufacturing industries

- Economic regulator
- Large contributor to GDP and employer
- Capital goods industry, which sells means of production to other industries
- Stock of buildings very large in relation to production of new
- Large role for public/statutory authorities
- Each job large in relation to firm
- Not one industry, but several
- Long time-scale. relatively inelastic to supply and demand in the short term
- Product custom-built
- Product often sold before it is produced
- Division between design and construction
- Poor public image
- Sells the process of construction and not the end-product
- Process of construction is not re-saleable
- Domestic trade
- Self-employment and skilled tradesmen
- Lack of training, research and development
- Weather
- Mass of small firms, through ease of entry into exit from industry
- Archaic management styles
- Backwardness

slow to produce and unimportant compared with the amount of housing, industrial and office stock already in existence. Given that it takes many months (and usually years) to design, gain planning approval, build and sell (or let) a new building, coupled with the fact that it is commonly agreed that only about 1 per cent of total properties are being produced by the industry, it can be seen that the industry cannot respond rapidly to large changes in demand for property.

In other words, the supply of property is fixed in the short term and only marginally adjustable over longer periods; there is said to be an inelastic supply. The product is also often a bespoke product which is paid for before it is completed. Certainly, some property is speculatively developed and sold when completed like every other product from baked beans to cars, but there is a common perception that clients like to be involved in the design and construction of their new buildings, rather than purchase a standard, mass-produced 'off-the-shelf' model. Property is not, then, mass produced, and both the resale of the building and economies of scale are difficult to achieve because of this individual nature of the building, and because of individualized state of the location site and its unique production problems, including ground stability, groundwater, site access and local working restrictions. The weather also plays a role, because the work environment is not controllable, unlike in a factory. Moves to standardize the process have taken place but within the commercial sector have largely been unsuccessful; similarly, attempts have been made to streamline construction, and to use new materials and techniques which minimize physical problems in relation to development, but these have not resulted in large improvements either.

Peculiar business practices include the traditional division between design and construction and the nature of the building firm. The design process is divorced from the construction process within the construction industry, despite a number of attempts to overcome this, including the Tavistock Report, Design-and-build procurement methods, and the Latham Report. The latter is the result of a review of working practices carried out by Sir Michael Latham and published as *Constructing the Team* (1994). The report calls for a reduction in antagonistic working and contractual practices through the implementation of 'partnering' – that is, negotiated arrangements – and a reduction in building costs of 30 per cent. Current practices are thus seen as expensive and argumentative. There are strong legal, cultural and financial barriers between the designer and the builder, which results in an antagonistic relationship between the two and a lack of practical feedback to aid the design process (known as buildability).

Construction firms are relatively small in size, especially when compared with the value of the building work which they undertake. They have little capital of their own, and have a tendency to enter and leave the industry through bankruptcy on a regular basis. This adds to the poor public image of construction firms and the industry as a whole. Most firms have a small number of high-value jobs on their books at any one time, and thus the success of each job is paramount. They usually employ flexible working methods, including the use of hire plant, the self-employed and subcontracting firms. Workers hired for their labour only, and for fixed periods, are known as 'the lump'. There are a few large construction firms and rather more medium-sized firms to whom much of these image problems do not apply, although they also tend to hire their workforce on the lump. The industry has a history of having a highly skilled craft workforce, allowing firms to avoid training expenses and employ workers on the lump. There is, however, an increasing struggle to maintain the supply of skilled workers, and there are worries about skills shortages. Undoubtedly, however, the use of short-term labour has provided the construction industry with an element of flexibility not found in other types of industry.

A major challenge currently facing the construction industry is that presented by PFI, which seeks to let one contractor take responsibility for all the processes of development, including design and build through to eventual management. This initiative places the industry contractors in a very different role from that traditionally undertaken in providing the building at 'Day 1'. Not only do construction firms avoid training costs, but the industry has a poor record in research and development, and in management and professional education. This leads to perceptions of the industry being archaic, using, as it does, old (labour-intensive) technology and out-of-date managerial practices. This led Ball (1988) to posit the 'backwardness thesis', asking whether construction was backward or merely different. He tends to support the latter conclusion, pointing to the acceptable profit levels achieved.

The above discussion is a qualitative discussion, based on perception by the public and the industry itself, and in the literary tradition of Hillebrandt (1988) and Ball (1988) in particular. It is not necessarily true. The Latham Report (1994) called for many changes, based upon the view outlined above, and action is being taken. The Construction Industry Board (CIB) was set up in the wake of Sir Michael Latham's review of the construction industry in order to carry out many of his recommendations. The board provides a focus for all sectors of the construction industry, its clients and government. It has ratified a business plan and will continue to operate until 1999. Working groups created by the CIB are producing codes of practice and guidance notes for the industry on how to make improvements throughout the construction process. The industry, its clients and government have set up a Whole Industry Research Strategy (WIRS) to implement new ideas, and the Technology Foresight Programme (created by a White Paper on *Science, Engineering and Technology*) has also identified opportunities for improvement in construction. Some firms within the industry are already at the forefront of good business practice in quality assurance, IT, business management and profitability, for example. The professional institutions have produced many discussion papers pointing to their future roles in the next century, and in this new property and construction industry. At the same time, old attitudes fade very slowly, and the common perceptions of backwardness, inefficiency and shoddiness provide a basic framework in which to understand the industry.

2.5 CONCLUSION

The construction industry has many unique features compared with other parts of a nation's economy. Certain studies allow a framework to be developed, which ends in a description of these idiosyncrasies. Perhaps surprisingly, although it is old, NEDO's (1978) flexibility analysis is still relatively valid in detail as well as in substance.

A more qualitative description, however, does suggest that change is happening, and that common perceptions about the industry should be questioned. In particular, its alleged domesticity, backwardness and individual nature of production need to be examined carefully.

2.6 SUMMARY
- Property and construction constitute a unique industry, which may be a sign of inefficiency and being out of date, or simply of being different.
- Construction is classified as a discrete division of the general industrial classification. The business of property, however, is included under several different headings.
- Industries need to exhibit flexibility in order to survive in a capitalist free-market system. Evidence drawn from two major surveys supports the view that the industry, as a whole, is flexible. Certain sections within it, however, are considerably inflexible to changes in demand.
- The underlying description of the 1978 NEDO report is still valid, and the case is that the construction industry remains individualistic in its characteristics.

FURTHER READING

Ball, M. (1988) *Rebuilding Construction*, London: Routledge.
—— (1996) *Housing and Construction: A Troubled Relationship*, London: HMSO.
Latham, Sir M. (1995) *Constructing the Team*, London: HMSO.
NEDO (1978) *How Flexible Is Construction?*, London: HMSO.
Turin, D. (ed.) (1975) *Aspects of the Economics of Construction*, London: George Godwin (contains, *inter alia*, Hillebrandt, P. M. (1975) *The capacity of the construction industry*).

EXAMPLE QUESTIONS

Below are questions relating to this chapter. For each chapter model answers have been prepared for some of the questions set; these are found in the Appendix.

2.1. What is property?
2.2. Define the property industry.
2.3. Describe the characteristics of property as a product.
2.4. Distinguish between the two actors in the use and ownership of property.
2.5. How important, nationally, is the construction industry?
2.6. How large a role does the public sector play within the industry?
2.7. 'The construction industry sells the process of construction and not the finished product'. Explain.
2.8. What are the characteristics of the products of the construction process?
2.9. List the resource inputs into the construction process.
2.10. How flexible is construction?
2.11. (a) What is the economic capacity of the construction industry?
      (b) How do we measure it?
      (c) What are its determinants?
2.12. How efficient and stable is the British construction industry?

2.13. 'The inadequate provision of housing at modest cost in contrast with that of, say, automobiles or cosmetics, can be considered the single greatest default of modern capitalism' (Galbraith 1989: p. 290).
'I will make housing the way we make cars' (Le Corbusier, trans.).
Compare and contrast.

3 A brief history of property and construction economic thought

OBJECTIVES

The objectives of this Chapter are to:

- describe the history of economic thought in relation to property and construction;
- analyse the role of the construction industry, the property profession and the built environment within that history;
- help the reader to recognize the importance of the social and political context of economists and their ideal;
- assist the reader to develop an understanding that ideas regarding economic 'truth' are a product of their time;
- draw conclusions for today's economic theories regarding the current positioning of property and construction economic thought.

3.1 INTRODUCTION

The history of economics is an important intellectual area of interest in its own right, but it has other useful functions. History provides the root of modern ideas, the base upon which the present is built. More importantly, the history of economics illustrates how actual economic systems operate, allowing us the benefit of hindsight and the possibility of examining the particular place of property and construction in these economies. Built environments are often the only remaining evidence of civilizations and their economic systems. The passage of time also provides a stable and neutral framework in which to develop an appreciation of the context of real economic situations. In the context of this book, an historical study of economic thought is included to provide an appreciation of how property and construction economics has developed as a discipline.

The importance of the history of economics results from the interconnectedness of the subjects. Economists do not simply appear as esteemed intellectuals providing complete and useful theories. Thinkers and their ideas are a product of their time, in particular the social, economic and political crises and events of their surroundings.

We have to be very careful because our thinking may not be as perfect as we would like to think. Burke warned of the dangers most eloquently when he wrote:

> You know what you know. Fifteenth-century Europeans 'knew' that the sky was made of closed concentric crystal spheres, rotating around a central earth and carrying the stars and planets. That 'knowledge' structured everything they did and thought, because it told them the truth. Then Galileo's telescope changed the truth.
>
> As a result, a hundred years later everybody 'knew' that the universe was open and infinite, working like a giant clock. Architecture, music, literature, science, economics, art, politics – everything – changed, mirroring the new view created by the change in the knowledge.
>
> Today we live according to the latest version of how the universe functions. This view affects our behaviour and thought, just as previous versions affected those who lived with them. Like the people of the past, we disregard phenomena which do not fit our view because they are 'wrong' or outdated. Like our ancestors, we know the real truth.
>
> At any time in the past, people have held a view of the way the universe works which was for them similarly definitive, whether it was based on myths or research. And at any time, that view they held was sooner or later altered by changes in the body of knowledge.
>
> (Burke 1985: 9)

Philosophers have long recognized the importance of society and its attitudes upon thinkers and the creation of ideas. Ideas are not the product of individual brilliance alone, but a product of a myriad of factors, which then mould the ideas. For example, Barnes and Bloor (1988: 21–47) argue that the history of science clearly shows that different scientists drew different conclusions and took the same evidence to point in different directions, despite their supposed identical methodology. They also point to the importance of extra-scientific influences in deciding their actions. These influences include payments and grants, political ideology and religious persecution.

A useful economic example of particular reference is provided by Gaffney and Harrison (1994) in their discussion on the corruption of economics. They argue that economic theories of the late nineteenth century are the product of landowners' desires to defeat the ideas of Henry George. George's ideas will be discussed later, but in essence he envisioned a society much like today's but with considerably lower levels of taxation on both individuals and firms. This, he argued, could be achieved through heavy taxation and nationalization of land, a move obviously detrimental to the owners of land. Thus, they (the landowners and influential people of the day) paid economists to create neoclassical economics, which is the predominant theoretical premise today. To Gaffney and Harrison (1994), then, modern economics is a consequence of Victorian landowners' desires to protect their vested interests, and not a serious intellectual study aimed at producing the most efficient use of economic resources for the general good. This view is contentious and not universally accepted, but it does serve to illustrate that the prevailing economic view of the Western world encompassed in neoclassical economics can be questioned.

3.2 THE BEGINNING OF ECONOMICS

It is simplest to state that economics began with Adam Smith and the publication of *The Wealth of Nations* in 1776. Certainly, Smith is regarded as the father of modern economics, but to assume this date for the beginning of economics would be to ignore 2000 years of human history and the factors that created Adam Smith and his ideas. It is necessary to go back much further, beyond even the Greeks and Romans, who are regarded as the creators of modern civilization, to the dawn of mankind and prehistory. When we study economic history, only written history is effectively being studied, since this provides the only evidence for constructing such a history, but certain factors can be described about the first humans and economics.

Primitive economics

In accepting the concept of economics in its widest context it is necessary to acknowledge the existence of what may be termed primitive economics. Once human beings began to differentiate the processes of carrying out work, the concept of economics was founded. This can be most simply represented in the family unit. Sahlins investigated the 'domestic mode of production' (Sahlins 1988). He referred to a convenient identification of the 'domestic group' with the family. This was a loose and imprecise definition which he used to investigate how traditional societies arranged the economics of the domestic unit. Sahlins portrays such 'stone-age economics' as belonging to a relatively affluent society in terms of both production and consumption.

Smith (1986) regards primitive economics from a different point of view. He uses traditional societies as an example of inefficient methods of working by arguing that a social division of labour is a far more efficient method of working. The division of labour will be examined in more detail later (in section 3.6). However it is worth noting at this stage that Smith is critical of early economic thought for not being rational and for relying upon social frameworks rather than notions of efficiency.

There are still examples of 'simple' economic systems operating in traditional societies. These are, however, becoming very scarce as modern communication methods introduce modern ideas and living standards. Despite Sahlin's (1988) arguments on the levels of affluence of primitive production methods, from what can be gathered through archaeological research life was generally harsh and short. A lot of romanticized discussion about more meaningful means of existence, or 'alternative' lifestyles, occurs but there is little evidence to substantiate the reality of this dream view of traditional societies and economics.

The major period of human existence is covered within this frame of reference. The simplest societies consisted merely of family groups, who collected whatever nature happened to provide for shelter (caves) and food (wild flora and fauna). Gradually, people began to organize, and sought to manage and improve upon nature. Domestication and farming provided a sedentary way of life which replaced hunting and gathering as a more productive technique. Increased production allowed a higher standard of living through increased consumption. It also allowed for specialization and for a social division of labour, the principle upon which modern civilization is founded. Higher production meant certain individuals – priests, thinkers, warriors – could be excused ordinary work altogether; it allowed for experimentation and risk; it allowed a smaller number of people to specialize in carrying out each task and become more productive than before; it allowed time for new business to be introduced; it allowed for leisure time.

Economics, in any complete sense, clearly did not exist in primitive societies. However, decisions about when activities should be carried out, and by whom, needed to be made by some process, and it is this process which can be regarded as the first economics.

Early civilizations

There is essentially little distinction between a primitive society and a civilization. However, when we examine the cultures of Babylon, Sumeria, Assyria, the Hittites and Egypt we can clearly recognize 'civilizations'.

From the viewpoint of economic history, however, detail is difficult to amass. The little information available is often difficult to translate, is not widely available and tends to be concerned with military exploits. It is possible to recognize increasingly centralized national units developing with the expansion of specialization. These national units provide evidence of a number of characteristics that are usually associated with economics. The existence of the state itself as a centre of control is the first example. From this comes the increased existence of trade over large geographical areas and the consequent development of an international market. The creation of money, a basic requisite of modern economics, can also be seen in this period. There are actually two main traditions of coinage, those of ancient Asia Minor and China. The first Western coins did not appear until about 600 BC and were made by the Lydians or Greeks. The concept of specialization was fully recognized and implemented as skilled workers founded cities with markets large enough to guarantee work. The building trades were among the first to develop as self-build was replaced by the employment of builders of varying specialisms, including stonework, carpentry and plumbing. Buildings themselves became a statement of economic prosperity and stability, showing not only a technical ability to build, but also the willingness and ability to pay for it.

Classic economics

The ancient Greeks and Romans are regarded by many as the founders of modern Western culture. In this vein they may also be regarded as important originators of modern economic theories. Arguably the two most important economists of the period were the philosophers Plato (427–347 BC) and Aristotle (384–322 BC). Plato, in his *Republic* and the *Laws,* was primarily interested in creating the ideal society. This model society was presented as an ideal state. The ideas do not particularly incorporate economic theories, instead concentrating particularly upon the social, educational and moral characteristics of this ideal state. Economic ideas are subsumed into the philosophical whole of Plato's republic. The republic is a strong hierarchical structure in which common economics is seen as very much an inferior intellectual area.

Aristotle is also interested in political constitutions and institutions. His ideas followed from those of Plato and in the *Politics* the clearest account of these ideas is found. In examining the formation of the political body, Aristotle places great emphasis on the economic unit of production. As a biologist, Aristotle is interested in the natural order of things. The natural order of things socially and politically is the *polis*, the city. Everything revolves around the fact that the city structure is natural. Just as political life takes place within the city, so does economic life. The city is seen as the most efficient form of economic production. Aristotle sees the city as a self-sufficient state, and foreign policy is seen as guaranteeing this self-sufficiency economically. Therefore the political framework of the *polis* is reflected by this desire for economic power and self-sufficiency. Just as the natural political state is the city or the state, so for human beings on a smaller scale the family is seen as the natural unit. Man is by nature a political animal and needs company. The natural state of this family is thus developed by Aristotle from a biological base, but creates the simplest economic sub-unit for production, the family. The family is seen as the unit through which production is achieved. One example of this is Aristotle's recognition of the concept of property, which 'is part of a household and the acquisition of property part of the economics of a household; for neither life itself nor the good life is possible without a certain minimum standard of wealth' (Aristotle 1962: 31). Property is thus a natural factor of the household, and it is through this property (Aristotle is looking particularly at slaves as property here) that the goods are produced that form the products sold on the market and thus create the economy of the *polis*.

Aristotle is also concerned with classifying types of economic behaviour. Initially this argument evolves around the concept of making money, which he seeks to keep as a completely separate classification from production which results in a profit. Here the social context of Aristotle's writing is clear, because moneymaking was frowned upon by the ancient Greeks. Aristotle's economic classifications are nomadism, agriculture, piracy, fishing and hunting. These classifications are regarded as means by which food for basic subsistence can be created.

In terms of economics, Aristotle's writings are far from complete, and the economic sections of his works are largely used to argue a particular philosophical line of thought. While his ideas are incomplete, the fundamental idea behind Aristotle's writing is that wealth should be sought, but only as a basis for livelihood and not for its own sake. He disapproves of the pursuit of unlimited riches and seeks to distinguish between commercial activity and the management of the household or state. For Aristotle, both household and state are natural, almost biological, bodies and thus they gain the greater part of his attention. Commercial activity remains separate from this. Commercial activity is accepted when it aids the biological growth of the household or state but where it is done merely to gain money is not seen as a good thing. Money is merely a system of exchange and Aristotle is quick to point out that it has no value in itself.

> And it will often happen that a man with plenty of money will not have enough to eat; and what a ridiculous kind of wealth is that which even in abundance will not save you from dying with hunger! It is like the story told of Midas: just because of the inordinate greed of his prayer everything that was set before him was turned to gold. Hence we seek to define wealth and moneymaking in different ways; and we are right in doing so, for they are (different); on the one

hand true wealth, in accordance with nature, belonging to household management, productive; on the other moneymaking, with no place in nature, belonging to trade and not productive of goods in the full sense.'

(Aritstotle 1962: 43)

This is exemplified, for Aristotle, by the concept that value is easily debased.
Those who seek to gain unlimited riches are seen as self-defeating because moneymaking has no limit and therefore getting money can have no end. Economics, for
Aristotle, is thus concerned with household management which has a limit, that
limit being the management of resources for the betterment of everybody within
the household. The household as a biological identity is some form of family
social or political unit. Ultimately it is the *polis*.

Aristotle and Plato, and indeed all Greek writers, were communitarians. Economic life in ancient Greece revolved around this social form. To discuss the
notion of communitarianism in Plato and Aristotle it is necessary to place the idea
in the specific cultural context of the history and philosophy of ancient Greece.
Greek communitarians established public life as the centre of the *polis*. The focus
of human existence was shifted away from the family and towards the community;
hence the magnificent festivals and displays, and the great public buildings for
religious and public purposes. It was surrounded by these buildings, in the *agora*,
that the Greek male spent his time. In contrast, his home was mean and unim-
pressive; it was not safe in a democracy to display a lifestyle different from that of
other citizens, and anyway a man's life was lived in public not in private.

Although it pre-dates the period of Classical Greece by centuries, the influence
of Archaic (or Homeric) Greece cannot be overemphasized. Homeric man lived in
a society of virtually autonomous small social units termed *oikos*, noble households under the leadership of a chieftain. The *oikos* was the largest effective social,
political and economic unit. The chieftain ensured prosperity and was responsible
for defending it in times of war. War was endemic, though generally on a small
scale. Heads of *oikos* could be called to assembly, but each was effectively left to
look after himself.

The psyche of greek society and philosophy is deeply affected by the writings
of Homer and the deeds of Homeric man. Homeric society is a results culture. The
society's highest commendation is reserved for those who can produce the desired
results, and for those qualities in them that appear to be most relevant to their production. Such a person is titled *agathos* and is strong, brave and successful; no
quality is of any use unless it leads to success. Good intentions are of no use in
themselves, they must lead to success. Such admired qualities are *arete*: strength,
bravery and wealth leading to or preserving success. Other qualities, such as justice and self-control, are less highly valued, although a wronged individual sets a
high value on obtaining redress for himself. In effect, the motivation for Homeric
man is concerned with what people will say about his actions, over which he has
no control.

The Greece of Plato and Aristotle had developed away from Homeric society.
The characteristic (and peculiar) element in their political life was the *polis*, the
city-state. Boardman *et al.* describe this as:

a community of citizens (adult males), citizens without political rights (women
and children) and non-citizens (resident foreigners and slaves), a defined body,

occupying a defined area, living under a defined or definable constitution, independent of outside authority to an extent that allowed enough of its members to feel independent. The land at large may have been virtually empty of residents or occupied by farmhouses or villages or even small towns, but there had to be one focal point, religious, political, administrative, around which usually grew up ... a city, the *polis* proper, usually fortified, always offering a market (an *agora*), a place of assembly (often the *agora* itself), a seat of justice and of government.

(Boardman *et al.* 1991: 19)

It is this physical base that allows us the first glimmerings of an understanding of Greek communitarianism; it was essential to the Greeks and provided them with their feeling of community, or belonging. Tied to this is the notion of independence, for however limited it was by treaty or tribute, there was always a sense of autonomy. Thus Greek communitarianism is not based on any notions of widespread democracy, but on the much more authoritarian principle of *polis*, where, at best, only a fraction of citizens were allowed to vote. All Greek action and thought was founded in this social construct.

Greek society was thus complex and dynamic. The Greek city was based upon a network of associations, and it was these that created the sense of community, of belonging. This was the essential feature of the *polis*, communitarianism. It does limit the personal freedom of the individual, but allows freedom within the public sphere. Liberal individualism is non-existent in Greek thought; it is a communism of the elite.

Roman civilization followed that of the Greeks both chronologically and culturally. Much of Roman religion, art, politics and economics was derived from the Greeks. The Romans' major contribution was in scope, in that the Roman Empire occupied almost the entire known world, and was responsible for a degree of economic management never seen before, and scarcely since. Sekunda draws our attention in particular to the complex economics required to maintain such military domination for some 500 years. 'The record which was achieved of maintaining a fully professional army of such a size for so long a period is a phenomenon of social, political and economic history scarcely rivalled by any other society in world history' (Sekunda 1994: 12). Running such a complex empire, albeit a largely decentralized series of semi-independent agricultural areas, must be recognized as a major economic achievement. The raising of revenue through taxation, the development of international trade, mass public road construction, and civic and military building programmes require a high degree of economic expertise. The great circus and gladiator games, perhaps the most evocative features of ancient Rome, are used by Mannix (1973) to describe the inventiveness and sophistication required to run such an economy, and to show how it failed. Mannix describes the state of the Roman economy as follows:

the Roman government was constantly threatened by bankruptcy and no statesman could find a way out of the difficulty. The cost of its gigantic military programme was only one of Rome's headaches. To encourage industry in her various satellite nations, Rome attempted a policy of unrestricted trade, but the Roman working-man was unable to compete with the cheap foreign labour and demanded high tariffs. When the tariffs were passed, the satellite nations were unable to sell their goods to the only nation that had any money. To break the deadlock, the government was finally forced to subsidize the Roman working-class to make up the difference between their 'real wages' (the actual value of what they were producing) and the wages required to keep up their relatively high standard of living.

(Mannix 1973:8)

For Mannix, the Roman economy was thus complete anarchy. The games were used to pacify the population and keep economic problems from the mind of the people, but became a drain as games became larger and lasted longer.

3.3 THE MIDDLE AGES

The Catholic Church dominated economic theory in the Middle Ages through its control of written language and its political use of religion. Practically the only literate people in the period were in religious service, and so the majority of extant written material is religious in itself or written by the Church for others. The Middle Ages were an extremely religious period, a time when a lack of belief or disagreement over religious matters led to excommunication, death and eternal damnation. Even kings dared not oppose the Church.

Economics thus clearly followed the teachings of the Bible and papal decrees precisely. Business was forced to follow these guidelines. In what was basically an agrarian economy operating within a feudal culture, a strict social hierarchy determined by birth, there was little economic dynamism to question or undermine this orthodoxy. Towns and cities were as yet only small, largely defensive, developments. Markets were localized, merchants in their infancy and coinage still not widely used. The majority of construction work was carried out by travelling craftsmen for either the Church or the local overlord. In addition, business success was determined, not by economic sense, but through divine will. Success was a reflection of one's humility and Christian virtues. This was true of all outcomes. Military histories of the period portray defeat as the wrath of God for wrongdoing and victory as divine support for the cause and leader. Strategy, troop numbers and quality, selection of the battlefield site and provisioning are all irrelevant to the outcome compared with the Will of God. Economic theory, similarly, is made both redundant and irrelevant by this divine judgement. Economic success was achieved by operating within the laws laid down by the Church and was guaranteed by God.

As the period progressed, the power of secular interest rose and that of the Church declined. Religion became fragmented and divided, and political rule became more centralized. Economies began to become more complex as urbanization spread, agriculture declined and manufacture increased. Social hierarchies were broken down. Transport infrastructure improved.

Mercantilism

Arising from the social, political and religious upheavals of the declining Middle Ages was a new class, the merchants. They were early capitalists, who bought goods in one area, transported them and sold in a new area, and then reinvested their profits in new merchandise. As economists, they were interested in the mechanics of trade, how prices were arrived at and how to hold value (in the form of gold). As Britain expanded they sought to use the nation's military and naval power to expand and protect their trade.

Mercantilism is the body of theory they developed, and it still has echoes today in its calls for protectionism (of national markets) and preservation of national confidence in the money supply (through accumulation of gold bullion).

3.4 THE SOCIAL CONTRACTUALISTS

Three philosophers of the seventeenth and eighteenth centuries developed social-contract theory. They are Thomas Hobbes (1588–1679), John Locke (1632–1704) and Jean-Jacques Rousseau (1712–78). Their general argument was that society was created (in theory) by a legal contract, and that social relationships were contractual and not based upon morality, loyalty, love, honour or any other factor. They proceeded to describe the mechanisms of a society formed in such a manner.

The historical period in which our three contractual theorists lived could be termed the age of the three revolutions. Each writer has been associated with one of these social upheavals. Hobbes's writing was interrupted by the English Civil War; Locke was heavily involved in the machinations of the 'Glorious Revolution', writing the two *Treatises of Government* (Locke 1990; originally published 1690) to justify the English Revolution of 1688; and Rousseau is frequently cited as a guiding light of the French Revolution.

Thomas Hobbes

Thomas Hobbes's principal work, *Leviathan* (published in 1651), revolves around his concept of the state of nature. All men are by nature equal, according to Hobbes, for even the weakest may find a means by which to kill the strongest, and prudence is merely that which experience teaches us all in its own time. For Hobbes, there are no natural inferiors (slaves) or natural superiors (masters). It is through this natural equality that the individual's freedom from political subjugation within the state of nature is derived. From this equality of ability and freedom comes equality of desire to achieve the same ends; unfortunately, resources to achieve those ends are limited and thus war must be fought by each natural man in order to achieve those ends. The state of nature is a constant state of war because war is a natural event. This leads to an environment Hobbes describes as:

> no place for Industry . . . no Culture of the Earth; no Navigation . . . no commodious Building . . . no Arts; no Letters; no Society; and which is worst of all, continuall feare, and danger of violent death; And the life of man, solitary, poore, nasty, brutish, and short.
>
> (Hobbes 1986: 186)

Hobbes recognizes as a fundamental right of nature the freedom of all men to use their power in whatever way they wish, in order to protect their own life. Laws of nature provide the fundamental rules to prevent man from alienating his own life, but the Hobbesian state of nature is essentially a negative one; it consists of an absence of impediments to any possible actions. Natural man has the right to every thing, even another's body.

Hobbes's view of natural man is thus very clear and very negative. Natural man is a bestial primitive, and a poor relation of modern social man. This model, however, is necessary to enable Hobbes to construct his *Leviathan* logically. He sees the need of a 'Power' to keep natural man from war, the contract being the social method of achieving this. The social contract saves natural man from his nasty and brutish existence, and thus Hobbes's social contract depends upon the acceptance of his view of the state of nature.

Scarcity is the primary system of allocation in Hobbes's state of nature, and economics becomes a simple survival of the fittest. The view that men are driven in their actions by the scarceness of their resources is a particular one, and one that seems to be at odds with the reality of that which occurred in early societies. A social contract arises because men enter into a 'contract' for the security of civil society, each giving up equal amounts of freedom from their natural rights, and each receiving equal rights under the contract. It is an essential part of Hobbes's radical individualism that everyone is equal in the state of nature. Hobbes clearly states this:

> Nature hath made men so equall, in the faculties of body, and mind; as that though there bee found one man sometimes manifestly stronger in body, or of quicker mind than another; yet when all is reckoned together, the difference between man, and man, is not so considerable, as that one man can thereupon claim to himselfe any benefit, to which another may not pretend, as well as he.
> (Hobbes 1986: 183)

Hobbes examines the creation of the social contract in some detail. Natural man has almost unrestricted freedom, but all men may transfer their rights, thus forming a 'contract'. This is an attempt to obey the fundamental law of nature, that every man ought to attempt peace and is consistent with the second law, that a man be willing to lay down his right to all things if others equally respect this. Only in this way can peace be maintained.

John Locke

Locke begins his first treatise with an examination of the arguments of the patriarchalists whose ideas stem from the argument that men have always had power since God gave it to Adam. Locke clearly defines the powers given to Adam, and thus to all men as his descendants, in his description of this 'fatherly authority':

> Law is nothing else but the will of him that hath the power of the supreme father. It was God's ordinance that supremacy should be unlimited in Adam, and as large as all the acts of his will; and as in him, so in all others that have supreme power. . . . This 'fatherly authority,' then, or 'right of fatherhood,' in our Author's sense is a Divine, unalterable right of sovereignty, whereby a father or prince hath an absolute, arbitrary, unlimited, and unlimitable power over the lives, liberties, and estates of his children or subjects, so that he may

take or alienate their estates, sell, castrate, or use their persons as he pleases – they being all his slaves, and he lord and proprietor of everything, and his unbounded will their law.

(Locke 1911: 8–9)

Locke is, however, profoundly critical of this line of argument. The power granted to men, according to the patriarchalists, is unbounded, as was seen above. The premise for this argument, Locke shows, is based upon the Bible's commentary upon the Fall, and, since this is Adam's fall as much as Eve's, would it be feasible to assume that God would then give such total power to Adam and all men in such circumstances? Locke clearly thinks not. Like Hobbes, Locke considers his notions of civil society in comparison with a state of nature. Women and men in the state of nature are 'all equal and independent' (Locke 1911: 119) since they are all made by God.

An individual's relationship to property facilitates his/her capacity for active political participation. Locke, however, also contends that although God gave the earth in common he intended it for the use of the 'industrious and rational' (Locke 1911), who appropriate it by their labour. The introduction of money allows the most industrious to hoard. In so doing some are able to accumulate limited resources, while others must sell their labour in exchange for their subsistence. Property is also a route to, and a sign of, one's rationality. The use one puts one's property to manifests the direction and industriousness of one's chosen path. Locke clearly denies labourers rationality (and hence an active role in the state) because of their lack of estate; they have not the time to raise their thoughts above the monotonous routine of survival. Locke's economic contribution is related to ownership; ownership of property and savings allows humans to be fully socialized and intellectual beings. This economic process is thus seen to be integral to creating civilized human beings.

Jean-Jacques Rousseau

Rousseau is also concerned with the state of nature as a precursor to modern civil society, although he is critical of those states developed by both Hobbes and Locke. His is a more sympathetic model. He begins his second discourse, *On the Origin of Inequality* (Rousseau 1986; original published 1755), with a distinction between two types of human inequality: natural and moral (political). In the state of nature only the first is present. Rousseau's natural savage is solely individual and truly pre-social. Natural man lived as an individual, without home or property, living from moment to moment with no thought of the future. He is a superior species: rugged and fit, suffering little sickness, and with a remarkable capacity for healing and recovery.

The human being is endowed with a well-developed faculty for self-improvement and a natural inclination to learn new skills, which encourage cooperation and the formation of communities. This leads to the development of a civil society. Civil society is necessary to establish order, but the rationality and benefits of this agreement are not universal. For Rousseau, it is a cunning device fabricated by the rich to institutionalize their power over the poor, and thus is natural liberty lost to, and corrupted by, civic servitude. In *The Social Contract* (originally published in 1762), Rousseau begins by reasserting this premise, and by further examining the change wrought on natural man by the socialization process of civic life.

> We no longer dare seem what we really are, but lie under a perpetual restrain; in the meantime the herd of men, which we call society, all act under the same circumstances exactly alike, unless very particular and powerful motives prevent them. Thus we never know with whom we have to deal; and even to know our friends we must wait for some critical and pressing occasion; that is, till it is too late; for it is on those very occasions that such knowledge is of use to us. ... Sincere friendship, real esteem, and perfect confidence are banished from among men. Jealousy, suspicion, fear, coldness, reserve, hate, and fraud lie constantly concealed under that uniform and deceitful veil of politeness.
>
> (Rousseau 1986: 6–7)

The Social Contract itself is a solution to this state of affairs: a 'good' agreement facilitates a moral equality that will transcend the disadvantages of civil society. It revolves upon the notion of the General Will, although this may not be the simple will of the majority. Public good and public interest are more than a mere aggregation of all private interests, and are thus dependent upon a transformation of human nature into one of enlightened self-mastery. This enlightenment of the corrupt individuals of *The Second Discourse* (Rousseau 1986; originally published in 1762) can be achieved only by the external involvement of a Legislator (Law Giver). His *Emile* (1991; originally published in 1762) also shows that correct education can save the individual from corruption. For Rousseau, economics can be either a means of promoting the good of the General Will or a means by which the powerful become corrupt and selfish.

3.5 THE PHYSIOCRATS

François Quesnay and the physiocrats are of importance to economics since they developed the first formal economic model as a description of the mechanics of a national economy: the *tableau économique*. The model was based upon Quesnay's experience as a physician, and followed a similar construction to the flow of blood in the human body. Quesnay's model is also likely to have been an influence on Smith.

3.6 ADAM SMITH

Adam Smith is regarded as the father of modern economics. He wrote the *Wealth of Nations*, regarded as the first economics book, in 1776. Although it has been argued that economics begins with Smith, most modern writers regard those before him as irrelevant. This is unfair, but most of the theories from this point will not be in this chapter on history, but in the subsequent chapters on practical theory.

Smith argued that an economy runs on self-interest. We are all selfish. The market translates selfish action into results which serve the common interest. He presents many examples of how producers provide goods to customers, not for charity, but in trade for goods which they cannot produce. Thus the butcher provides meat to customers in order to purchase eggs, milk and other items from these customers. Smith presents his market as a simple barter system within a small village. This is partially because of the time in which he was writing, but also to present the argument clearly.

Smith is often a contradictory author. This is because he was the first real capitalist economist. It is often said that he supported capitalism yet disliked capitalists. He was clearly in favour of a market without constraint. He also demanded efficient production methods, most notably the division of labour, whereby work is divided into simple repetitive tasks. At the same time, he was aware of the social problems associated with capitalism, particularly unemployment caused by the use of more efficient employment practices and the drudgery of work which has been deskilled under the division of labour.

The division of labour aims to create a more efficient work process. It does this by splitting a job of work into a number of simple, repetitive tasks. Those doing these tasks become more specialist, and thus more efficient at completing the task. Output rises as a result, which in turn provides the impetus for further task fragmentation and specialism – but with each task becoming, of itself, less skilled. This process, known as deskilling, is the primary drawback of the system; a complete, skilled job is transformed into a series of mundane, boring repetitive tasks. The social division of labour occurs when there is a simple rearrangement of the job of work; a technical division of labour occurs where this reorganization is determined by the introduction of machinery or new technology.

3.7 THE CLASSICAL SCHOOL

Adam Smith's ideas developed into the classical school of economics as the study of macro-economics theory was continued. The primary motive of the school was to extol the virtues of capitalism over competing economic practices, and to investigate and describe the workings of the new system. It tends to express what today would be regarded as very rigid views on the poor of the capitalist system. Poverty is seen very much as a result of low morals and laziness. Significant classical economists were Thomas Malthus, David Ricardo, John Stuart Mill and Karl Marx.

Thomas Malthus

Malthus was concerned about a number of economic problems facing the classical school, but is primarily remembered for his *Principles of Population* (Malthus 1973; originally published in 1803). It was his assertion that population growth has a tendency to outstrip the ability to create the resources to feed it. According to Malthus, population growth rate is a geometric progression (1–2–4–8–16–32–64), while resources increase at an arithmetic rate (1–2–4–6–8–10). Malthus's solution, as a church minister, was to encourage marriage and sexual abstinence in order to avoid massive overpopulation and starvation.

David Ricardo

David Ricardo's theory of rent provided an enormous contribution to the foundations on which much current theory of valuation practice is based. Ricardo was
interested in the relationship between costs and values. In looking at the factors of
production–land, labour and capital–he noted that analysis of costs *into* production
did not reflect the ways in which the rewards for the output were distributed. So
capital costs into production might be low but result in high reward. From his studies has come a development of the way in which rent could be determined for land.
Under his thesis the economic rent that a tenant could pay for the right to farm land
was connected to its productive capacity. Rent essentially is a residual element; as
more improvements to land take place, so the rental capacity increases. However,
Ricardo's theories ignore two major factors affecting values. First, Ricardo was
dealing with land in agricultural use only. Taking the theory and applying it to land
put to secondary (industrial) or tertiary (service-sector) uses presents new and different constraints – principally those connected with planning and consents. Second, Ricardo was concerned with interrelations between factors of production and
variations in input; he was not concerned with the prospect of competing uses or
users for the land. Thus the distorting effects of level of demand as a determinant
of value did not form a principal part of his theorizing.

Although from the perspective of the late twentieth century the theories of
Ricardo seem very removed from the major concerns of property professionals,
for whom the prevailing theoretical preoccupation is with market economics, the
work of Ricardo is still important on two grounds:

- The valuation of some types of property is derived not strictly from market-
  economic principles but from the notion of individual profitability in the hands
  of an operator, thus calling down on Ricardo's thinking.
- His works were influential in shaping the views of economists who were working at the same time or later, principally Marshall, whose work marks the move
  to the neoclassical school.

John Stuart Mill

J. S. Mill was the author of arguably the first economics textbook, his *Principles
of Political Economy*. He recognized a brutal unfairness in the classical system,
but appealed for patience and hope, since it would improve in time and capitalists
would become more benign. He also reaffirmed the principle of utilitarianism.
This identifies utility as that property of any object which causes happiness.

Karl Marx

Marx is both an economist of the classical school and an enemy of the classical
school. Methodologically, he adopts much of their philosophy, but he is an advocate of revolutionary socialism. In order to overthrow the system, however, he
must understand it. Marx argues that capitalists have a primary need to keep wages
down in order to maximize profit which they seek to retain. They cannot, however,
spend this excess because they are forced both by competition and by greed to
reinvest and strive with each other to raise the productivity of labour. Marx sees

the capitalist world (of nineteenth-century Europe) as one of grim poverty and sides with the workers to overthrow the system. He regards capitalism as flawed, and believes it contains the seeds of its own destruction since its economic rules are unfavourable to the masses of the working class. Marx is merely working to hasten this revolutionary change.

For Marx, social justice is a palliative. In his view, the abolition of private property through common ownership of the means of production, distribution and exchange is the only means of achieving justice.

3.8 THE NEOCLASSICAL SCHOOL

The neoclassical school established the real acceptance within Western economies of capitalism and market principles, and it sought both to explain its evolving characteristics and to defend it from its opponents. Arthur Marshall's (1920) work is a clear example of a strong defence of capitalism. He seeks to make capitalism acceptable by showing it in an agreeable light. Profit is portrayed as the reward for waiting to spend one's money, and the normal rate of profit is equal to the supply price of capital (the interest rate). The real costs of production are seen as being the efforts of the worker (rewarded by a wage) plus the sacrifice of the capitalist (rewarded by profit). Marshall sees the blossoming of peace and prosperity as all classes benefit from the implementation of these economic rules which produce the greatest possible total wealth. He does recognize certain blemishes within the system but argues that if everyone accepts this system, everyone will benefit.

Some argue that the strength of Marshall's convictions and the way they were expressed lacked rigour and were complacent. Some were Marxists, but other critiques were developed. Thorstein Veblen was profoundly critical of any system that placed monetary value above any other source of value, and ridiculed the so-called gaudy ostentation of the rich. Joseph Schumpeter was rather more theoretically critical. He disliked the rigidity of neoclassical theory. Capitalism, for him, is a dynamic and vibrant system which cannot be described by the static, fixed models of Marshall and his compatriots. Another critique was prepared by Henry George, who championed social justice and economic efficiency. He argued that this could be achieved by raising public revenue from the natural resource of land. Taxes on income could be abolished by taxing land.

George argued that land was distinct from capital, following the lead of the classical economists, who recognized the three basic factors of production as land, labour and capital, that each was necessary for economic activity and that they formed a coherent system. Land was different, as George looked to a sympathetic traditional relationship between human beings and land, and also to the simple fact that land is naturally occurring, is not manufactured and is not owned by economic distribution. Property rights in land originate in its initial distribution by military, legal and political factors. George's economics offers much: social justice, economic efficiency, a well-funded state and no income tax. His proponents argue that his economics were defeated politically by neoclassical economists funded by worried landowners to overwhelm his argument by a mass of counter-argument through publication, education and bribery. Certainly, even today his theories offer a non-socialist alternative to modern capitalism, and an appealing alternative for property professionals who know the value of land and the development uses possible on it, and who would thus play a major role in the practical mechanics of implementing Georgist policies. However, at the time he was writing, his views found little support and they have not been revived in any serious way since. Modern economists have tended to follow in the mould of the market economics propounded by Marshall and his followers.

3.9 THE KEYNESIAN REVOLUTION

Keynes provides a defence of capitalism but one tempered by his recognition of the failings of the free market system. His aim was to examine economic theories in order to devise a means to save it from destroying itself. Keynes saw poverty in the midst of plenty, caused by fundamental defects in the capitalist system. These problems were, in his opinion, capable of solution.

Keynes highlights the difference between saving (refraining from consumption) and investing (increasing the stock of productive capital). Both are forms of accumulation, but they may not be connected. Saving involves spending less on consumption, reduces market sizes and profitability of investment. Investment involves employing extra labour to produce extra goods. The very nature of private enterprises causes them to get out of gear. Investment tends to be too low and is therefore wasteful of resources by causing unemployment. Economic rules need to be amended to ensure that wealth continues to grow. Keynes was thus against waste, short-term stupidity and unnecessary profit. Keynes's rules are, however, only concerned with obtaining the extra production, and not with distributing it. The connection between savings and investments and the consequences of money flowing into one rather than the other are examined in greater detail in Chapter 8.

3.10 MODERN ECONOMICS

In the last twenty years, the most commonly held economic belief has been adherence to the principles of 'the market'. This **economic determinism** relinquishes all responsibilities to the adjudication of the market, which in its most pure form would be the sole forum for issues to do with the distribution of scarce resources. In particular, if a totally free-market economy were to prevail, issues of morality, social justice and ethics would tend to be excluded because they are seen as subjective illusions without useful substance. Since the outcomes of the market, whatever their perceived degree of inequality, cannot be foreseen or predicted, they cannot be subjected to a moral critique. The reliance on a market system that excludes such individual moral opinion leads to much of the discussion and criticism that currently occurs in the field of economics. The argument revolves around whether economists can be allowed to ignore social and ethical consequences or whether they can be allowed to impose such factors upon an economic system; in short, whether wider social considerations must take priority in resource allocation, thus requiring some intervention in the operation of the market. Thus, as was outlined in Chapter 1, issues such as the running of the health service (should it be on a needs or demand basis?) and the finance of prisons (using public or private money) are concerns of both the political and the economic debate. The difficulty is in separating out political stance from economic.

When studying economic theory, learning is in the context of ideologies. All economic theories contain political judgement and make decisions about which issues are important and which are not. Economists must be careful not to select theories purely on the basis of political ideology, and not to be misled by the propaganda which shrouds the actual ideas. For example, Karl Marx is often treated as either an oracle or the butt of cheap jokes, *without actual regard to his written work*. Common parlance associates Marx only with communism, yet he was one of the most profound economists of his day and his theories have influenced all serious economists since – whether or not they concur with his political views.

When talking about modern economic theory, the problem of prejudging ideas is more severe because it is impossible to have the benefit of hindsight and the political viewpoint behind the theory may be very difficult to isolate.

Milton Friedman

Modern theories of the market are typically associated with Milton Friedman's *Monetarism* and his attack on state regulation and Keynesian economics. Friedman concentrated on macro-economic theorizing and in particular advocated the use of control of the money supply as a means of economic control, rather than the use of direct interventionist techniques such as legislative interferences with, for example, the housing market (through rent control) or by planning law (to control land uses). Politically, Margaret Thatcher and Ronald Reagan are regarded as the ones who introduced this theory into reality. Both sought to reduce direct control of the economy and encouraged the use of monetarism to stimulate economic performance.

Monetarism depends on tight central control over the supply of money, and relies on the removal of the state from the provision of public services and its replacement by the private sector. The measures taken to implement monetarist policy which concern property and construction include the privatization of assets (see Chapter 2 for the relationship with the construction industry) and the freeing of financial money flows (see Chapter 7).

Social and environmental economics

Alternatively to the monetarist views, the ideas of the social contractualists have been renewed in an effort to accommodate the continued existence of the market with the concept of social justice. Contract replaces community by accepting the natural inequalities of the market and seeking methods to ameliorate them. This contract creates individual rights for just and fair treatment, but also creates obligations, particularly to future generations.

Another major field of economics, which is also concerned with responsibility to future generations, is environmental economics. Environmental economics offers a critique of most other schools of economic thought, but has a particular focus on neoclassical theories as the dominant ones. The basic premise of environmental economics is concern for the natural world, and a demand that it be valued in its own right and not merely as a consumable resource. It adds a warning to its argument, that the very planet is in danger if action is not undertaken immediately.

E.F. Schumacher

Schumacher (1974) is usually regarded as the foundation for the movement in his arguments for appropriate technology, sustainable development and small firms. He demands the use of a technology which is appropriate for the country in which it is operated, a sensible planning of resource use to aid its conservation and the reduction in size of firms to enable them to be run flexibly rather than as faceless, uncaring bureaucratic units. The emphasis of environmental economics is on 'Mother Earth' or 'Spaceship Earth' as a finite living space, not as an infinite rubbish dump. Within property and construction there is a fundamental contradiction between environmental economics and construction, in that by its very nature construction is concerned with the transformation of a natural environment into a built environment. Debate is then possible only on reducing and recycling consumption of materials, otherwise the profession would be redundant.

Beyond market economics?

It is conceivable that a 'New Age' of economics has dawned as people are increasingly replaced by computers. The primary reason behind this is the predictability of computers operating through machine code as their reaction can be guaranteed by knowledge of their programming. People are not so predictable. Program trading in international markets thus becomes a 'global casino' run by computer and creates an increasingly computerized single world market in all commodities. This also changes traditional definitions of money, the symbol of value. Now, money is computer money, a series of electrons flowing down a copper wire or light flashing down a cable. Money is the computer message; it is information.

Finally, two semi-fantasy models of economics must be examined. The first is **anarchy**, an anarchy caused traditionally by atomic and/or bacteriological annihilation from a third world war, or, more fancifully, invaders from outer space. Today, it is thought most likely to be caused by environmental collapse. Much literature and cinema has been produced on this subject. The primary result of such a disaster is the collapse of central government and, with it, law and order. Rape and pillage follow as people begin to degenerate into barbarians. Martial law is declared by the military, until it too falls apart. Extermination of populations is authorized in an attempt to control epidemics or starvation. Out of this mess arise the survivors. Fighting for scarce resources (food) and sheltering in vacant buildings, groups of people band together for defence. Economics is about survival. The cities are now redundant, and these people drift out into the country in order to establish farming communities where they can grow their own food and create a defendable space. Civilization thus begins again.

The second mythical model is the opposite, and is portrayed as domination by a centralized state, or **big brother**. Academically, Burnham's *Managerial Revolution* and, fictionally, Huxley's *Brave New World* and Orwell's *1984* provide typical examples. Influenced by the efficiency and regulation of Nazi Germany and Stalin's Communist USSR, the future can be portrayed as an increasingly centrally controlled, bureaucratic and impersonal nation-state. This is typically represented by an austere, repetitious and dominating built environment. Here economics is about control – whether such control is exercised at the level of the nation-state or of a larger unit.

3.11 CONCLUSION

Economics is not the product of modern societies, and some most profoundly argued ideas have their roots in ancient history. Certainly, Adam Smith's *Wealth of Nations* provided a new and increasingly rational perspective on economic theory, but it was not the first. Economics, however defined, was needed by the earliest human groupings to enable them to ascertain needs and wants, and seek efficient methods of satisfying them.

Throughout the history of economics, the construction industry and property people have served as the providers of means of production, and as consumers of surplus to provide built environments.

3.12 SUMMARY
- Economics has existed since human beings grouped together and had to make decisions about production and consumption of food and shelter.
- Modern economic thought can be said to begin with Adam Smith.
- Property, and the creation of buildings, has always been a major part of economics.
- Economics has historically fallen into two major categories: those in favour of capitalism and those against capitalism. More recently in Western Europe the notion of capitalism has not been seriously questioned.
- Economic theories are affected by the time period in which they were devised. Economic ideas do not simply materialize.
- Table 3.1 summarizes the chronology of the history of economics.

Table 3.1 A history of economics

1	Prehistory	
2	Early civilizations	
3	Ancient Greeks/Romans	
4	The Middle Ages	
5	Mercantilism	
6	The social contractualists	Thomas Hobbes
		John Locke
		Jean-Jacques Rousseau
7	The physiocrats	Francois Quesnay
8	Adam Smith	
9	The classical school	David Ricardo
		Thomas Malthus
10	The classical school divided	Karl Marx
11	The neoclassical school	Alfred Marshall
12	Against the status quo	Henry George
		Thorstein Veblen
		Joseph Schumpeter
13	Keynesian 'revolution'	John Maynard Keynes
14	Modern economics	Milton Friedman
		E. F. Schumacher
15	Beyond the modern	Environmentalism

FURTHER READING

Barber, W. J. (1967) *A History of Economic Thought*, Harmondsworth: Pelican.

Clarke, L. (1992) *Building Capitalism*, London: Routledge.

Colander, D. and Coates, W. (eds) (1993) *The Spread of Economic Ideas*, Cambridge: Cambridge University Press.

Galbraith, J. K. (1989) *A History of Economics*, Harmondsworth: Penguin.

Routh, G. (1989) *The Origin of Economic Ideas*, Basingstoke: Macmillan.

Smith, A. (1986) *The Wealth of Nations*, London: Penguin.

EXAMPLE QUESTIONS

Below are questions relating to this chapter. For each chapter model answers have been prepared for some of the questions set; these are found in the Appendix.

3.1 'Economics began with Adam Smith,' Is this true?

3.2 Assess the 'schools of thought' and their relationship to capitalism.

3.3 Given that Marx seeks to understand 'the system' in order to overthrow it, examine the contribution of Marx to our understanding of economics.

3.4 'Alfred Marshall provides a complacent defence of capitalism; John Maynard Keynes provides a disillusioned defence.' Discuss.

3.5 Who are the current icons in economics?

3.6 How relevant is all of this history to construction and property economics?

3.7 Describe and explain what you regard as the major strands of construction economic thought that have developed since the writings of Adam Smith.

4 The theory of the market and its application to construction and property

OBJECTIVES

The objectives of this chapter are to:

- define a market in economic terms, and examine the different categories of market;
- examine how the theory of the market operates in relation to price determination for a good or service;
- analyse how applicable such theories are to construction goods and property services;
- examine in detail the special characteristics of the property market and compare these with the economic model of the market.

4.1 MARKET TYPES

At its simplest, a market is the geographical location where buyers meet sellers. At the time of Adam Smith the market perhaps still existed in that form. Today markets are so vast and complex that it is impossible for such a single place to exist. However, economists think of the market existing in such a form through modern mass communication and computer technology; the market is a virtual market. Some markets are fixed places – such as a retail market in a town centre – but they are really only subsets of larger markets, for example for the national total of retail goods. With the influence of global integration the retail market can in fact be considered not just on a national level but internationally.

Markets may also be very fragmented; for example, the market for houses is split between new and second hand, and between property type (flat, house, bungalow), location and price. Between these markets there is some interaction – for example, someone looking for a house may eventually buy a bungalow – but they are also differentiated.

A market is defined by the number of buyers and sellers operating in it. The following market types are commonly recognized by economists:

- **monopoly**, where there is one seller;
- **monopsony**, where there is one buyer;

- **duopoly**, where there are two sellers;
- **oligopoly**, where there are a few sellers;
- **monopolistic competition**, where there are a number of sellers;
- **perfect competition**, where there are so many sellers and buyers that no single participant can materially affect the operation of the market.

4.2 THE MARKET PRICE

In order to understand how prices are set it is necessary to consider the neoclassical-school concept of supply and demand, and to expand the ideas set out in Chapter 1.

Prices are calculated by considering the supply and demand possibilities for a **single** good at a **specific** time. Each supply-and-demand curve considers all possible production outcomes for only this one period of time, and any changes mean that a new graph must be drawn. The lines are usually curved because this better represents the mathematical relationship of supply and demand, and price and quantity, at the extremes of production possibilities. However, straight lines are simpler.

A supply-and-demand graph has 'price' on the vertical axis and 'quantity' on the horizontal axis. A demand curve is drawn to show consumer behaviour in the market and a supply curve to map out supply decisions of the firm. These are intended amounts of demand and supply, what people will buy or sell at various prices. Figure 4.1 shows a simple representation of this. In this case the price at which goods will be sold will be at price P1, because intended supply is equal to intended demand. Q1 is then the realized demand and is also the realized supply, as manufacturers will produce Q1 amount of goods and consumers will buy Q1 amount of goods. The price is always at this equilibrium, where supply equals demand, so that everything that is produced is bought.

In creating a supply and demand graph, there is an implicit assumption that perfect competition exists. This model is accepted by most commentators and thus

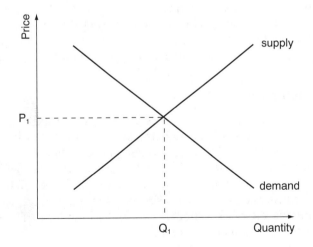

Figure 4.1 Supply and demand

implicitly there is the expectation that the property and construction industries operate under perfect competition. This contention is now examined.

4.3 THE NEOCLASSICAL ECONOMIC MODEL OF PERFECT COMPETITION

Neo-classical positive economics describes the linkages and relationships of a system of economic variables and units which are in general equilibrium. These units are individuals, firms and countries. These variables feed, either directly or indirectly, into each other. They continuously adjust until their values are mutually compatible. There is then no further impulse for adjustment as a steady state will have been reached. In the real world of growth and continuous change this equilibrium may never be reached, but economists hold that the system is always tending towards it and that the operation of the free market, unconstrained by government interference, will result in the optimum allocations to ensure economic efficiency.

There is a mechanism by which this general equilibrium of apparently independently moving variables is reached. The term for this mechanism, which describes the adjustment process of the economy, is the theory of perfect competition. This theory consists in the assumptions about the way this adjustment occurs. All these assumptions are necessary in order for the system to work as this theory suggests. The assumptions are:

- multiplicity of separate economic actors;
- homogeneity;
- perfect knowledge and economic rationality;
- no barriers to entry;
- marginal adjustments.

Each will be considered below in relation to construction and property. In the sections which follow we will examine each of the assumptions necessary for the perfect-competition hypothesis to operate and in turn raise objections to the ability of the markets in the UK to experience perfect competition. Later in the chapter we will re-examine the notion of a perfectly competitive market in relation to the particular characteristics of the land and property markets.

Assumption 1: multiplicity

A multiplicity of separate economic actors is assumed to exist. Each actor is insignificant in relation to the aggregate being studied. A mass of individual consumers must be added together to make up aggregate demand. All of these actors have to act independently of one another, and in the knowledge that, alone, they cannot influence directly the economic conditions in which they find themselves. Thus all prices, for instance, have to be taken as given in the short term, although they are adjustable via the market mechanism in the long term. The result of all these actors responding separately to a certain price may be such that the aggregate level of demand is changed, and therefore price or output changes, but the individuals cannot know this, nor can they predict or plan it. For perfect competition to exist it is not enough that those who demand the product cannot affect its price in the short term; it is essential also that the suppliers are sufficiently numerous that they must, on entering the market, take the price as given. Their individual contribution to competition must thus be insufficient to have any impact on price in the short run.

It is often argued that the stock market is an example of a market acting under the conditions of perfect competition, for in this market there are indeed many participants and knowledge of prices which adjust in relation to supply and demand in a continuous process.

Reality

For consumers, the assumption of independence is invalidated by advertising, so that firms do not have to take demand as given, but can work to affect its level, form and composition.

Despite the break-up of the large publicly owned utilities into smaller private-sector companies, many goods and services are supplied by an increasingly dominant handful of large firms, which together produce the bulk of a given industry's output. A good example of this has been the development of the massive food retail chains, where the 'big five' dominate the sale of food in the UK in a way which is in great contrast from the predominance of small grocers in the past. This is called oligopoly. The level of such concentration in any particular industry may vary, but will still not conform with the assumption of multiplicity. Such firms are not helpless, and they are not faced with a given set of conditions to which they can only blindly react. They have autonomy, the ability to pursue strategies and to manipulate their environment. Thus their response to any given change will not tacitly follow the path which the theory describes; nor can their reactions be predicted with the degree of confidence that the theory assumes.

Within the construction industry a number of such oligopolies exist, particularly in the materials-production sector and those firms able to construct large mega-projects. In commercial property the influence of certain categories of investor (the institutions) may significantly affect market operation. If the institutions decide they no longer wish to invest in (buy) certain categories of building, then demand is significantly affected. (Detailed illustrations of this phenomenon are developed by Dubben and Sayce 1991; Fraser 1993; Scott 1996.)

Assumption 2: homogeneity

The assumption is that, for perfect competition to exist, the products in the market must be homogeneous: that produced by each manufacturer is identical to that produced by the next. For the purposes of aggregation of individual units it is necessary to know that one is adding like to like, otherwise one gets not an 'aggregate' but merely a 'mixture', not all parts of which can be assumed to react in the same way or to cause the same responses in others.

Reality

There are few examples where homogeneity can truly be claimed. Certainly one shareholding in a company is identical to another shareholding in the same company – one loaf of bread may be much like the next (though even that is debatable). However, for most goods and services there is differentiation of product, and indeed this is precisely what producers advertise; they will seek to identify their product as dissimilar to that of their competitors, thus ensuring that they can likewise differentiate on, for example, price.

Within the construction and property fields it is even harder to substantiate any claims to homogeneity. Building firms are heterogeneous in type, form and size, and therefore likely to respond differently to the same set of circumstances. The products of the industry are not homogeneous. Even within the same broad type of product (say, housing), not all houses are similar, or substitutes for one another, as far as consumers are concerned. In particular, any product of the industry is fixed in space: a house in Lancashire is not a good substitute for – that is, the same thing as – a house in Surrey.

Much building output is also produced for custom-built or bespoke markets. Such buildings are built as 'one-offs' for individual clients. There is no repetition, no mass production and there is often secrecy over production methods. To some extent, **techniques** in building can be repeated, and firms can learn from their mistakes, but there is a limit to this.

Each of these markets constitutes a little subsystem of its own. Each has to be in equilibrium for the whole economic system to be. Below we consider in more detail the characteristic of land and property markets as offering an example of a market in which heterogeneity is most pronounced.

Assumption 3: perfect knowledge and economic rationality

All economic actors are supposed to have the same single objective. This objective is the maximization of their utilities and the achievement of the maximum possible degree of satisfaction of their economic wants. For consumers, this means that each starts off with a different 'structure of preferences'. These are decided by the individual's circumstances and taste. Consumers then pursue a rational strategy so that, given their resources, they satisfy these preferences to the greatest extent possible.

For producers, it means that each is a profit-maximizer and that all decisions are aimed at maximizing the profit gained from their business. Financial return, tempered only by notions of risk, is the only legitimate objective for economic rationality. In order to be assured that they do maximize their profit (or return) both producers and purchasers must be assumed to have perfect knowledge of what other products are available and of the level of demand.

Reality

In order for this assumption to hold, all parties to the proposed transaction require perfect knowledge of the options available to them. They need to know the price, availability and utility of every commodity on the market. Prospective purchasers (consumers) need to know their own minds – exactly how much more they prefer two apples to one banana, a car to a convenient railway station, a garden to an extra bedroom, a Pulp CD to an Oasis CD, etc., ad infinitum. Moreover, all possible combinations of these characteristics are assumed to be available, at some price or other. This assumption is quite simply unrealistic. While the large investor may have very clearly defined objectives and know precisely what strategy it will adopt towards buying, for most people the decision process is tempered by many other things, from fashion and taste to the availability of finance to make a purchase.

Similarly, firms are supposed to know the price they can get for their output because this is assumed to be 'given' by the market. They must also know their costs both for each level of output and for each possible product. Only then can they decide on their optimal output. However, as already noted, many firms can affect the pricing structure of a product from 'day one' of entering the market. In other cases the level of price is not purely the result of interaction between supply and demand, for government intervention does take place. For example, in the recent past the government has had a social objective of increasing levels of home ownership; thus it used tax incentives in the form of relief against mortgage repayments to increase the demand for houses. As no tax relief was available against rental payments this had an impact not only on demand but also on the comparative levels of rent/purchase prices that people could afford. More recently government has reduced the tax-relief element, and this was a contributing factor to the decline in house prices experienced over the early years of the 1990s.

Lastly, for perfect knowledge and perfect competition to exist each actor must know the future, since decisions made now have ramifications later in time. The future is, of course, unknowable, and although the last decade has seen the rapid growth in development of forecasting techniques, the results have not led the authors to believe that the future is yet predictable.

Assumption 4: no barriers to entry

This assumption states simply that there are no barriers and that any firm can thus swiftly and without significant costs change the market within which it operates. The position for new business is that it can start up and compete alongside existing businesses immediately and 'on a level playing field'. Each firm is thus able to move easily between markets and industries to take advantages of any changes in consumer preferences. Differences in rates of profit are thus eliminated in the long run because entrepreneurs can shift production to more profitable industries, which will then reduce the profit level there. Investment is assumed to readjust very quickly to new conditions.

Reality

Once more it is possible to see that objections can be raised. For some products there are very few barriers to entry; it takes little time or capital, for example, to set up as a window cleaner, since premises are not needed, materials (a ladder and cleaning materials) are cheap and readily available, and knowledge can be distributed to the potential market cheaply (adverts in local shops and newspapers). However, such opportunities are few and far between. Most new businesses require considerable capital in the form of premises, materials and publicity – even if they do not need specialist technical knowledge. A management consultant may be able to enter the market quite cheaply by working from home, but without specialist knowledge (i.e. skilled labour) the product (his/her advice) will not command a price to cover the necessary costs.

In the property and construction industries there are considerable barriers to 'entry' or movement of capital. Barriers are created by the following:

● land ownership;
● technical specialization;
● vertical integration of established firms;
● client-selection procedures;
● collusion between firms.

(i) Land ownership

The market for the purchase and sale of land is not a typical one. Most existing property developers own **land banks**, a reserve of land prepared for building. The purchase of land and the negotiation of planning and building permissions on it are a complex affair, done on the basis of previous experience and informal networking. New firms are excluded easily from purchasing land and preparing it for development. In addition, the legal complexity involved in land transfer, and the taxation and professional fee costs incurred on land transfer, affect the market operation. Land banks also require finance, typically bank finance, and for this to be available the company generally has to show that it has a good 'track record' of previous activity. Thus getting started is hard; it requires that others take a view that your venture is likely to succeed.

(ii) Technical specialization

Like all industries, construction is a technically complex industry, and the process of building involves specialist technical knowledge and specialist managerial experience. New firms cannot just decide to commence building. They need knowledge, experience and the ability to utilize them. Similarly, with the whole development process of land, it takes time to assemble or develop the skill base required. Mention was made in Chapter 2 of the length of time it takes to increase (or decrease) the supply of property professionals.

(iii) Vertical integration

Vertical integration is the degree of diversification a firm exhibits, both over its material inputs and over the distribution and sale of its outputs. A simple example would be a building firm owning a brick manufacturer and an estate agency – that is, the means to produce and the means to sell the production. This may disadvantage a new competitor without such resources. Within the construction and property industries there are many instances of companies in which vertical integration exists. The changes in the contractual arrangements made over the last two decades to ensure new buildings come about (or are procured), have moved toward a 'one-stop shop' approach to designing and building, and reinforced the market advantage to firms who have vertical integration.

(iv) Selection procedures

Clients select building contractors on a number of criteria, not just price. These include previous work done for the client, reputation, size of firm and similar work done elsewhere. New firms will not be able to satisfy these criteria. The impact of government standards and regulation compounds these issues. For example, quality assurance and environmental standards are often made tendering prerequisites, yet these are difficult for new firms to attain immediately. With the introduction of the Private Finance Initiative (PFI) the pre-tender requirements of organizations are so stringent that criticisms have been levelled at the initiative on the basis that it is possible for only a very few companies to meet the requirements.

New methods of procuring buildings may also exclude new firms. In recent years there has been a growth in using design-and-build contracts. In such cases the contractor is chosen because of a mix of the proposed price and design. This makes comparison of bidders difficult and more subject to aesthetic whim. The design team's reputation is paramount in selling a scheme, and new designers will face barriers.

(v) Collusion

Existing firms may collude over prices and/or share of the market and will not take kindly to new firms upsetting their arrangement. Collusion is illegal, but industry folklore contains examples. Little tangible evidence exists of such practices, but in any industry in which statistical information is limited and which exhibits the characteristics of flexibility detailed in Chapter 2 the opportunity exists for 'inside' information to be put to the use of restricting competition. Collusion is normally set up to control price and it is not just the construction industry that is prone to such practices. Perhaps the most celebrated cases of collusion have been found in auction rooms, where dealers set up 'rings' to ensure that the prices of certain items are not bid up in the auction room so that the nominee of the ring can buy cheaply and do a subsequent deal outside the room. Such practices are always illegal but are very hard to detect. In recent years the government has sought to regulate them out of existence in the money market by requiring investing organizations to set up self-regulatory bodies (see Chapter 7).

Assumption 5: marginal adjustments

Marginal adjustments relate to what is called **the continuity of functions**. When economists draw a demand or cost curve, called a **function**, they are implicitly assuming that, in practice, a whole array of marginal adjustments (to output and price) are possible. Thus output can be at *any* precise level and can be adjusted by a series of infinitesimal amounts, with a pause each time so that the reaction to such changes can be observed.

For the purposes of prediction, economists also require that the functions made up of this series of points be smooth and continuous. Ideally, they would like straight lines or curves of simple mathematical properties. For example, in Figure 4.2 curve A, with equation $y = mx + c$ (straight line), and curve B, with equation $y = x^2 + c$ (simple smooth curve), where c is a constant, are perfect for economists, allowing them to predict results simply from changes in input. The importance of this continuity of change is that the changes can be used to predict. Any relationship that does not show the ability to react to change in this fluid manner will result in a curve or line that is not smooth or straight, and implies that prediction will not be exact and that relationships are not built on only two or three variables but are the result of numerous interactions. The more complex the perceived relationship, the less it is possible to develop causal links and understanding.

Reality

If economists have a curve, C or D, to deal with, as in Figure 4.3, they are immediately faced with a problem. They can no longer predict whether output will rise or fall with a rise in price from P_2 to P_1. They are forced to assume that the real world behaves in such a way as to give smooth or regular curves. These they term

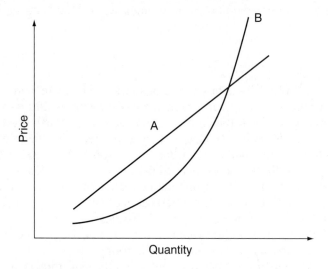

Figure 4.2 Ideal economic curves.

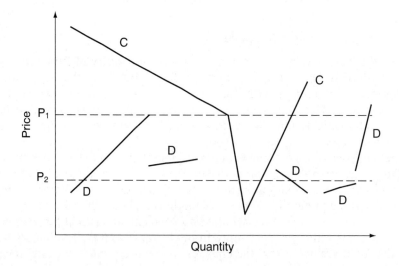

Figure 4.3 Real-world economic curves.

demand functions, **production functions** and **cost functions**. Because of this general assumption, economists are forced to assume the principle of constant returns to scale. This means that unit costs are assumed, over the range of potential outputs, to be constant irrespective of the level at which output is set. There is, however, very little evidence to suggest that this is often the real case. If there are not constant returns to scale the structure of an industry will be unstable; there will be an advantage in being as large or as small as possible. The average costs and efficiency of the industry will vary with the size structure of its constituent firms. Each firm's size will be unstable as it continuously strives towards giantism or fragmentation.

4.4 SUPPLY FOLLOWS DEMAND

The implicit mechanism of supply-and-demand theory is that supply follows demand or, alternatively, that demand creates a supply. This seems sensible. In the property industry, for example, demand for commercial property creates supply via the money that will be brought forward to supply the funding for the development. However, some commentators have suggested that supply follows money. Demand itself is not enough. There are social consequences to following money, in that some sectors of demand (notably housing and health) may not be financially attractive; highly profitable luxury goods will thus be supplied instead of necessities for the poor. Some economists argue that this is the 'savage world' we live in; others argue for economics with social justice. Even where supply follows demand in a way which is both economically predictable and socially acceptable, problems can occur. With the property market the **time lag** involved in the development process means that the mechanism is at best imperfect.

4.5 SHIFTS IN SUPPLY AND DEMAND

Demand is determined not only by price, but also by taste (affected by fashion, advertising and social conditioning), the number and price of substitute goods, the number and price of complementary goods, income and expectations of future price changes.

A demand curve is constructed on the principle of *ceteris paribus*, an assumption that other things remain equal. In other words, all determinants mentioned above remain constant and only price changes. Movement along the demand curve thus represents a change in the quantity demanded. For example, Figure 4.4 represents an increase in demand (from D_1 to D_2). When a different determinant changes, an entirely new demand curve must be constructed as this represents a change in demand.

Supply is also not determined purely by price, but also by the costs of production, the profitability of alternative products that could be produced, the profitability of goods in joint supply that must be produced to sell the goods, the aims of producers, expectations of future price changes and natural or unpredictable events such as strikes, the weather and wars. Supply curves are constructed in exactly the same way as demand curves. A change in supply necessitates a new supply curve, while a change in the quantity supplied is represented by a movement along the curve.

It is also useful to consider supply and demand in relation to time. For example, the supply of land is essentially fixed; no matter what the demand, supply cannot be increased. Figure 4.5 represents this. The supply of land is said to be inelastic (see section 4.6 below), in this case perfectly inelastic. It is possible, however, in the long term to increase the supply of land through land reclamation and changes in use of land, especially agricultural land.

This idea becomes clearer in studying property, for example housing. In the

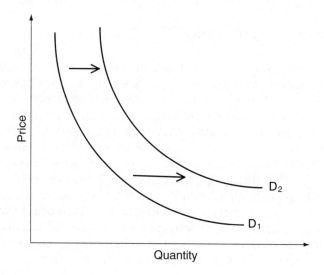

Figure 4.4 An increase in demand.

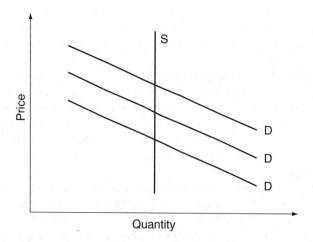

Figure 4.5 Supply of land

short term, housing supply is fixed (as shown in Figure 4.6) due to the long period of time it takes to build housing and the existing nature of the housing stock. In reality it is unlikely that housing supply is perfectly inelastic, but merely inelastic as shown in Figure 4.7, since new housing is continuously being built and housing can be created through changes in property use. In the long term, however, supply can react to demand elasticity as new buildings are built over the longer period, more building is started and construction times are speeded up. Supply is as in Figure 4.8.

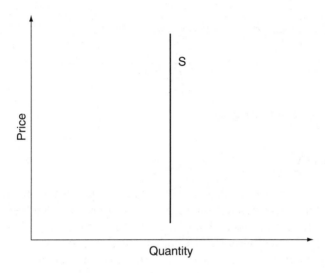

Figure 4.6 Supply of housing (perfectly inelastic)

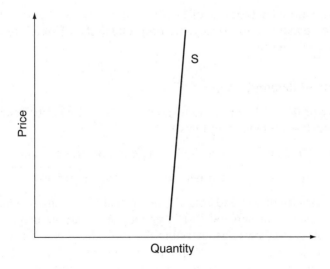

Figure 4.7 Supply of housing (inelastic)

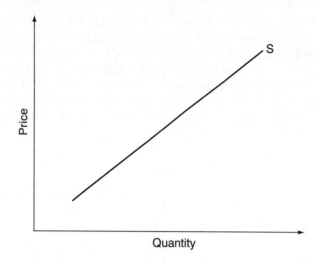

Figure 4.8   Long-term housing supply

4.6 ELASTICITY

As the price of a good rises theory states that the quantity demanded will fall. However, the relationship is not the same for each product. The degree to which demand will fall is a product of its responsiveness to change. The measure of responsiveness is termed **elasticity**. Chapter 10 relates the theory of elasticity to the property and construction industry. The formula for elasticity is:

$$\text{Elasticity } (\in) = \frac{\text{Proportionate (or percentage) change in quantity}}{\text{Proportionate (or percentage) change in the determinant}}$$

There are four particular types of elasticity in common use: **price elasticity of demand**, **price elasticity of supply**, **income elasticity of demand** and **cross-price elasticity of demand**.

Price elasticity of demand (P$\in_d$)

Price elasticity of demand shows the responsiveness of 'quantity demanded' to a change in price. It is defined as follows:

$$P\in_d = \frac{\text{Proportionate (or percentage) change in quantity demanded}}{\text{Proportionate (or percentage) change in price}}$$

Where price elasticity of demand exists it means that a very small change in price will produce a change in demand that is greater. An example of price elasticity might be in relation to a new consumer durable. Typically, when it is first produced the price is high, but if a few more suppliers enter the market and reduce the price just a little many more purchasers are attracted. This in turn may trigger off the response of bringing yet more suppliers into the market, forcing prices down still further. Alternatively, if new suppliers do not enter the market the increase in demand may push the price back up to the original level.

Price elasticity of supply (P$\in_s$)

Price elasticity of supply shows the responsiveness of 'quantity supplied' to a change in price. It is defined as follows:

$$P\in_s = \frac{\text{Proportionate (or percentage) change in quantity supplied}}{\text{Proportionate (or percentage) change in price}}$$

In a similar vein we can measure the responsiveness of demand or supply of a product to changes in determinants *other than* price. Two useful examples both apply to demand: income elasticity of demand and cross-price elasticity of demand.

Income elasticity of demand (Y$\in_d$)

Income elasticity of demand measures the responsiveness of demand to a change in consumer incomes (Y). It is defined as follows:

$$Y\in_d = \frac{\text{Proportionate (or percentage) change in demand}}{\text{Proportionate (or percentage) change in income}}$$

Cross-price elasticity of demand (P$\in_{d_{ab}}$)

Cross-price elasticity of demand measures the responsiveness of demand for one good to a change in the price of another good – either a substitute or a complement. It is defined as follows:

$$P\in_{d_{ab}} = \frac{\text{Proportionate (or percentage) change in demand for good } a}{\text{Proportionate (or percentage) change in price of good } b}$$

For the sake of simplicity, we will focus on price elasticity of demand and price elasticity of supply.

- Price elasticity of demand is determined by the number or closeness of substitute goods, the proportion of income spent on the good and the time period over which people can become acclimatized to price changes.
- Price elasticity of supply is determined by the amount that costs rise as output rises, and by the time period. In the long run elasticity will increase because of improved techniques and greater capacity.
- Elasticity is measured in percentage or proportionate terms. This allows a realistic assessment of how big a change is and allows for comparison.
- Elasticity is positive or negative. Price elasticity of supply and income elasticity of demand are normally positive, while price elasticity of demand is usually negative.
- The value of the figure determines whether demand (or supply) is elastic or inelastic.

Elastic (∈> 1). This is where a change in a determinant causes a proportionately larger change in demand (or supply). In this case the value of elasticity will be greater than 1, since we are dividing a larger figure by a smaller figure.

Inelastic (∈< 1). This is where a change in a determinant causes a proportionately smaller change in demand (or supply). In this case elasticity will be less than 1, since we are dividing a smaller figure by a larger figure.

Unit elastic (∈= 1). Unit elasticity is where demand (or supply) changes proportionately by the same amount as the determinant. This will give an elasticity equal to 1, since we are dividing a figure by itself.

● 'Necessities' tend to be price inelastic and luxury goods have high elasticity.
● Demand for construction projects tends to be highly elastic because of the major expense of property, the reliance of customers on interest rates, and the ability of existing stock to meet their needs through refurbishment, sharing and not forming new households.
● Supply of property, on the other hand, is relatively inelastic due to the long procurement and construction time period of the good.

4.7 COMPLEMENTARY GOODS

Complementary goods are a pair of goods which are consumed together. As the price of one goes up, the demand for both goods will fall. Thus the price of a complementary good is a determinant of demand. For example, if the cost of petrol rises the number of cars bought will fall, despite there being no change in the price or production of cars. With property, if the demand for retail goods falls, the demand for premises in which to carry out retail trade will likewise fall, causing a drop in rental values.

4.8 SUBSTITUTE GOODS

Substitute goods are competitive goods. A pair of goods which are considered by consumers to be alternatives to each other are said to be substitutable for each other. As the price of one rises the demand for the other will rise.

Figure 4.9 represents this interplay between a good, a substitute good and a complementary good.

4.9 THE SINGLE EUROPEAN MARKET

One of the most debated examples of a market at work is the Single European Market. While the bulk and immovability of the construction and property output have been shown to create a traditionally domestic national market, the increased importance of the Single European Market cannot be ignored. While the actual buildings may be permanent in location, the process of constructing them, the means of financing them and the clients buying or letting them are all increasingly international. The Single Market has far-reaching effects on both political and economic matters.

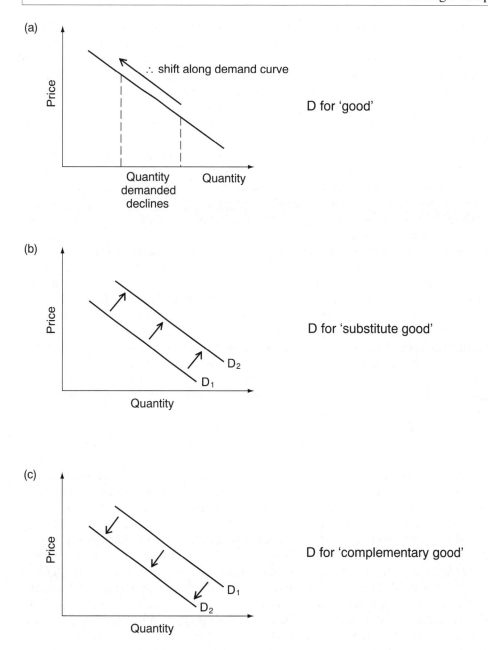

Figure 4.9 Substitute and complementary goods.

The European Union can be regarded as consisting of a number of predominantly similar nations, characterized as capitalist Western democracies of a primarily Christian nature whose history is united through their occupation by the Roman Empire, the development of feudalism and centralized monarchies, and the Industrial Revolution. Linguistic and other cultural differences are outweighed by similarities and a number of common causes such as political freedom, the creation of private property and the importance of the market economy. These causes need to be defended and expanded militarily, economically and politically. Individual nationalism causes some problems over unification, but the need for general legislation tends not to be seen as a theoretical problem, but as a problem of implementation. The abolition of internal borders to create the so-called 'Schengenland' (currently Austria, Belgium, Denmark, France, Germany, Greece, Italy, Luxembourg, Spain and Portugal) creates, for the purposes of travel, a single national unit.

These political discussions, however, are dwarfed by economic debate over monetary union. The creation of a single currency (the European currency unit or Ecu) is seen as a symbol of the replacement of economic control by national governments by a less representative single European 'super-government'. In addition, in Great Britain it is also seen as an attempt to impose a different ideological stance on the British government by arguing for more regulation and socialist manipulation of the free market. The argument against a single currency is primarily that the actual initial conversion rate would be very difficult to establish and that individual countries would lose their **monetary sovereignty**. By giving control of monetary policy to a European central bank, a nation would lose the right to devalue its currency and to set its own interest rate to suit domestic need. Increasingly, tax rates would need to be equalized and fiscal policy would be centralized. In other words, each country would lose its ability to manage its own economies, a complex political issue. In essence, of course, governments have tended to do this already. It has been recognized for some time that individual countries have lost much of their economic power in an increasingly world market and are seen as pawns in a much larger economic game. The debate thus becomes increasingly one of a free-market economy versus a regulated 'federal' European economy.

The advantages of monetary union are that a single currency will eliminate the threat of currency fluctuations, make cross-border transactions cheaper and help tourism by reducing currency exchange. A European central bank should create a less inflationary environment in Europe than national policy-makers influenced by public opinion. Monetary union should prove beneficial to the property and construction industries by allowing easier and cheaper transactions and encouraging investors away from profiting on currency trading and into investing in property and the built environment. It can also be argued that the world capitalist economy has always had, and needs, a dominant currency: sterling from 1800–1917; the US dollar since 1918. There are fears that the US dollar is now in terminal decline, the Japanese yen is not strong enough given the small size of the Japanese market, and China is still too undeveloped. A European currency would fit the bill perfectly. Thus, world economic prosperity (within this argument) is dependent on a single European currency unit.

4.10 THE STOCK MARKET

The stock market also provides an example of a market. The financial markets probably approximate most closely to both Adam Smith's and the neoclassical school's concept of the market. Because of the mass of daily trading and the rapid transfer of these business dealings and data generally, the money, commodity and financial services markets provide an almost perfect market. Indeed, the perfect-market theory argues exactly that.

Neither construction nor property offers these same market characteristics, but each obviously provides commodities and financial characteristics which form part of a prospective perfect market. Property professionals, in particular, may find themselves heavily involved in this market when examining and comparing the financial and investment opportunities of property.

4.11 CONCLUSION

The market is the primary tenet of neo-classical economics and is of major ideological and practical importance. The reality, however, is that evidence of the ability to apply market-economic theories to provide solutions to specific economic problems is less substantive. Perfect competition has been shown to be – if not irrelevant – less than fully applicable to the construction and property market sectors, and this undermines the value of neo-classical economic theory as a sole supportable tenet. Other market types are more valid in the real world but any modern study of economics must recognize the central location of the market.

Markets are places where buyers and sellers can interact, where prices are determined and where firms obtain their information of what, and how much, to produce. However, with the technology giving increased possibilities for markets to become non-tangible things, not space- and location-specific, the implications for the notion of property markets become enormous.

4.12 SUMMARY
- There are many types of market, although the perfect market of perfect competition is most widely assumed useful.
- The assumptions of perfect competition are not fully applicable to construction and property markets.
- Elasticity measures responsiveness to supply and demand for a good or service.
- Most goods and services have both complementary and substitute goods and services.

FURTHER READING

Armstrong, P., Glyn, A. and Harrison, J. (1991) *Capitalism Since 1945*, Oxford: Blackwell.
Dicken, P. (1992) *Global Shift*, London: Paul Chapman Publishing.
Dubben, N. and Sayce, S. (1991) *Property Portfolio Management: An Introduction*, London: Routledge.
Fraser, W. D. (1993) *Principles of Property Investment and Pricing*, 2nd edn, Basingstoke: Macmillan.
Scott, P. (1996) *The Property Masters*, London: E. & F. N. Spons Ltd.

EXAMPLE QUESTIONS

Below are questions relating to this chapter. For each chapter, model answers have been prepared for some of the questions set; these are found in the Appendix.

4.1   What is a 'market'?

4.2   Describe the different types of market and the competition which occurs within them.

4.3   Explain the terms 'normal' and 'supernormal' profits.

4.4   What determines the price of land?

4.5   Do you think that a premier division footballer should be paid £20 000 a week? Why or why not?

4.6   Explain 'elasticity'.

4.7   Examine the economic structure and organization of the construction industry in the UK.

The construction and property firm

5

OBJECTIVES

The objectives of this chapter are to:

● define, in economic terms, a firm;
● define and describe construction and property firms;
● examine how in reality firms react to the market;
● examine how in reality firms react to the market mechanisms described in Chapter 4.

5.1 INTRODUCTION

Neoclassical economists introduced 'the firm' as the primary unit of study. This recognises their emphasis on micro-, as opposed to macro-, economics. Within their models, only the firm is able to determine what to produce, how to produce it and how much to produce. The firm is taken to be any business unit; they are all the same. Thus 'a firm' could actually be a professional surveying office, a brick manufacturer, a plant hire-firm, a labour-only subcontractor, a general contractor or a house builder. The economic rules are said to hold for all these firms equally, whatever goods or services they are producing and selling.

5.2 THE FIRM

The major issue of concern to a firm is its profit, as without profit it cannot invest for the future. It is not necessary to create profit to stay in business in the short term or to pay salaries and wages, as these are deducted before profit is reached. However, to stay in business in other than the short term it is necessary continually to invest: in people, in plant and machinery, and in technology. Without such investment the level of competitiveness of any firm is bound to decline over time as it falls behind its competitors. Firms are said to be profit-maximizers; that is, they seek to ensure that their profits are at the maximum possible value. In order to maximize profits, firms have to come to decisions concerning their operating levels. These are determined by their costs and the demand for goods.

The demand curve for the market under perfect condition is represented in Figure 5.1. However, an individual firm's demand curve is horizontal, as shown in

Figure 5.2. This is because an individual firm is unable to determine the selling price for its goods. This price is given by the market. The firm is said to be a **price taker**. Whatever quantity of goods or services is produced, the price for the firm is dictated by the market. The perfect-market model assumes that there are neither economies nor diseconomies of scale. Profit is determined simply by the mass of goods (or services) sold and the efficiency of the firm in relation to the efficiency of competing firms.

Chapter 4 showed the objections to this simple situation. Firms do not operate under perfect competition, and thus their profit, cost and production possibilities are more complex. The simplest alternative is the monopoly. A monopoly is where there is only one firm in the market, producing a product with no close substitute. Figure 5.3 shows the demand curve for firm and market; they are the same,

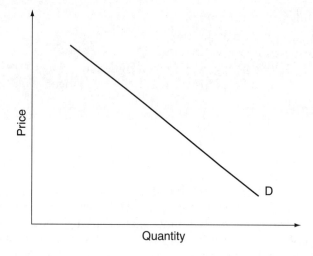

Figure 5.1   Demand and the market

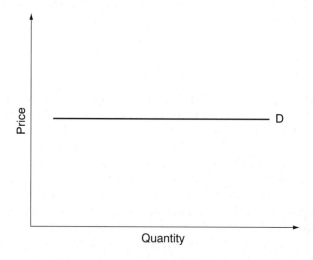

Figure 5.2   Demand and the firm

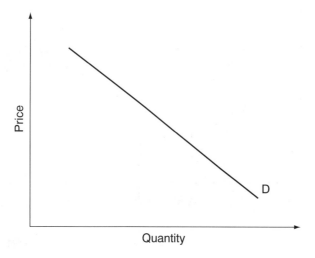

Figure 5.3 Demand in a monopoly: the firm is the market

because firm and market are the same. There are no monopolies in construction and property. However, certain oligopolies may exist. An oligopoly is where there are only a few firms in the industry. Where these firms collude they become equivalent to a monopoly as they act as one. Collusion is illegal, but *may* exist in construction and property.

A monopoly is called a **price maker**, since they create their own price and do not accept that determined by the market. Monopolies are the only sort of organization that is in a position to make supernormal profit in other than the very short run. They do not face competition so they do not have the incentive to innovate or search for greater efficiency. For these reasons, monopolies are generally thought to be unsuitable for market-led economies, and governments may take steps to discourage their formation. In the UK the work of the Mergers and Monopolies Commission is to ensure that firms do not reach such a stage of expansion through the process of merger or takeover that they are able to set prices in a way that influences market price to any significant extent. However, monopolies do not exist only in the private sector. The rise of the welfare principle in the UK and the recognition that the market could not always allocate resources in an optimal, *social* as opposed to *economic*, way led to the setting up of state monopolies to run certain key industries, such as health, coal, steel, water and parts of the transport industry. Current political ideology, however, perceives the advantages of state control over price to be fewer than the benefits of promoting competition, and hence through the pricing mechanism encouraging increasing efficiency and reducing price to a level of equilibrium. This has resulted in the breaking up of many of the major monopolistic industries.

However, it is now necessary to see the impact of a monopoly on the model previously established for the market. Figure 5.4 examines this and introduces some new concepts. In perfect competition, average revenue is equal to marginal revenue because demand is given at the market price. This is represented in Figure 5.5. The more complicated form of Figure 5.4 is due to the nature of costs.

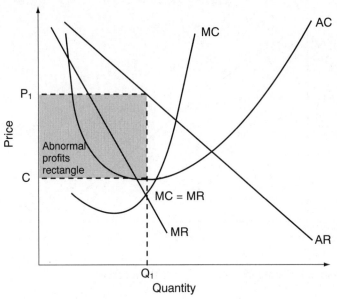

This situation is called 'monopoly equilibrium'
Total revenue (TR) is $P_1 \times Q_1$
A firm can:

- predict volume of sales from price;
- predict average cost of units from expected volume of sales;
- calculate total cost (TC) = average cost $\times$ Q;
- calculate profit = TR − TC;

Thus, monopolies choose P to give a maximum profit.

Concepts
- *Marginal cost (MC)* is the additional cost in producing an extra unit of output. If an extra unit is not produced, MC = 0.
- *Marginal revenue (MR)* is the extra revenue gained by selling more units at a lower cost per unit. It is necessary to reduce the cost per unit to increase the quantity sold.
- *Average cost (AC)* is the mean cost per unit.
- *Average revenue (AR)* is the mean revenue earned per unit sold.

Figure 5.4 Monopolies as price makers

The firm operating outside perfect competition faces both economies and dis-economies of scale. This means that the size of a firm holds advantages and disadvantages, and that firms are not merely at the whim of market forces, but can affect them. Firms operating under such imperfect competition are said to operate in either oligopoly or monopolistic competition. Monopolistic competition is similar to perfect competition in that there are large numbers of firms and unrestricted market entry (at least in the long run), but different in that firms may differentiate their products and have down-sloping demand curves. Product differentiation is further refined within an oligopoly, where competition is becoming less price-based, and is based more on the design, location, quality and 'extras' (known as value added) of the goods and services. Oligopoly markets need a determined strategy. Figures 5.6 and 5.7 show the result of these changes on the cost structure of a good, clearly showing that there exists an optimum production strategy within imperfect competition. It is this mechanism which so complicates Figure 5.4.

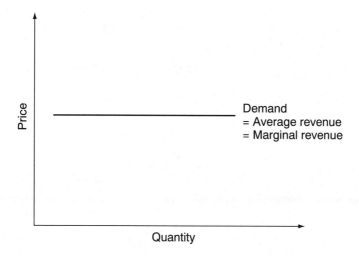

Figure 5.5 An ordinary firm acting as a price taker

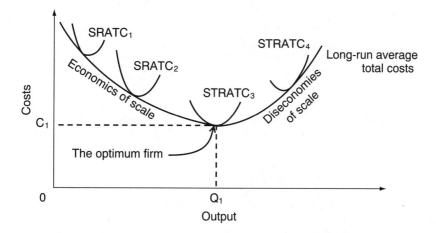

Figure 5.6 Total costs

Thus, firms must use a number of strategies to compete in an imperfect market. On the one hand, they can predict the optimal output in order to achieve the lowest unit cost and, on the other hand, they must ensure that their product is unique by selecting a variety of characteristics to make up the product so that it is impossible for customers to compare products purely on the basis of price.

For example, a housebuilder will produce houses of a particular design, in a particular location, with particular furnishing offers and a mortgage payment offer. Alternatively, a plant-hire firm will offer the plant, but also a maintenance agreement and an insurance scheme. Indeed, in every walk of life evidence is adduced of producers seeking to promote the 'uniqueness' of their product. The homogeneity espoused by perfect competition is rejected by those producers who exercise any oligopolistic or monopolistic abilities to have an impact on price.

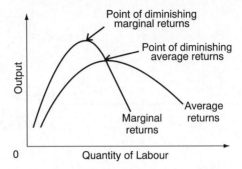

(a) diminishing marginal returns and diminishing average returns to labour set in

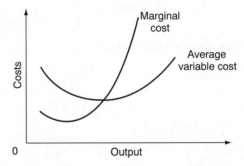

(b) these can be translated into money costs as the marginal cost (MC) curve and the average variable cost (AVC) curve

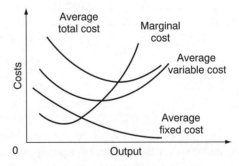

(c) the average total cost (ATC) curve is obtained by including average fixed costs (AFC) and average variable costs (AVC)

Figure 5.7 The derivation of the firm's short-run cost curves

Note: The total cost (TC) of producing a particular output is made up of the cost of employing both the variable and the fixed factors of production. This can thus be expressed as the identity:

$$TC = TVC + TFC$$

Likewise, average total cost (ATC) can be written as:

$$ATC = AVC + AFC$$

In practice, either through product differentiation or through market differentiation (e.g. location), very many firms are able to exercise some degree of price-making. Hence, for example, in some areas of the country the commission charged by an estate agent for the sale of a house may be considerably lower than that charged by an agent operating in another part of the country where there are few estate agents to compete for the work.

5.3 FIRM STRUCTURES

All firms, including those in construction and property, can be described in terms of their organizational, legal and economic characteristics. The first two of these measures for analysis, arguably, are not matters for an economics text. However, it is argued that they are relevant in that legal and organizational structures of firms have an impact on their ability to respond to change, their attitude to profit and their restrictions on trading ability.

Organizational structures

Firms are organized in a variety of structures, usually hierarchical. It is not really the scope of an economics textbook to look at managerial issues, but these obviously affect the economic efficiency of the firm. In particular, the ownership of the firm will affect the degree of its economic rationality. Economics assumes firms to be profit-maximizers, but ownership may affect this. While managers are interested in profit, it has been suggested that they also have other interests, such as awarding themselves bonuses in the form of bigger company cars, better dining and leisure facilities, and other perquisites. In addition, it is suggested that they seek to increase a firm's prestige and image, rather than its profit. This may be true for small unquoted companies, but with firms that have public share ownership attempts by directors to reduce profits by artificially increasing salaries are likely to be resisted by shareholders who naturally seek maximization of profit and hence capitalization of assets.

If property and construction organizations are examined, the characteristics noted earlier in the book (Chapter 2) can be observed again. It was noted that many of these firms are small in size, and these, especially those owned solely by one person or family, are also said to operate on non-maximization principles. In particular, these firms are thought to operate from a love of the industry in which they work, and aim to gain pleasure from running the firms and from carrying out construction work. However, within property development this is often not the case, with the desire for profit being almost the only motivation. Property development is a process that is notoriously risky, as the demand for the product can fluctuate over a short timespan, whereas the production process is lengthy. Thus not only are firms often very profit-oriented, but they are also often short-lived if the development process results in a product for which demand has decreased during the project period.

Firms not operating as profit maximizers are termed profit-satisficers. They aim to achieve satisfactory levels of profit. However, it is difficult to arrive at any satisfactory definition of what may be deemed to be satisfaction level.

Legal structures

Prima facie, legal structures have little economic impact. Firms are legally created as sole traders (one owner), partnerships (joint owners), private limited companies (a number of shareholders) and public limited companies (shareholders of varying numbers, whose shares are traded on the stock exchange). However, the impact of the legal structure can be large. For example, a firm that changes legal status from private limited to public limited will alter its ability to raise finance and thus may increase its potential ability to undertake work; similarly, the implications of being a sole trader or a limited company can be large, as the respective tax liabilities are different and this will affect costing structures.

Economic structure

There are a number of ways of describing the economic structure of firms. The entrepreneur is a most important figure in modern economics. As a figure of dynamism constantly seeking openings in the market, much faith has been placed in the entrepreneur in revitalizing the economy. In reality this faith may sometimes have been misplaced, but the entrepreneur is still an important figure as someone with innovative ideas able to have an impact on the manner in which not only his or her own business operates, but also that of the competition.

Two important examples of entrepreneurial figures who have single-handedly affected the running of industry sectors are Richard Branson, whose Virgin empire revolutionized the music and aviation industries and now appears set to create new levels of competitive pricing structures within the rail network, and Anita Roddick, whose campaign for environmentally friendly cosmetics production through the Body Shop successfully differentiated her business from that of her competitors and set a new agenda for consumer demand within the industry.

Within the property industry there are many instances of entrepreneurs affecting the operations of markets. In the 1930s the skills of Edward Erdman and other commercial estate agents with entrepreneurial flair were largely responsible for the development of the sale-and-leaseback style of transaction which introduced the major financial investors to property as a means of investing money for the first time (see Scott 1996), while the legacy of the entrepreneurial skills of Harry Hyams and other developers in the 1960s (see Marriott 1967) were influential in producing for the first time office developments specifically as investment vehicles for financial institutions.

The career of an entrepreneur begins with simple survival, while slowly establishing a power base. General ambitions will then be crystallized into specific objectives. Matters of finance will grow increasingly important, leading to a shift of interest to purely monetary concerns. Perhaps the most critical characteristic of the entrepreneur is singleness of purpose. Entrepreneurs are forever seeking opportunities. They do not wait for them to arrive, but are actively making things happen. The essence of entrepreneurial activity is trading, i.e. buying and selling. Successful entrepreneurs have direction and determination, recognize opportunity and are able to plan resources to achieve it. The seeds of failure are age, the need for constant innovation, the steady supply of new, younger entrepreneurs and success itself (which cloaks complacency and discourages constructive criticism).

In the construction industry, the primary distinction in the economic structure of firms is between the speculative developer and the general contractor. At the micro-economic level of the firm clear differences in forms of circulation and use of capital between contractors and speculative builders exist. Similarly, different forms of competition and production exist.

Speculative developers

The speculative developer follows the normal method of economic production but is regarded as the unusual form within the industry. A developer designs a project, constructs it and then sells (or lets) it. The entire production is paid for before sale. Speculative developers are price makers because they price differentiate. However, speculative developers do not always work in this way. Although they will endeavour to forward sell developments (that is, arrange the sale of the completed building(s) before starting work), this will not always be possible. At times when prices are perceived to be rising fast the developer will seek not to sell until completion, thus taking advantage of the extra pricing possible. Conversely, if demand is low it might not be possible to arrange forward sale. In such instances the developer has either not to embark on building, with, therefore, a prospect of going out of business, or to commence development in the hope that economic conditions will improve by the time the development is complete. In these circumstances the speculative developer is a price taker, rather than a price maker.

General Contractors

General contractors operate in the contracting system, where there is a separation of design from construction such that the contractor plays no part in design. The contracting system can be clearly divided into the following parties: client/landowner/building owner, designer, contractor. The contracting system operates where the client intends to own the building; the speculative system aims to sell it to someone else.

Contractors work in a competitive environment to obtain work. They normally tender for work on terms of price, although, as noted earlier, factors other than money, such as track record and quality processes, may form part of the landowner/client decision-making process. They not only compete for the work, but will also compete for resources to do the work. Speculative builders, on the other hand, compete for sites which, once acquired, guarantee the potential for work generation. They compete for customers by price competition or, more usually, product differentiation on location, design and specification.

General contractors compete around 'the market price', but the concept is dubious in speculative building, except in geographically constrained markets, where they are price takers although, even here, they can choose specific locations within a given region. Speculative builders are able, more than general builders, to move outside the notion of a 'market price' because they can differentiate their product – thus creating in effect a different market, for which a different structure of market price can prevail.

Faced with a slump, speculative builders are likely to reduce volume produced. In fact, speculative builders' output varies more than that of contractors, who have no control over their total output. Economies of scale would imply that speculative builders would seek to maintain high output by cost-cutting if necessary. But profitability varies enormously and it is this that affects output. Speculative builders are also highly dependent on bank finance; if this dries up output falls. There may also be a lack of land. In a boom they run their land banks down, while in a slump they will, subject to their financial standing, build up their land banks. This moderates output in a boom because they are not willing to pay boom land prices. However, many small speculative builders enter the market only in booms and are dormant in slumps. This is normally because they lack the available financial reserves to strategize the timing of their purchases and during a slump bank finance is either unavailable or too expensive. They, therefore, must buy land in the boom. In a downturn the construction period lengthens, and in upturn the construction period shortens. Speculative builders aim to develop sites slowly but properties quickly, thus ensuring that they obtain a return quickly on the money they expend on the construction process.

Speculative builders have two types of capital accumulation, recorded profit and writing up of the value of assets (land), but contractors have only recorded profit and must aim to achieve a minimum level of output to pay overhead costs at all times. They do not shut down operation in slumps, although they may diversify to keep their workforce employed.

5.4 THE PROFESSIONAL FIRM

Professional firms are a unique category of firm. Like all firms, they have a series of business objectives, but they do not have a single economic objective. Professional firms are not profit-maximizers; they are profit-satisficers. Professionals have not traditionally been interested in the pursuit of profit for its own sake; they see themselves as a vocation, serving the public interest and working at an interest, which they skilfully and enjoyably complete. Profit merely serves the purpose of ensuring that the firm survives and all employees are paid appropriately.

Unlike building firms, professional firms have tended to operate as sole traders and partnerships. They have remained relatively small and favoured informal organizational structures. This has maintained their relatively off-hand attitude towards economics. Like the general contracting firm, the professional firm is an obstacle to the complete supremacy of the forces of perfect competition that were examined as the foundation of neo-classical economics. Professional firms are not simply firms that employ professional people. The firms themselves are also members of professional institutions. In other words, for example, surveying firms are chartered surveying practices and building firms are chartered building firms. The result of such membership is that firms must obey certain external codes of practice and procedure, which are beyond those required by the market. Such regulations include items such as restrictions on advertising, which may appear trifling but seek to maintain professional stature, but also rules on the handling and banking of clients' money.

The general nature of these obligations is related to ethics. Professional firms and professional people have professional ethics. This moral code of behaviour is a supra-market phenomenon; that is, professional ethics transcend the one-dimensional demands of the market. These ethics are codified into professional codes of conduct, but also form informal controls on behaviour through social pressures from peers and colleagues. Such formal and informal codes may be seen to inhibit market activities.

Professional firms, however, seek to restrict market forces in a much more obvious manner. They have traditionally been price makers. They have achieved this through the use of fee scales. Fee scales are a statement by the professional body of the fee that may be charged by the profession for work. These fees are binding; no firm may charge less (or more) than this amount, and no client may attempt to negotiate an alternative price. This is a monopoly situation. The professions were allowed to determine fee scales in this way because they were committed to offering a first-class service to both clients and the public at large. Such an arrangement also encouraged non-price competition, termed **product differentiation**, so that clients could analyse competitive bids and choose the service offering the highest-quality service.

Fee scales operated in favour of the general social good, but expected the individual clients of the professions to pay for this. The Conservative government of 1979–97 and the 1980s ideology of the free market strongly disapproved of monopoly power and such forced price maker economics. They therefore abolished fee scales and replaced the monopoly with open competition. Professional firms were thus converted into price takers; they had to accept the market price for their work.

However, professional firms reacted in the manner of other firms shown in Chapter 4. Competition was not simply on price terms, but in terms of quality and the individual characteristics of service offered by individual firms. The government had hoped that professional firms would maintain quality and compete on price. This has not happened. The profession has seen rapidly declining income with falling fees for its work, especially in the long building and property recession of 1988–1997, and increased complaints about the quality of work undertaken. Professional firms have reacted against the perfect market in exactly the same manner as other firms.

Most recently, the Latham review of the construction industry, *Constructing the Team* (1994), has suggested a compromise. Its main emphasis is a move towards partnering and away from simple price competition. This would encourage the return of quality work, while preventing the perceived overcharging of the previous system of standard fee scales.

5.5 THE ECONOMICS OF THE PROFESSIONAL FIRM

Theory has failed adequately to recognize the qualitative differences between the organization and management of a professional private practice (firm) and of a purely business enterprise. The problem stems from discussion as to what professional surveying, architectural and building practices believe are the basic characteristics which make them professional chartered surveying, architectural and building practices. The supposition is that the ideology of professional firms:

● is different from that of the 'general' firms recognized in traditional theories;

● has come under increasing pressure to change (and perhaps change permanently) in the recent recession.

Professional firms are faced with twin obligations: those of professional integrity and those of the customer and market forces. This makes the economics of the professional firm rather different from the simple price calculation described for other firms. Traditionally, the two obligations have been achieved together, since professional firms guarantee professional work and, thereby, quality and general customer satisfaction. For individual surveyors, architects and similar professionals, professionalism has resulted in carefully designed career routes with assistance and understanding from their employers; after all, notions of firm professionalism depend upon employed professionals who are obeying externally laid down strictures of professional conduct.

Surveying and architecture have traditionally been portrayed as consisting of a plethora of small firms. Firms are small, with a few partners who see themselves as responsible not only for the firm itself, but also for its employees. This was achieved via continued professional development (CPD) assistance, education and training (RICS Assessment of Professional Competence (APC) in the case of surveyors, for example) flexible working, responsibility, social and welfare interests. Professional surveying, architectural and building practices can thus be portrayed as a unique organizational subset of the typical firm (business unit) represented in traditional organization literature. These practices have evolved over a long period of time within a strong professional history and have retained much of the fundamental essence of these times. This history can be seen by the traditional reliance on Victorian business organization (partnerships), and is tied to that period's strong views on professionalism and the obligations inherent therein. In modern times the ideal of both the partnership and the professional has changed, and, while there is clearly no suggestion that firms are old-fashioned, architecture and surveying still retain many relics of this past.

It is for this reason that the 'small' surveying, architectural or building practice in some way retains in its very nature those Victorian ideals that are traditionally regarded as typical for such practices. It is also for this reason that notions of professionalism can be tied to the 'small' firm, which represents the sole trader/partnership legal structure, and operates on flexible and ad hoc organizational principles. Ball recognizes the contradictory philosophy of the professional firm to economic norms, when he states that in surveying, 'like other Victorian professions, ideological emphasis was placed on service rather than quick profits and on quality rather than the scale economies that could be derived from standardized high-volume turnover (Ball 1988: 59–60).'

Ideals of professionalism are fundamentally delineated within this heritage. Traditional definitions of professions–which recognize them as specialized authorities based upon a superior knowledge of a body of theory, governed by controlled entry within a code of ethics and a monitored self-discipline–can be applied only within this Victorian framework. The surveying profession, as a profession, cannot be separated from its own professional culture, which is firmly rooted within the culture of Victorian Britain. Any definition of surveying professionalism must recognize the essential status of this culture in the workings of that professionalism within the firm. Ball acknowledges this when he identifies the typical duties of the quantity surveyor (QS) firm: 'When quantity surveyors perform independent advisory roles they take on few management functions, because of the potential contradictions between the objectives of a profession and the needs of a productive enterprise' (Ball 1988: 62). He proceeds to identify this as the major source of conflict that existed within surveying between contractors (who used to be represented by the Institute of Quantity Surveyors–now defunct) and private QS firms (represented by the RICS). The issues raised at the time are examples of the reluctance to erode traditional professional values by an acceptance of neo-classical economic necessities. Similar issues can be identified within all the professions such as the abolition of fee scales to open up competition on price terms and lessen the importance solely of quality as a measure of output; the various recent amendments to the 'Rules of Conduct', such as in advertising, the allowance of limited liability and membership; and the redefinition of what constitutes a chartered ('professional') firm in terms of membership of its partners or board of directors.

Duality has increasingly been challenged. There is a clearly emerging contrast between the demands of 'the market' and those of professional ethics. In periods of recession the simple aim of economic survival severely undermines notions of professional ethics. Response to change is increasingly pro-market and takes the form of conformity to supply, demand and price-determination issues. Whether professional firms can continue to transcend such basic economic questions will be a major area for future discussion within the construction and property profession.

5.6 CONCLUSION

According to traditional neo-classical economic theory, all firms have one aim: profit-maximization. The sole purpose of a firm is to maximize its profits. More recently, this purpose has been questioned from two perspectives.

First, it is suggested that, in the real world, profit maximization is not easy to achieve. While profit is the firm's objective, its simple maximization is not. For example, it is suggested that shareholders and managers have different views on what profit is. Managers may seek to expand the business, purchase better premises, order new furniture or award themselves better pay, while shareholders may seek higher dividend payouts. Accounting conventions also make it difficult to ensure that a firm is maximizing its profit. It is usually accepted that firms are profit-satisficers, aiming to make a level of profit to satisfy all parties.

Second, many commentators object to the right of firms simply to maximize their profit without regard to any other factors. They argue that as firms operate in societies they must accept the cultural and social codes and etiquettes of their hosts. This opinion is criticized by the neo-classical economists, who argue that it makes firms less efficient and that they should not be expected to involve themselves in such activities. However, it is clear that legislation already forces business to accept certain cultural values; for example, however profitable using slave labour on a building site might prove to be, it would not be allowed in the UK. There are many other less obvious areas, however, where legislation is replaced by voluntary codes of conduct and self-regulation. Within the built environment professions and the financial services sectors, for example, such codes of conduct monitor business behaviour and members have to observe compliance – even if it reduces their profitability.

Firms aim to make profit in order to ensure their survival. This is their business. Firms may, however, also serve other additional purposes. Individual entrepreneurs setting up their own business often do so for empowerment and the right to work for themselves. The firm is, for them, both work and enjoyment, in addition to the profit which their labour will earn. This ideal is often found in construction and property firms, where many business owners, partners and managers work within the industry and profession because they obtain a high level of personal fulfilment from the challenges provided by the working environment.

Thus, firms can be defined in terms of their economic, legal or organizational structure. Economic structure is determined by market structure: firms are price takers or price makers.

Contracting builders resemble price takers, competing by tender for work, in which the lowest bidder will win. Speculative builders are price makers, able to outflank the market through product differentiation.

5.7 SUMMARY
- Firms are more important economic units than is assumed under the theory of perfect competition.
- Firms may be price takers or price makers, depending upon whether they operate in the contracting or speculative system.
- Firms have economic, legal and organizational structures, resulting in complete inter-notions.

FURTHER READING

Ball, M. (1988) *Rebuilding Construction*, London: Routledge.
Fellows, R., Langford, D. A. and Newcombe, R. (1991) *Construction Management in Practice*, Harlow: Longman.
Marriott, O. (1967) *The Property Boom*, London: Pan Books.
Reekie, W. (1991) *The Economics of Modern Business*, Oxford: Blackwell.
Scott, P. (1996) *The Property Masters*, London: E. & F. N. Spons Ltd.

EXAMPLE QUESTIONS

Below are questions relating to this chapter. For each chapter, model answers have been prepared for some of the questions set; these are found in the Appendix.

5.1 Describe the 'firm'.
5.2 (a) What are price takers and price makers?
    (b) Which construction firms are which?
5.3 What are the aims of a business? How far are the aims of a professional firm the same as those of a general building contractor?
5.4 Explain the economic structure of professional firms. Why might the structure differ from that of a property company?

The nature and functioning of the real property market

6

OBJECTIVES

The objectives of this chapter are to:

- introduce the nature and particularities of the property markets;
- consider the concept of an 'efficient market' and compare the property market to this;
- distinguish between land markets and property markets;
- explore the factors, economic and otherwise, that drive demand for property;
- explore the distinction between property as an investment asset and property as a means of production;
- consider constraints on the supply of property.

6.1 INTRODUCTION

Chapter 4 introduced the concept of the market and set out the conditions that economists have assumed to exist in order to establish the notion of a 'perfect market'. It is widely accepted, even by the most ardent advocate of market economics, that no such thing as a perfect market exists. If the stock market is often quoted as being the closest approximation to a perfect market, the real property market is the converse and is generally accepted to present a very special market, which, although not 'perfect' in the economic sense, nonetheless has been held to be 'efficient' at least to some extent (see Brown 1991).

In this chapter the notion of 'efficiency' in economic terms is introduced, and both this and the 'perfect competition' assumptions are examined in relation to the UK real property markets.

6.2 PERFECT MARKETS AND EFFICIENT MARKETS

We have already seen that a perfect market is defined as one in which:

- there are many buyers and sellers;
- there is a homogeneous product;
- there is a central marketplace; and
- there is no possibility of any one participant affecting the market.

Under perfect market conditions price will always result from the simple interaction of supply and demand. However, it has come to be recognized that no perfect market exists. Even the stock market, which perhaps comes closest to conforming to the conditions set out above, is not perfect. Thus in recent years economists have become more concerned with the notion of market 'efficiency'. Markets can be assessed in respect of efficiency at three levels: weak-form, semi-strong and strong (or full) efficiency.

A market is said to be **weak-form efficient** if prices reflect all published *past* performance information; **semi-strong** if not only past published information but *other* information is reflected in prices; and **fully efficient** if the pricing mechanism takes account of *all* information, including information on future performance. Generally the property markets, for which published information is very sketchy in comparison with other commodities, is not thought to be efficient, although Brown (1991) has argued that it meets the criteria for weak-form efficiency. Most other commentators have considered that the paucity of data for analysis, which has been regarded as a characteristic of the property markets in the past, renders them inefficient.

6.3 REAL PROPERTY

The nature of real property

'Real property' is the term given to land or land and buildings to distinguish them from 'personalty' or personal property, which is mainly moveable items such as personal effects, consumer durables, etc. While it is usually obvious what is, or is not, real property as opposed to personal property, sometimes disputes can arise, as for example with the fixtures and fittings found in many buildings. Thus, clearly, a freestanding wardrobe in a house would fall into the category of personal property, but a fitted wardrobe might very well be regarded as belonging to the building as a permanent fixture and hence be included in the term 'realty'. Examples of items that have given rise to dispute in the past have included panelling, wall hangings and garden statues! It might be thought that the distinction is unimportant, but the value (or market price) of a property can be affected very significantly by whether or not certain items of fixtures and fittings are included.

Land tenure

Within the UK the basic legal principle controlling land and property ownership rests on the notion of ownership by the crown. No individual or company actually owns any land; what people and organizations do own is a legal or equitable 'right' in the property. Thus when people talk of buying a property what they mean is that they purchase a 'bundle of rights' in that property – or what is termed an 'estate' in land.

(a) Freehold

The highest estate in land in England and Wales is freehold in possession (feuhold in Scotland), which gives the owner full rights of ownership and occupation. Technically the rights exists both upwards to the sky and downwards to the centre of the earth. In reality the rights are hemmed round by restrictions placed by operation of the law, and some rights, such as mineral rights, are normally reserved to the Crown. Whilst interference in the right to use land as one wishes might seem an imposition, society has, over the years, come to accept the principle that individual freedoms must be curtailed for the common good. Thus, for example, it is generally accepted that consent must be obtained before any development takes place on owned land, a legal restriction introduced in a comprehensive way for the first time by the Town and Country Planning Act 1947.

A more vexed question, however is that of compensation for appropriation by the state of land by way of purchase, which is compensatable, or by the restriction of rights, which generally is not. Similarly contentious is the question of whether financial gain arising to an individual by action of the state – by, for example, allowing development – should give rise to a liability for taxation.

(b) Leasehold

It has already been stated that the highest estate in land is freehold in possession. Frequently however, the ownership and the occupation are separated. The most usual legal instrument for creating this is a lease. A lease will detail the nature of the relationship between the owner (freeholder) and the lessee, including:

- the length of the term;
- the repairing liability;
- liabilities for improvement;
- the rent and provisions to review same;
- arrangements for the lessee to sell;
- arrangements in the case that the lessee defaults.

For large commercial buildings, it is common for the lessee, in turn, to create other shorter leases within the terms of the 'head lease' or to let out part of the property. In this way, hierarchies of interests in land can be created. Each may or may not have an economic value. The value of a leasehold interest will arise where the rent paid to the freeholder (or head lessee, as the case might be) is below the current rental value. This can happen for various reasons. The most common are:

- the rent paid was set a long time ago and there are no provisions in the agreement for it to be reviewed;
- the tenant has made improvements to the property.

Later in the chapter we consider some of the things which influence the predominant form of land tenure–that is, either freehold owner-occupation or freehold and leasehold.

(c) Other interests

The only interests in land that are recognized as 'legal estates' are freehold and leasehold. However, in the law of **equity** other interests in land are recognized which will bind the **legal estate** owners. Examples of these include:

- **rights of way or access**, which may either be created expressly or be implied through long usage;
- **easements**, which give rights to one landowner over adjacent land in other ownership;
- **profits a prendre**, which are rights to take, for example to catch fish in a lake.

While these are generally insignificant, their presence can sometimes be very detrimental to the ability to use and develop land.

(d) Legal charges

As land is generally regarded as a valuable asset, either as a resource and means of production or as an investment which will command a price, it is often used as security for loan purposes. The loan commonly takes the form of a legal mortgage, in which the lender acquires a charge over the title to the land and the borrower is obliged to pay back the debt over a period of time. The payback either is on the basis that the debt only is serviced by way of interest payments until the term date at which the whole of the capital must be repaid, or is structured so that the capital sum is paid off gradually over the term so that the debt-service element decreases as the term progresses.

With the former type of mortgage the payments are lower through the initial period of the loan, as only the interest is payable; but with the second type as the debt capital reduces, so does the level of interest, and the overall costs decrease comparatively. Mortgages set up for **residential purchases** can be of either type and are generally taken over a twenty- or twenty-five-year period. If a debt-only arrangement is entered into the home buyer will commonly also purchase a term assurance policy, the premium payments for which will be invested by the assurance company so that when the mortgage debt capital is due for repayment the term policy matures and is sufficient to pay back the debt. Such arrangements became very common in the 1970s and 1980s as tax relief was granted on the interest payments but not the debt repayment. However, with the gradual reduction of tax advantages such schemes have reduced in popularity.

For **commercial purchases** mortgage arrangements are commonly interest only and may be for much shorter terms. However, where large-scale developments are being funded, the exact nature of the mortgage or other financial arrangements is usually individually negotiated, and may be complex. Some general principles are observable, and for an examination of these the reader is directed to Dubben and Sayce (1991) or Isaac (1994).

6.4 THE PROPERTY MARKET

It is clear that a perfect property market does not exist, so the more pertinent question is, does '*a* property market exist', or is it so fragmented as to constitute not one, but many markets acting largely independently, and if so in what ways can we disaggregate it?

The first distinction to make is between the land market and the market for developed property – or the property market.

The land market

The land market is dominated by the concept of supply, determined both physically and in planning terms. While the supply of land is, for all practical purposes, fixed in physical terms, the supply of land available for any particular use depends on the planning position. For each area of the country the relevant Local Planning Authorities produce plans indicating in general terms the permissible uses for land in their area. Thus they will make provision for land for, *inter alia*, residential and commercial uses. This does not guarantee that any development proposal brought forward in compliance with the general provisions of the plan will be approved, or that any non-conforming use will always be refused. It does, however, provide a framework controlling supply in general terms. The plans are reviewed from time to time to take account of changing social needs and priorities, but it is inevitable that the supply of land for particular uses will not necessarily be in economic equilibrium with the demand for the developed 'product'.

Where demand outstrips the supply in any location the effect will inevitably be a rise in land prices, and the consequent impact on the cost of producing the finished building. Politically, such a rise in prices may not be acceptable, and in recent years the pressure to provide land at prices which will result in 'affordable housing' has been an issue of both debate and research.

The political dimension to the operation of the land market has also taken the form of various attempts to impose taxation on financial gains arising from the sale of land for development. The theoretical argument for the imposition of tax is that the imposition of planning controls is for the general good of the community, but it is acknowledged that the effect is to restrict supply. Thus, to release land for development by the granting of planning permission is to give value to the land in the hands of the landowner. However, the argument goes, such release in value arises from the action of the community, in the shape of the local planning authority, not out of any work, investment or labour on the part of the landowner. The gain in the owner's hands is thus in the form of a 'windfall gain'; in equity the gain should be returned to the community. Whether such an argument is acceptable or not depends on the reader's political view, but it must be held in mind that if the principle of interference with legal rights by way of planning controls is accepted as fair and equitable an unfettered free market in land does not and cannot exist. This will inevitably result in anomalies in land values.

Since the Second World War legislation in respect of taxation of development gains has been introduced on several occasions. The first attempt, related to the introduction of general planning controls, was abandoned in the mid-1950s; in the 1960s betterment levy was introduced and subsequently abolished, while the

1970s saw two attempts: the Development Gains Tax and the Development Land Tax. Neither lasted for longer than a few years and the only tax on development gains since the mid-1980s has been capital gains tax, which, although it catches windfall gains, is at a relatively low level (30 per cent) and aimed at all gains, however arising.

Taxation, or indeed the prospect of such taxation being introduced, has always had a significant impact on the working of the land market. At times of high taxation the experience has been that landowners, hoping that taxation will be reduced in the future, are unwilling to bring land forward for development. This reduces the supply of land for building and if the demand for the product (be it houses or commercial property) is high, land prices will be forced up and so will the prices of the built product.

Characteristics of property as a product

Fundamentally, the total supply of land is (almost) fixed. However, given the potential to change the use to which land is put and the ability to develop it, the supply in any 'user' sense is not fixed in other than the short term. With advances in agricultural and land-reclamation techniques, supply for food production can be enhanced, but currently more social concern is expressed at the loss of productive land for development and subsequent despoliation. Within the urban setting perhaps the chief determinant of land supply is the prevailing planning-control system.

As a product to be 'marketed' some of the characteristics which set property apart from other products include:-

- each parcel of land is heterogeneous;
- it can often only be traded in large inflexible units;
- it may be inflexible in its use (i.e. fit for use by only one occupier);
- trading is frequently slow;
- the costs of transaction tend to be higher than with other products;
- it needs to be managed;
- ownership implies ongoing costs of holding;
- given the requirement for management, it can provide the opportunity for restructure to release value and facilitate further trading;
- it is possible to have other than absolute ownership (i.e. partial ownership or restricted ownerships can be created and, in most cases, traded);
- no central marketplace exists;
- the level of knowledge regarding transactions is low;
- there is an imprecise pricing mechanism and imperfect knowledge of the pricing mechanism;
- unlike most other products, ownership may not be linked to consumption.

Consequently, what does exist is a series of markets, which are normally structured according to use, location and tenure (fragmented or total). An interesting development in the property markets since the early 1980s has been a trend of divergence: at one level markets have become increasingly specialized, while at another there has been a move towards a global property market.

Land: resource or investment asset?

There are, in essence, two major reasons why people seek to own land: first, for the benefits of occupation and, second, for the purpose of investment. Other reasons can be identified, namely for development or trading (the value-added or value-released distinction is important here), and to this some would add for speculation.

(a) Occupational demand

The requirement for shelter is a basic human need, identified by Maslow (1954) as being second only to the need for food and sleep. From this very basic approach, however, it is necessary to distinguish need from demand in economic terms. Where an economy is driven by public ownership of assets the design and development of property will focus on the needs of the occupier, as perceived by the state; where, however, it is a free-market economy, economic demand becomes the overriding control. In reality, in most EU member states the economies are mixed, with at least some state intervention affecting the design and location of building development. This will produce anomalies in the pricing mechanism, which seeks to reconcile effective demand with the supply stock, and this may become a driving force in the investment market for property.

Factors affecting occupational demand for property include:

- use of the property (in planning and physical terms);
- location;
- design and fitness for purpose;
- accessibility;
- costs-in-use;
- flexibility;
- potential for improvement/development;
- legal constraints and fiscal implications (taxes on occupation, grants and incentives, etc.);
- finance availability, structure and cost;
- availability of supply;
- cost;
- social acceptability (environmental concerns, taste, etc.).

The ranking of these criteria will depend upon individual occupier requirements, the type of property under discussion and the market conditions prevailing.

It is possible to divide the occupational market for property into broad categorizations, as follows:

- residential;
- office;
- retail;
- industrial;
- agricultural;
- leisure.

The **residential** market, for example, is by its very nature location-sensitive, and professionals working in this sector of the market will tend to operate in a small geographical area.

Within the sector generally, common trends can become established, but the markets operate sufficiently separately, both on the demand and supply side, that generalizations can provide a distorted view. Occupational demand may be dictated by price, location, condition, internal configuration and aesthetic considerations, although it is not a well-researched area in terms of the literature.

The **office** market is likewise fragmented, so that property analysts will differentiate between location and age (generally analysis is only between prime, other new and second hand). Within the last decade, however, many developments have taken place which do not fit the standard criteria of 'an office', e.g. business park, science park and high-tech enterprises. Structurally these may be specified as offices, but they may also include areas fitted out for production activity.

The **industrial** sector is traditionally divided between the heavy-industrial market, general industrial, light industrial and warehousing. A very recent development here is the development of a segregated market in distribution centres, pivoted on accessibility to high-speed rail, ports and airports. Occupational demand will be price and location sensitive although design features are critical.

The **retail** market is perhaps the best example of recent disaggregation, with high-street shops, shopping centres, out-of-town centres, hypermarkets and supermarkets all forming distinct groupings. Of all property types it could be argued that high-street shops are the most location-sensitive, with identifiable nodes of highest occupational demand, from which values radiate downwards.

The **agricultural** market, which may or may not be taken to include woodlands, has recently been affected by diversification within the countryside, and demand for agricultural land may now reflect not only the 'grade' of the land in agricultural terms but also the quality of the buildings and the holding's potential for recreation (e.g. golf, country parks, tourism/holiday).

Leisure property is a little-documented and understood market, but it is developing fast as leisure becomes a more important part of consumer spending, driven by rising real incomes and more sophisticated lifestyles.

(b) Summary on occupational demand

To summarize the above: land has no intrinsic value. Value exists only where the land has a 'beneficial use' – that is, a use in occupation, or a potential to offer use in occupation. If occupational demand is weak or lacking the rent or price that the property can command in the market is lowered. However, the market is distorted by legislative interference, the existence of a heterogeneous stock, supply considerations and imperfect knowledge, so the pricing mechanism is not efficient.

What tenure?

Occupational demand can be satisfied in two basic ways: ownership allied to occupation, or occupation on the basis of a tenancy, lease or other contractual relationship with the owner. Whether a market develops to become dominated by owner-occupation or not will depend on:

- custom, culture and practice;
- legal framework;

- tax incentives or disincentives;
- finance and funding;
- occupier preference and policy;
- investor attitudes.

Thus, for example, if we examine the residential sector in the UK, the combination of restrictions on private lettings combined with tax relief on mortgage interest payments has resulted in a predominance of owner-occupation. Within commercial property markets the need to release cash for the business, combined with a desire to operate flexibility in terms of location, has meant that many retailers, in particular, seek to occupy without consequent ownership.

Factors necessary for the establishment of an investment property market

The separation of ownership from occupation to create an investment market requires not only an underlying occupational demand from those wishing to rent rather than purchase, but also the following:

- a suitable supply of property investors;
- accepted and acceptable vehicles for leasing/tenancy;
- the availability of finance to back investment purchase;
- an acceptance that property is a suitable home for investment funds;
- the availability of knowledge and data.

- **A suitable supply of property investors**. Investors may be individuals, corporates, property companies or institutions. Since the late 1970s the interest or otherwise of the financial institutions has been critical in the performance of the property investment markets (see Chapter 8).
- **Accepted and acceptable vehicles for leasing/tenancy**. Given that the lease or tenancy is the interface between landlord and tenant, it is important that the nature of the agreement is one that is acceptable to both parties. Within the major EU countries differing patterns of acceptability exist, with the UK being notably out of line with most other countries (see Dubben and Sayce 1991).
- **The availability of finance to back investment purchase**. In the case of all but the institutions, some of the large corporations and the very wealthiest individuals, there is a necessity for financial backing, hence the very large influence on the property market of the attitudes of bankers. Since the late 1970s the financing of property purchase has become very sophisticated, with development being funded on structured deals which comprise a mixture of debt and equity funding. As a generalization, the banks have been the prime generators of debt financing, with financial institutions providing equity funding.
- **An acceptance that property is a suitable home for investment funds**. The acceptance of property as a suitable home for investment funds depends on two things: perception and performance. If property is to be regarded as a desirable investment it must be shown to display the qualities that are required by investors. Obviously these vary between investors, but as the commercial property investment markets are dominated by the institutional investors their requirements are critical.

● **The availability of knowledge and data**. Knowledge of performance is critical to the investment decision. Within the equities and stock market this does not present a barrier to investment; electronic trading and large volumes of transactions daily mean that investors can track their investments with ease, and know precisely how they are performing in absolute terms and against indices. Property is different. Not only are there comparatively few transactions, even in a strong market, but the measurement of property performance to date is at best an inexact science.

Summary of investment market requirements

If investors are seeking opportunities to maximize their returns at acceptable levels of risk they are interested in acquiring assets which are appropriate within their portfolio and which are expected to give adequate performance, set against acceptable levels of risk. While the level of existing occupational demand is an important issue, it is not the controlling factor. From this it is apparent that the investment market operates, if not independently of the occupational market, then under different constraints. Accordingly commercial properties which fulfil the basic criteria of acceptability as an investment vehicle have a dual market – that for occupation and that for ownership.

6.5 PROPERTY: A DUAL MARKET

From the analysis above it is clear that sometimes the conditions exist for an investment market to become established and sometimes they do not. In the UK it has become the tradition that the commercial (shops and offices) markets are dominated by investment ownership, whereas the residential and industrial markets have a dominance of owner-occupation. With houses there have been government incentives (in the form of mortgage relief) and a financial structure which supports home ownership. Not only that, but home ownership has been seen politically to be socially desirable. Industrial units are often owner-occupied as they are specialized in design and equipment, so that they would not appeal to more than one or, at most, two tenants.

Where an investment market exists for a particular type of property a 'dual market' can be said to exist: at one level the market is about rents and occupational demand; at the investment (or freehold) level the market is determined by the numbers of investors who see property as attractive as compared with other mediums of investment.

Rental values

Rent is the annual price paid for occupation of property. The amount paid will vary according to the actual nature of the tenancy or lease agreement between owner and occupier (for example in respect of who pays for repairs and insurance, and the length of the term). Agreements commonly include clauses calling for the rent to be reviewed to take account of changes in value and money. In periods of inflation the period for which the rent is fixed without review can significantly affect the rent agreed.

There are two major determinants of rent, however:

- **The strength of occupational demand**. In accordance with Marshallian theory, the law of supply and demand will determine the rent (price) paid for the property. If demand increases without an increase in supply (and bear in mind that supply in the case of property is fixed at least in the short term until new developments can take place), then rents can be driven up very quickly. Similarly, rental levels can fall quickly. In the City of London office market during the first years of the 1990s rent fell by over 50 per cent in a period of only one year.
- **The economic surplus**. For many types of property (such as offices) the cost of rent is just one of the overheads a business has; it is thus difficult to see a direct relationship between the accounts of a business and the level of rent that can be paid. However, with some other types of property (notably petrol filling stations and hotels) there is a very direct relationship between the nature of the property and the rent that a tenant can afford to pay. Indeed, in such cases the rent is determined more in accordance with Ricardian (1971) theory as a economic 'surplus'.

Imperfections of the market

It has been noted above that the property market is not generally regarded as either efficient or perfect. Indeed, it is often quoted as an example of an imperfect market. The reasons for this are complex but can be summarized as follows:

- **Imperfect knowledge**. The lack of a central marketplace, and indeed the fragmented nature of the market, combined with a paucity of published comprehensive information regarding transactions, predisposes towards imperfection.
- **Time lags**. Property may be regarded as having a fixed supply, but this is not quite accurate. While at any given time the stock of, say, houses is fixed, that supply will change over time. Land may be fixed in terms of its area, but the ability to build new units and convert or redevelop old properties means that, providing the necessary consents can be obtained, supply will react to changes in demand. However, it can take a long time on average for supply to react. Whereas a small housing scheme can, given favourable planning, be brought 'on stream' in a year or less, some major developments take several years to bring to fruition. Because obtaining land and consents can be very time-consuming some developers try to build up land banks in *advance* of anticipated demand so that they can react more swiftly than their competitors.
- **Dominance of stock of real property over price**. One of the major characteristics of the property markets is the dominance of existing stock over price. Whereas with most commodities stock production is normally short in time-span, the complexities in terms of planning and financing, combined with the length of the construction process, mean that short-term changes in demand for property cannot result in quick responses by supply. Indeed, as outlined above, the greater community needs, as expressed through the planning process, may mean that supply will not react to increases in demand. Inevitably, the relative inability of supply to respond to demand means that price, the interaction between supply and demand, will be dominated by the nature of the existing stock pile.

6.6 CONCLUSION

In this chapter we have introduced the property markets. It has been seen that, compared with the markets for other economic goods, the land and property markets have special characteristics. Among these characteristics, the time lag before development occurs and the interference with a free market by legislative interventions such as planning, are very important. Another characteristic is that the markets operate on two 'planes': that of occupation and that of investment. The differing goals and objectives of both sets of owners can lead to idiosyncratic behaviour in the markets, for example where patterns of demand for investment property, which are driven by the performance of investments in other media (such as gilts and equities), do not coincide with patterns of occupation demand, which are driven by a range of economic and social factors.

The land and property markets are thus seen to be complex in their construction and operation. It has to be accepted that they are not fully understood by economists. Since the late 1960s violent swings in both operational and investment demand have produced great volatility in prices. One of the main factors driving demand at both levels is the availability of finance for purchase (particularly mortgage finance for residential) and the recognition, or otherwise, that property represents a sound investment medium, particularly in the commercial sector. Thus linking factors are the role of money and the other avenues of investment.

6.7 SUMMARY

- The general understanding is that the property markets are not efficient in economic terms; data is incomplete and inaccessible in many ways. However, it has been argued that, despite this, there is evidence that for commercial property a degree of efficiency does exist.
- The nature of the land market in particular is that supply is, at least in the short term, fixed, although the current system of planning controls over land use and development means that there is flexibility in supply. However, the restrictions on changes in supply mean that prices are very sensitive to changes in demand. Because of this, the land market has been particularly vulnerable to manipulation through the taxation system.
- Property markets are generally considered in terms of the property type and each may display differing characteristics at any one time. The slowness of the planning and the construction processes makes the level and nature of existing stock the dominant force in price determination.
- Within the UK, land ownership and occupation may be combined, or separated through a system of leaseholds. The tradition is, for reasons both historical and economic, that residential property is predominantly owner-occupied, whereas commercial property is often a 'dual market'.
- Where a 'dual market' exists, the factors which affect demand for property as an investment and property as a resource may differ. This means that, although occupational demand lies at the root of economic value of property, in the short tem investment value may appear to move independently of occupational demand.

FURTHER READING

Brown, G. (1991) *Property Investment and the Capital Markets*, London. E. & F.N. Spon Ltd.

Colander, D. and Coats, A.W. (eds) (1993) *The Spread of Economic Ideas*, Cambridge: Cambridge University Press.

Dubben, N. and Sayce, S. (1991) *Property Portfolio Management: an introduction*, London: Routledge.

Fraser, W.D. (1993) *Principles of Property Investment and Pricing*, 2nd edn, Basingstoke: Macmillan.

Isaac, D. (1994) *Property Finance*, Basingstoke: Macmillan.

Marriott, O. (1967) *The Property Boom*, London: Pan Books.

Plender, J. (1982) *That's the Way the Money Goes*, London: André Deutsch.

Ross Goobey, A. (1992) *Bricks and Mortals*, London: Century Business.

Scott, P. (1996) *The Property Masters*, London: E.&F.N. Spon Ltd.

EXAMPLE QUESTIONS

Below are questions relating to this chapter. For each chapter, model answers have been prepared for some of the questions set; these are found in the Appendix.

6.1   'The property market is noted for its inefficiency.' Do you agree with this contention? Give reasons for your answer.

6.2   What are the major factors that determine the development of an investment market in land and buildings? Give your views on whether UK-style investment markets might emerge in Central Europe.

6.3   'Land is in fixed supply; therefore demand is the sole price determinant of land.' Why might this statement be regarded as inaccurate and oversimplistic?

6.4   Why should the heterogeneous nature of property result in an imperfect market?

6.5   Choosing examples drawn from different sectors of the economy (e.g: industrial manufacturer, high-street retailer and financial services company), explain what economic factors might affect their demand for property, and in particular discuss whether they would prefer to occupy as tenant or freeholder.

6.6   What factors affect rental value? Are they the same as the determinants of capital yields?

7 The state and property economics

OBJECTIVES

The objectives of this chapter are to:

● define the state and its economic role;
● examine how the state affects construction and property economics;
● describe the methods and reasons why the state may elect to intervene in the economy;
● explain how and why the construction industry has been used as an economic regulator;
● examine the nature of economic cycles;
● introduce the application of the theory of economic cycles to property and construction.

7.1 INTRODUCTION

From the early chapters it is apparent that no economic textbook can ignore the role of government in influencing the workings of the nation's economy, even where 'market principles' are avowed.

In order to examine the economic relationship between the state and the construction and property industries, it is first necessary to confirm certain definitions. In particular, the concepts of 'the state', 'the nation' and 'the public sector' must be delineated. Chapter 3 showed how important the concept of a central authority has been in maintaining peace, raising money and constructing built environments. In the UK the economy has been traditionally run as a 'mixed economy', which means that both the private and the public sector have been involved in economic production. Since the late 1970s the role of the state as landowner and as industrial entrepreneur has declined with the privatization of publicly held industries and landed estate, but nevertheless the state, both as national body and as local authority continues to influence the working of the economy in general, and in respect of construction and the property markets in particular.

7.2 THE STATE

Max Weber provides a much-quoted definition of the state. He defines it as that agency within society which possesses 'the monopoly of legitimate violence'. This is a simple idea, but within a democratic society is not strictly accurate, for the state is capable of acting as an agent only for the people by whom it has been elected. Thus the power lies, not with the organ of state, but with the electorate.

While it is true that society cannot allow private or sectional violence, it does not (or cannot) forbid conflict. Therefore conflict must be resolved through a central authority, to whom are granted a number of sanctions to maintain order, the ultimate of which is force. This central political force is the state. Weber's definition can be seen to be relevant to the modern centralized 'Western' states that concern this book, but it should be noted that application of this definition to other historical and cultural settings is more problematic.

Chapter 3 explained how Hobbes, Locke and Rousseau called into existence a single central authority termed variously Monarch, Power, Dominion, Legislator or Law Giver. They feared that social evils would befall humankind without such a force, in particular violence and destruction of private property and individual liberty. While today such a situation seems very peculiar, that is because the need for the enforcement of such ideals is unconsciously accepted in our universally applied law and order, general taxation and social conditioning. These are monitored and controlled by the democratic process.

However, despite the undoubted importance of the sanctioning role of government within the UK, it is not generally recognized as the user of legitimate violence, but as the seat of law and of justice. It is from such roots that its use of the economic arises, in particular to ensure social justice. It has also become increasingly important as the vehicle through which economic controls are exercised.

The state provides the stable framework in which economic, social and cultural prosperity and peace may occur. This stability stems in part from the state's monopoly on violence through its military and police enforcers, and is embodied through legislation embodying a citizen's rights and duties. In part, however, this stable framework has been achieved by the relative success of the state as a controller and initiator within the economic process, which has been seen to be associated with increased standards of living.

7.3 THE NATION

The concept of the nation depends upon an understanding of the state. Gellner provides two in-depth definitions:

> In fact, nations, like states, are a contingency and not a universal necessity. Neither nations nor states exist at all times and in all circumstances. Moreover, nations and states are not the same contingency. Nationalism holds that they were destined for each other; that either without the other is incomplete, and constitutes a tragedy. But before they could become intended for each other, each of them had to emerge, and their emergence was independent and contingent. The state has certainly emerged without the help of the nation. Some

nations have certainly emerged without the blessings of their own state. It is more debatable whether the normative idea of the nation, in its modern sense, did not presuppose the prior existence of the state.

What then is this contingent, but in our age seemingly universal and normative, idea of the nation? Discussion of two very makeshift, temporary definitions will help to pinpoint this elusive concept.

1. Two men are of the same nation if and only if they share the same culture, where culture in turn means a system of ideas and signs and associations and ways of behaving and communicating.
2. Two men are of the same nation if and only if they *recognize* each other as belonging to the same nation. In other words, *nations maketh man*; nations are the artefacts of men's convictions and loyalties and solidarities. A mere category of persons (say, occupants of a given territory, or speakers of a given language, for example) becomes a nation if and when the members of the category firmly *recognize* certain mutual rights and duties to each other in virtue of their shared membership of it. It is their recognition of each other as fellows of this kind which turns them into a national, and not the other shared attributes, whatever they might be, which separate that category from non-members.

(Gellner 1993: 67; emphasis on original)

The nation is also a recent creation, and one which can be seen to be a product of nationalism. When general social conditions provide standardized, homogeneous, centrally and locally sustained, all-pervasive cultures a situation arises in which geographically well-defined and intellectually acknowledged unified cultures provide the unit with which people ardently and willingly identify themselves. This unit is the nation. It is thus a product of both will and culture.

The concept of the nation-state as a strong political and economic force is increasingly subject to question. Not only has the European Union rendered Britain less politically and economically isolated, but the increased globalization of world trade towards a single world-market has left all individual nations' economic power diminished. This has led some to suggest that nationality can be considered as a commodity that may be bought and sold, so that individuals may elect to choose their nationality. In addition, this evolutionary change in both economic power and cultural integrity, by undermining the previous definition of the state, leads to a further inference that the nation becomes little more than a bureaucratic relic, a unit for statistical data collection and dissemination, but of little practical value.

7.4 THE PUBLIC SECTOR

As a home of legitimate violence, unified culture and a general will, the state/ nation requires a mechanism to carry out its obligations and duties. This mechanism has traditionally been a bureaucracy; a codified set of procedures carried out within a hierarchical organizational structure by politically neutral and technically and professionally competent employees. This is the public sector. It allows the state to act in its role of fundamental initiator and controller of value, culture and political decision-making. It is the means by which government policy (economic, social, cultural) is implemented, and the means by which government data are collected.

7.5 THE STATE AND PROPERTY

In relation to property and construction the state has two roles:

- as a guarantor of (private) property rights.
- as a purchaser of property and a subscriber to the services of the construction process.

In order to have a property market and economic activity within the property sector the state has to guarantee the concept of private property. The construction industry, on the other hand, merely manufactures the property product and need not operate in a market economy. In guaranteeing property rights the state must employ property professionals to advise it and carry out policy. It also operates in the property and construction markets as a purchaser of products and a seller of services both within its own property sector and as a means of supplying health, education, housing, defence and other services demanded of it.

7.6 THE STATE AND THE ECONOMY

The State has a dual role in the national economy:

- As the manager of the economy, termed **economic regulator**.
- As a player in the economy, acting as both a supplier and a purchaser of goods and services.

After the First World War, and to a greater extent after the Second World War, there was immense pressure upon the British state to provide health, housing, education and work. Previously the nation-state had been a political construct with only macro-political issues while following Adam Smith's *laissez-faire* economic policy. In the twentieth century this was not enough. Two world wars had economically bankrupted the British state, requiring it to raise large sums of money through taxation. Those returning from fighting made increased demands from a greater political awareness. To satisfy these political needs the state became a provider of health, housing, education and a guarantor of minimum social standards. In doing so, it became a large employer (of doctors, nurses, teachers, social workers, urban professionals and the like). The nation thus became a major economic player.

The state was also politically pressured to guarantee the economic well-being of its population in general. It thus attempted to manage the economy; it acted as an economic regulator. Today's political climate generally assumes that such intervention in the economy is self-defeating and that a well-managed economy is one which is left alone. In this way, the provision of health, education and housing, amongst other things, can also best be provided by private enterprise. This apparently ignores the fact that the private sector has historically failed to do this and the changing expectations of people regarding provision. The shift away from the state as economic superpower has left institutions such as the pension-fund companies as the only bodies capable of playing a major economic role. Some believe that they should be more involved in planning and investing in infrastructure projects for the national economic well-being.

7.7 THE ECONOMICS OF THE STATE

As has been shown, there are two points of view about the state's role in economics. The predominant political opinions all stress more reliance on private organizations, and less reliance on central-government provision. Within this viewpoint, most usually termed **monetarism**, the only role that the state is to play is that of supplying a basic legal and cultural framework in which economic activity can safely occur.

It is important to recognize that this is only a recent position, and one that has proven impossible to achieve so far. Despite privatization and the influx of private-sector provision of public services, governments have still found themselves committed to large expenditures and extensive services. Revenue has to be raised to pay for these goods and services. Income is raised through the sale of these goods and services, and from taxation. Governments thus must act as ordinary businessmen, examining market opportunities and reacting to economic events. The status quo of the economy has proven very difficult to shift away from the state. For this reason alone, it is important to study the economics of the state, but there is also the strong tradition of deliberate state involvement.

Government and the state manage the economy for political, social and cultural reasons. The mechanisms by which they do this are thus important. Governments actively manage the economy by the application of Keynesian economic principles, through a mechanism called the **multiplier effect**. This allows them to encourage steady economic growth by removing money (saving) in boom times and spending money (investing) in slumps. Monetarists believe this is unnecessary and that such government manipulation is either useless or dangerous, and this view must be remembered when studying the theory. Keynesians believe that an economy's natural equilibrium is at an unacceptable level, particularly with regard to unemployment. Keynesians see unemployment as a factor to be controlled; monetarists see only money supply as an important factor.

7.8 THE KEYNESIAN MULTIPLIER

One of the greatest supporters of the validity of the state as economic player was Keynes. Keynes advocated the use of government intervention to provide economic stimulus. The principle developed by Keynes was the theory of the multiplier. The Keynesian multiplier offers governments a major economic tool for managing the economy. The multiplier effect states that an initial increase in aggregate demand of £X leads to an eventual rise in national income that is greater than £X.

Simplified, Keynes's analysis of economic recession blames it on a low level of aggregate demand. If the government increases aggregate demand, firms will respond by producing more and using more labour and other resources, and thus paying out more incomes to households. Household incomes will rise, people will spend more and so firms will sell more. Firms will respond by producing more, using more labour and paying out more income to households, who will consume more. And so on. There will thus be a multiplied rise in incomes and employment. This is known as the multiplier effect. Figure 7.1 outlines this model. The process does not go on for ever. Households will pay tax to the government (to repay the original investment), save more and buy imports. Imports remove money from the multiplier circle and thus reduce the multiplier's ability to increase national income. Figure 7.2 shows the multiplier applied to the construction industry. The multiplier has often been applied to construction, although the lengthy construction period makes the industry far from ideal. Its major advantage, however, is its domesticity.

The primary problem with the multiplier as a means of national regeneration is that it requires a domestic market. In other words, purchases must be made from domestic manufacturers, retailers and distributors. In a global economy this is unlikely. However, for some years, it has been suggested that the construction industry provides a perfect vehicle for Keynesian policy since it is a domestic industry and also produces worthwhile outputs, such as houses, hospitals, schools and roads. The extent to which construction offers such a domestic market is now seriously questionable. For example, material suppliers operating in the UK may

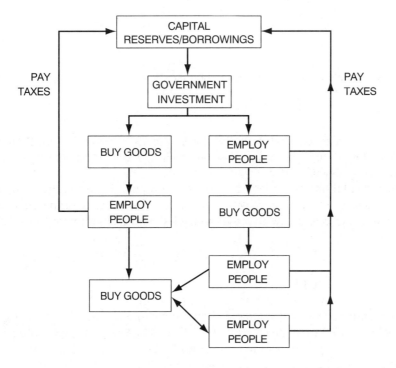

Figure 7.1 Simple model of a 'virtuous-circle' Keynesian multiplier

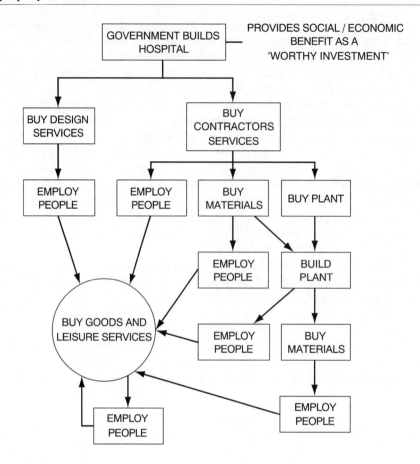

Figure 7.2 Simple model of the construction industry as multiplier

no longer be British, the materials trade deficit in 1995 being £1.46 billion. Membership of the European Union also prevents any discrimination against other members' businesses.

A second solution was to suggest that the European Union offered a protected domestic market of adequate size. Plans were drawn up to implement such a regeneration and employment programme, but political infighting has, to date, halted enactment.

7.9 BUSINESS CYCLES

It is a generally accepted fact that capitalist economies undergo cyclical growth, commonly referred to as business cycles. The Keynesian multiplier utilizes such cycles. There are arguments as to the various types of cycles, whether they are regular (and thus predictable) and over what timescale they occur. Two things are certain: that capitalist economies have grown over time; and that the growth is not continuous but occurs through a series of booms and slumps. Figure 7.3 represents this process.

At point A, the bottom of the slump (or trough), the economy is in recession. Investment levels are low, unemployment is high and confidence is poor. However, this makes costs low and creates the opportunity for high profits. The efficient firms have survived the recession, and industry is leaner and more efficient. Output rises and job opportunities increase as these efficient firms take advantage of both the loss of less efficient competitors and the increased profit levels. Confidence in the economy increases and capitalists are tempted by the profit levels to increase production. The economy passes through point B in a virtuous circle in the boom to point C, the peak of the boom. At this point overconfidence has taken over, speculation on increasingly unlikely projects causes financial loss and bankruptcy, and banks (and other lenders) start to act extremely conservatively in lending and in the calling in of loans. This crisis of confidence in a vicious circle of self-fulfilling prophecies of doom and gloom causes the economy to collapse in a slump (point D) to a new trough (point E), where the process begins again. Note the new trough (E) is at a higher growth level than the previous one (A), as the next peak (F) above the one before (C). Thus the economy grows over time.

This inherent cycle is what governments tried to control, or manage, by use of the Keynesian multiplier. When the economy is in slump governments invest in order to induce confidence, create employment and produce goods to spend wages on in a virtuous circle. When the economy is in boom governments disinvest in order to reduce overconfidence and maintain sustainable employment levels so as to avoid excessive wages causing profit levels to collapse. The aim of government was to ensure growth within a narrow band boom or slump (Figure 7.4) or, ideally, straight-line growth (Figure 7.5).

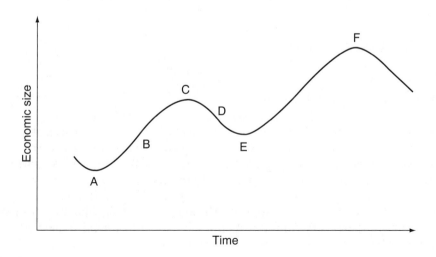

Figure 7.3   The business cycle

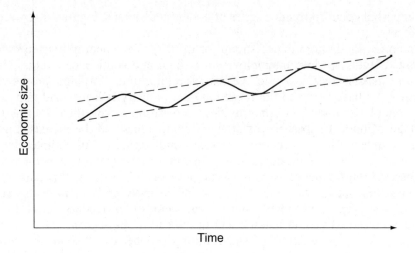

Figure 7.4 Managed business cycle

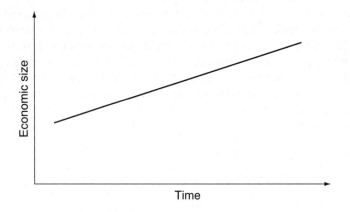

Figure 7.5 Idealized economic growth

7.10 BUILDING CYCLES

It is a generally accepted fact that a building cycle exists which consists of a series of peaks and troughs with an approximately twenty-year frequency. Parry Lewis (1965) is the architect of the empirical evidence that makes this such a universally recognized occurrence. His book principally covers the economic history of the construction industry in Britain (chiefly England and Wales). It amasses a wealth of statistical information on construction (from pre–1700) and attempts to analyse the output of the industry from this within the correct historical framework. The data is attributed, usually, to import and production totals, tax duties and local authority records. The history is roughly divided into the following periods: 1700–1832, 1832–64, 1870–1900, 1910–40, 1950–2000.

Construction during the earlier periods was primarily affected by three factors: harvests, war (and the fear of war) and credit. In the 'subsistence economy' of that time, Lewis suggests, the effect of bad or good harvests is of prime importance, affecting both the national economy and individual incomes and wealth. In addition, government intervention in both its main identified forms dictates the equation of investing in construction. At a time when there was little or no standing army, war resulted in a massive increase in government borrowing to pay the increased ranks of troops and war effort in general, raising interest rates and absorbing all available credit, as well as causing shortages of men and materials. Interest rates were also (in) directly controlled by law, as the governments seem to have attempted to control the economy in order to protect the gold reserves.

The increasing industrialization of the country leads to an increased importance for workers' housing and the railways, as does the generally increasing level of 'public' works. The inclination of people to improve their housing in good times rather than reduce it in bad is quoted as responsible for a dampening in the cycle. As incomes rise people seek better housing, and a rising marriage rate implies increased population size and therefore housing demand. By this time (*circa* 1850) eighteen-year building cycles which transcend the trade cycle had long been recognized. The reasons for this transcendence are given as: demography (affected by harvests, migration and the extended family concept); the long period of production which results in a 'sluggishness' in the industry regarding the supply of credit, labour and materials; the 'stickiness' of rents; exogenous events (basically harvests, war and the supply of credit).

An increasing amount of regional information becomes available in the mid-nineteenth century due to the emergence of local authority building bye-laws and the creation of first temporary and then permanent building societies, which provided a new source of funds for building, and encouraged saving and investment.

Speculation became increasingly rampant as the industry built for the market rather than building to needs. This led ultimately to collapse as investors invested over-optimistically and lost heavily abroad, and banks found themselves unable to meet their obligations. It was found even then that the plague of the industry was the 'cowboy' builders, who worked totally on credit, which was freely available in a boom and then disappeared overnight in a slump. Indeed, records note the distress of clients whose buildings collapse, before or shortly after completion as a regular occurrence.

The industry gradually became increasingly regionalized and the regional demand depended very much on the regional industries. The industry was also becoming more economically sophisticated in that supply became more linked to demand and consideration was increasingly given to demand factors such as costs of production, rents, the levels of migration, the number of empty properties available for use, changes in housing standards demanded by occupiers or legislation, and alternative investment opportunities in other markets.

After the First World War the cycle was influenced by new exogenous factors related to an increasingly complex national economy, identified as the need for urban renewal, a transport revolution, an increase in supply and demand for consumer goods, and the rise in local authority housing. Indeed, the period was characterized by a politicizing of construction, and of housing in particular, by the formation of government policies and direct intervention. The particularly interesting point drawn by Parry Lewis, is the continuance of the same basic influences as in 1700, but with perhaps a shift in emphasis. Post-Second World War there was a rapid rise in the variety of buildings produced and this caused problems in measuring the output of the industry. Parry Lewis concluded that output can be increased by altering the mix of building types produced and that it varies with the unit of measurement. The period also witnessed an economy affected by heavy military expenditure and a rising population demanding more consumption goods. There was a need for a massive replacement programme due to the war and an expectation of 'homes fit for heroes', but also a general increase in living standards, resulting in an improvement in the definition of substandard buildings. One of the principal results was the introduction of new materials and labour-saving methods, with a booming industry unable to cope with demand.

While the empirical research in the work ends at 1960, the description of the workings of the cycle is equally valid today. The period 1960–96 has seen a boom based on growth in the service sector leading to massive office development and a recession resulting from banking problems and import growth. The early part of this period (1960–70) saw a concentration of development, in part based on reconstruction of city centres following war action. Hence shopping centres, designed for the first time to accommodate the car-borne shopper, and offices to house the burgeoning service industries, themselves founded on increasing real wealth, were the subject of much development activity. However, the strong resultant demand for materials after previous supply patterns had undergone trauma due to the war led to the introduction of, for example, system building and the use of poor-quality, ill-seasoned timbers. Also, the requirement to produce buildings quickly encouraged the use of concrete and, in particular, the new, quick-setting cements, such as high alumina, which later were associated with building failure.

Following the property collapse of the mid-1970s, the boom in building in the 1980s was associated with a return to greater use of traditional materials, if not for structural components, at least for finishes, although increasing awareness of the environmental agenda in Europe has promoted both building design and use of materials which are sustainable and energy efficient. Although this shift towards environmental conscience in building has developed, it is still not possible to assess in economic return terms whether financial incentive to 'be green' exists. For the moment the greening of construction appears to be politically–rather than construction-industry or economically–led. However, this is a generalization and many examples exist of individual owner-occupied developments which were constructed with sustainability and energy conservation in mind, and the leading professional bodies (for example the RICS and the CIOB) are attempting to lead practice and put the economic case. Building cycles with periodic 'dips' in activity, while they may create economic problems, provide the opportunity for collective reassessment of techniques and may stimulate research for the next boom period.

7.11 PROPERTY CYCLES

The most recent research has been aimed at identifying and describing a property cycle. This has been presented as a different cycle from those discussed previously, relating to a different sector of the industry.

Definition

Property cycles are recurrent irregular fluctuations in the rate of all-property total return. They exist in other indicators of property activity, but with varying leads and lags against the all-property cycle. The cycle is an amalgam of the several distinct components of the property industry, namely occupier markets, the development industry and investment markets.

Property in the economy

The commercial property market has for a long time exhibited periods of boom and slump. Its importance in the economy has also long been recognized. The London Business School suggested that in 1989 the commercial property market in the UK contributed as much as 10 per cent to GNP and was equivalent in size to the entire gilts market. These findings have subsequently been verified, and it is currently believed that property contributes up to 40 per cent of the asset base of many organizations. The commercial property cycle is argued to feed directly off the economic cycle. Fluctuations in output and employment drive the occupier markets through the demand for space; changes in the financial climate have an impact on property yields and investment allocations.

The massive capital, labour and other resource investments in constructing buildings which stand idle provide an example of the profound and lasting impact of ill-timed development and ill-informed urban planning and management. The property cycle has other, less obvious, effects on key sectors of the economy. These affect occupiers, lenders, borrowers, the government and society.

Occupiers

Property occupiers are affected by the economic cycle because economic efficiency is impeded by building scarcity and expense in economic upswings when new property is most needed to provide for expansion. In downswings, vacant buildings represent a commitment of wasted investment which could have been put to more productive use.

Lenders

For those who lend on property, particularly in the cases of the secondary banks in the 1970s and the major clearing banks in the 1980s, market crashes impose strains on liquidity and capital adequacy which take years to clear, and in the meantime the banks limit lending to more fruitful investments.

Borrowers

For the majority of industrial and commercial companies, who borrow against property assets, market crashes place stress upon their balance sheets, diminish their creditworthiness and threaten their continued existence.

Government

Central and local government is affected because inappropriate development incentives and mistimed infrastructure spending become heavy burdens on public funds.

Society

The public at large is affected because the products of the property market are major elements of urban fabric and economic infrastructure, and the product is often messy and noisy to construct. The success of personal-pension and life-assurance schemes also partly depends on the performance of commercial property.

A property cycle model

A model developed by the University of Aberdeen and Investment Property Data-bank suggests three phases of the cycle:

- **Phase one**: during the early stages of an economic upturn, rental growth is dampened by the surplus of space left over from the recession and the previous boom. The demand recovery stops rents falling but does not push them up dramatically. This phase lasts as long as it takes for the unoccupied space to be absorbed.
- **Phase two**: continued economic expansion faces a shortage of space: rents begin to rise rapidly and trigger development starts. Since these developments are not going to reach the market for a year or more, the second phase of rapid rental growth is likely to be as long as a typical economic upswing. Shortage of space will often worsen, and rental growth will accelerate right up to the peak in the economy. As this happens, developers reacting purely to current market conditions will be encouraged to start more and more new development.
- **Phase Three**: the third phase is likely to begin with weakening or falling demand as the economic recession begins. At the same time, buildings triggered in the early part of phase two will be completed. The consequent fall in rental values puts a sharp stop to development schemes in the pipeline, though the surplus of newly completed space continues to rise as the schemes started at the peak of the boom become operational, but are unused due to the economic recession.

7.12 CONCLUSION

The state operates as a guarantor of rights and as realizer of the general will of its residents. This allows it to provide the stable platform upon which an economy can operate–a secure, permanent legal framework of private property. In addition to this, the State operates within the economy–as a supplier and purchaser, and as a regulator or manager.

Modern governments do not believe that the economy should be managed by them, because it is self-regulating and able to find its own equilibrium. Economic regulation, via the Keynesian multiplier, has been discredited in their view. Business cycles, including the building cycle and the property cycle, are endemic to capitalism and inevitable.

The construction industry was extensively used as an economic regulator by Keynesian economists, but was not a perfect tool because of the time lag between inception and completion. Its primary advantage was that it provided useful infrastructure projects–roads, hospitals and housing for example. Despite the attempts by many governments to remove itself from the economy, it is still a major buyer and seller both in general and in construction and property goods and professional services.

7.13 SUMMARY
- The state exists as holder of cultural values and has control over exercise of power and enforcement.
- The state is a major player in the economy, both directly and indirectly.
- The construction industry has been regarded as an important industry in managing the economy.
- Regulation of the economy can take place through the use of macro- and micro-economic measures; one of the most important ways in which this translates is through the 'multiplier effect', first identified by Keynes.
- Business cycles of boom and bust occur; building and property cycles also exist.

FURTHER READING

Friedman, M. and Friedman, R. (1985) *The Tyranny of the Status Quo*, Harmondsworth: Penguin.
Gellner, E. (1993) *Nations and Nationalism*, London: Blackwell.
Hillebrandt, P. M. (1975) 'The capacity of the construction industry', in Turin, D. (ed.) *Aspects of the Economics of Construction*, London: George Godwin.
—— (1988) *Analysis of the British Construction Industry*, London: Macmillan.
Key, T., McGregor, B., Nanthakumaran, N. and Zarkesh, F. (1994) *Economic Cycles and Property Cycles: Understanding the Property Cycle: Main Report,* London: Royal Institution of Chartered Surveyors.
Parry Lewis, J. (1965) *Building Cycles and Britain's Growth*, London: Macmillan.
Stewart, M. (1986) *Keynes and After*, Harmondsworth: Penguin.

EXAMPLE QUESTIONS

Below are questions relating to this chapter. For each chapter, model answers have been prepared for some of the questions set; these are found in Appendix A.

7.1   Is inflation always a problem? Why or why not?
7.2   Compare public and private monopolies. Which should governments prefer and why?
7.3   Examine the limitations of GNP as a measure of welfare. Describe other measures.
7.4   How important, nationally, is the construction industry?

7.5   How large a role does the public sector play within the industry?
7.6   'The construction industry is used as an economic regulator.' Discuss this statement.
7.7   How does the UK construction industry relate to national and international economics?

The private sector and the financial markets | 8

OBJECTIVES

The objectives of this chapter are to:

- define the concept of investment and explain the need for financial markets to facilitate the lending and borrowing of funds between investor and borrower;
- explain the role of and importance of money, the definitions and the theories behind the effect of changes in demand and supply of money, as well as how the government uses the control of interest rates to constrain inflation as part of its monetary policy;
- highlight the role of the banks, and especially the Bank of England, within the money market as financial intermediaries;
- explain the role of the stock exchanges in facilitating the movement of funds between lenders and borrowers;
- introduce the nature of investment and briefly describe the qualities and the various investment opportunities available to the investor, including financial assets such as equities and gilts, cash and tangible assets such as real property.

8.1 INTRODUCTION

In a developed economy such as the UK's there are people and organizations whose income is greater than their need to spend money on immediate consumption. This excess money could be used to acquire tangible assets such as machinery, new premises, homes or furniture. However, there are those who choose to make their surplus funds available for lending in return for payment (i.e. interest). In the UK a structured financial system has been set up to enable such people to lend their surplus funds easily and with expert help.

Lenders will require incentives to part with their surplus funds. These may include, first, the ability to obtain their surplus funds back quickly and easily, i.e. liquidity, with minimum risk of losing their capital, and, second, return on their funds in the form of interest payments. The size of the return is often traded for liquidity; for example, if a loan is short term it is more liquid than a longer-term loan and therefore will require a lower rate of interest.

Lenders then have to decide how to lend their surplus funds. They can deal directly with borrowers, but this is inefficient and risky, or they can use one or more organized markets where lenders buy liabilities issued by borrowers. The money market is one such organized market, where financial institutions such as the Bank of England, commercial banks, discount houses and merchant banks operate. These will be described both with respect to their role for lenders and borrowers and with respect to the influence they exert on the supply and demand of money and the determination of interest rates. The stock exchanges of London, Tokyo and New York are examples of organized capital markets, and are used by individuals, corporate companies and governments who wish to borrow funds.

Alternatively, lenders could use intermediaries such as banks, building societies, pension funds or insurance companies, who create attractive assets for lenders, e.g. a bank deposit account, a pension or life-assurance policy, which cannot be traded but only returned to the intermediary. Similarly, intermediaries create liabilities for borrowers, such as loans, or use the organized markets to buy securities. Non-bank financial intermediaries such as insurance companies and pension funds, unit trusts and investment trusts will be examined in the next chapter.

Borrowers can be individuals, industrial and commercial companies, governments and financial intermediaries. For example, an individual wishing to purchase a house and requiring a loan of £60,000 is unlikely to find another individual prepared to lend that sum. However, a building society acts as an intermediary by taking surplus funds as deposits from many lenders, paying interest to the lenders and using the deposits to loan the individual borrower a mortgage of £60,000. This system benefits both lender and borrower, so that one person's investment is another person's consumption.

This chapter looks initially at money, and the demand and supply of money, to examine how interest-rate levels are determined. The financial institutions operating within the money market–such as the Bank of England, discount houses, commercial and merchant banks–are described in relation to their role in the economy and how they work within the money market. The various media opportunities are then briefly introduced. This then leads on to the capital market, i.e. the Stock Exchange, where financial investments such as securities can readily be purchased or sold.

8.2 THE ROLE AND IMPORTANCE OF MONEY

As the saying goes, 'money makes the world go round', and it is certainly at the heart of business activity within the City of London. It has developed from the bartering of goods and gold, through coins as an acceptable medium of exchange, to later progress into banknotes, and now the use of cheques, credit cards and even home banking by computer.

The prime function of money is to be an acceptable medium of exchange to provide the owner with a flexible and general purchasing power for goods at any time or place with anyone he/she chooses. Second, money should allow for the comparison of prices of different goods or services. Third, it should provide a liquid store which can accumulate in value. Last, it should be able to act as a deferred payment, i.e. buy now and pay later. In order to serve these functions it should

have a constant, or at least stable, value. Inflation reduces the usefulness and efficiency of money to the point where hyperinflation can render it almost useless. It
should also be of an acceptable quality which is easily transferable, divisible,
portable and durable.

8.3 SUPPLY AND DEMAND OF MONEY

The following section represents a simplified version of the supply and demand for
money; for a more in-depth account of the various theories on this topic, reference
should be made to a pure economics text.

Supply of money

Economics is now so complex that it is important to track the movement of money.
In the UK the Bank of England is responsible for the creation of notes and coins.
However, money is not just cash. The government has introduced definitions of
money supply which have changed over the years. The nation's money supply is
currently defined in two main aggregates, e.g. M0 and M4. A summary of the
UK's official measures can be seen in Figure 8.1. M0 comprises the public and the
banks holdings of notes and coins and the banks' deposits at the Bank of England,
and is the oldest official measure, having existed since 1981. The money supply
can, however, include packages offered by financial institutions, shares, units in a
unit trust and property holdings. While notes, coins and bank deposits serve as a
medium of exchange, other financial assets act as a store of value. However, bank
deposits form the major part of the money supply. M4 contains bank and building-
society deposits, which make up approximately 96 per cent of M4; therefore any
change in the bank and building-society accounts will automatically change the
stock of money, which in turn may affect demand for money, output and prices.

   One theory is that the supply of money can be affected through the creation of
bank deposits by making a loan or purchasing a security. Banks are profit-making
organizations whose aim is to lend money at a higher rate than that at which they

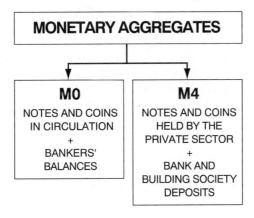

Figure 8.1   The monetary aggregates

borrow. A loan and a security are bank assets as they earn interest and therefore make a profit for the bank. Customer deposits are liabilities which are needed to enable banks to create loans. As the interest rate rises the banks will want to lend more money and hold less money as they will be losing the profits they could otherwise obtain from the higher interest rate. Banks are able to give credit or loans by relying on the fact that their customers will not all want to withdraw their deposits at the same time. Banks are allowed to loan up to 75 per cent (this figure can vary) of their total deposits and the remaining 25 per cent is called the banks' 'reserves'.

For example, a bank lends money on a loan to an individual who uses this loan to buy services from a tradesman. The tradesman then places his payment for the services he has provided into his bank account, increasing that bank's deposits. The tradesman's bank will then use its deposits to create more loans to other customers to buy other services or goods and the number of transactions will increase. A loan will therefore increase the deposits of 'banks' as a whole. Therefore the higher the interest rate, the more money banks will want to lend, increasing bank deposits and the money supply (see Figure 8.2). An increase in bank lending raises profits and increases the supply of money. However, a bank can lend money only if people wish to borrow, and people will wish to borrow more money only if interest rates are low. As interest rates rise the demand for bank lending decreases, and vice versa.

The Bank of England holds all the reserve assets of the deposit banks and manages the Government's account. The public-sector borrowing requirement (PSBR) is the quantity of money the public sector has borrowed after taking into account its total expenditure and revenue. The public sector consists of central and local government and public corporations. Total expenditure includes expenditure on goods and services, grants, interest payments and the finance of losses arising from nationalized industries. Total revenue includes taxes, council taxes, interest

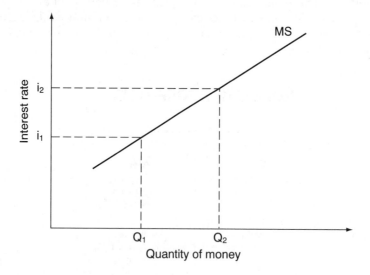

Figure 8.2 The supply of money
Note: MS = money supply

received, repayment of grants and profits from corporations. Thus, when government grants to the private sector exceeds revenue from the private sector to the government, the banks' reserves at the Bank of England will increase, raising the money supply. Likewise, if government revenue exceeds expenditure to the private sector, bank reserves decrease and the money supply falls. In the more usual situation where government expenditure exceeds revenue the government will have a public-sector borrowing requirement (PSBR). The PSBR tends to increase in times of poor economic performance since tax revenues fall and expenditure increases as benefits to those out of work rise. When the economy recovers, tax revenues increase with higher levels of earnings, spending and profits, resulting in reduced benefit payments and a lower PSBR. At the time of writing, the government is attempting to reduce the PSBR by increasing indirect taxation and restraining expenditure.

The monetarists believe that if this deficit (PSBR) is financed by creating more money, i.e. increasing bank reserves and the money supply, then inflation will follow. Alternatively, the PSBR can be financed by borrowing through the sale of securities such as Treasury bills or National Savings, or by running down the stock of liquid assets. These approaches will not increase the money supply. Thus the PSBR can ultimately create changes in the money supply if it is not fully financed by the sale of securities.

Demand for money

The demand for money is the quantity of money people wish to hold. According to Keynesian theory, there are three main reasons why people hold money. The first is the transactionary motive to make transactions for everyday purchases, and the second is the precautionary motive to provide a liquid store for emergencies to meet unforseen expenditure. The quantity of money held for both these motives will vary directly with income. The third motive is for speculation, to be able to shift money to assets where a return is expected. The speculative reason for holding money will depend on the interest rate. There are two main views behind this last motive. First, the higher the rate of interest, the more attractive bonds are to hold, so investors wish to hold less money and invest in bonds. Second, the higher the rate of interest, the more likely it is to fall, enabling bond holders to make a capital gain. (Bond prices move in reverse to interest rates, so falling interest rates result in rising bond prices and vice versa.) Therefore a lower quantity of money will be demanded at higher interest rates as investors will wish to invest the money and benefit from the higher returns. Likewise, the lower the rate of interest, the less attractive bonds are to hold as investments, as interest rates would be expected to rise, resulting in a fall in bond values and a capital loss to the investor; there would therefore be a greater demand to hold money (see Figure 8.3).

The equilibrium rate of interest

The Keynesian view is that the equilibrium rate of interest will occur where the quantity of money demanded is equal to that supplied (see Figure 8.4). Thus at an interest rate above i_1 the money supply (MS) exceeds money demanded (MD) and therefore people will try to buy bonds with their excess money. This will increase

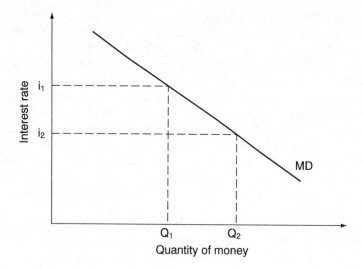

Figure 8.3   The demand for money
Note: MD = money demanded

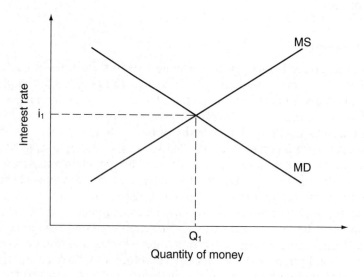

Figure 8.4   The equilibrium rate of interest
Notes:
MS = money supply
MD = money demanded

the price of bonds and cause interest rates to fall until the equilibrium rate is reached.

Changes in supply and demand

An increase in the money supplied shifting MS_1 to MS_2 will cause interest rates to fall from i_1 to i_2 and vice versa (see Figure 8.5).

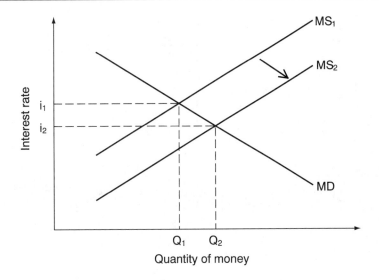

Figure 8.5 Changes in the quantity of money supply
Notes:
MS = money supply
MD = money demanded

Changes in the general price level

Demand for money is expressed in terms of real purchasing power, so an increase in the price level given a certain quantity of money will have the effect of reducing the real value of the money supply; thus there is an excess of demand for money at the original interest rate. People will therefore try to sell bonds or withdraw bank deposits, resulting in a fall in the price of bonds and a rise in interest rates. Thus an increase in the demand for money will also have the same effect, inducing bond sales or bank deposit withdrawals, leading to a rise in interest rates.

If the supply of goods and services is represented by GNP and is fixed, but the demand for these goods and services is negatively sloped (as more money can buy more goods and services at lower price levels), then at lower price levels more money is demanded (see Figure 8.6). If demand for goods and services increases (shift in the demand curve to the right) due to an increase in the money supply, then, given a fixed stock of goods and services Y (i.e. GNP), price levels will rise (causing inflation). This shows a relationship between changes in the supply of money affecting demand for goods and services and inflation. Inflation can be defined as the sustained rise in the general level of prices; the reverse is deflation. In the UK inflation is measured by the retail price index (RPI) and the current government policy is to seek price stability, i.e. low inflation.

There are two schools of thought on the causes and control of inflation, the Keynesian and the monetarist approaches.

(a) The Keynesian approach

The Keynesians believe that an increase in the quantity of money supplied will lead to price increases but argue that a rise in the money supply is not the exclusive

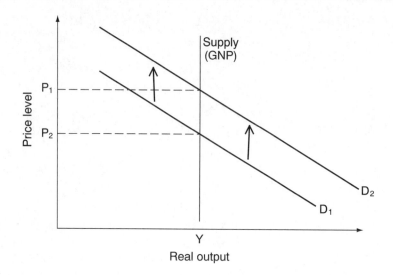

Figure 8.6 Changes in the general price level

cause of inflation – aggregate demand can be increased by government, companies and consumers generating a rise in prices. This is often referred to as the wage–price spiral, whereby an increase in aggregate demand for goods and services leads to an increase in demand for labour. In order to attract new labour, firms have to offer higher wages. This leads to an increase in the costs of production, which is passed on to the consumer via increases in prices, i.e. inflation. This leads to a demand from labour for higher wages, which, if a firm cannot afford them, results ultimately in unemployment. The Keynesians see the effects of controlling the money supply on unemployment as significant, and their policies suggest controlling either consumer credit through higher interest rates or costs through income policy.

(b) The monetarist approach

The quantity theory of money formalized by Fisher suggested a relationship between the supply of money and the price level. During the 1970s research by Professor Milton Friedman proved that an increase in the money supply was followed by an increase in prices (Friedman and Friedman 1980), although there was a time delay of up to eighteen months. The monetarists believe that, under the quantity theory of money, an increase in the money supply so that supply exceeds demand will lead to a rise in demand for financial assets and goods, leading to a fall in interest rates, and will in the long term cause a rise in prices, i.e. inflation. To control inflation the government must control the money supply (in the short term) in order to decrease economic activity and increase unemployment – but only in the short term. Any increase in the quantity of money supplied should be matched only by real growth in real output in the long term. In addition, monetarists argue that government policies should allow for the free operation of markets with minimal intervention by the government, which will then result in higher national incomes and lower unemployment.

However, during the 1980s the Conservative government sought to control inflation through its monetarist policies by setting targets to control the supply of money. They consistently failed to achieve their targets, which resulted in much political embarrassment. During the early 1990s targets for money supply were given a lower priority. Despite the various economic theories on the causes and control of inflation, the government controlled inflation during the late 1980s and early 1990s through the manipulation of interest rates. One could argue that this has controlled the supply of money and influenced the level of demand for investment and consumption by consumers, but unfortunately at the cost of high unemployment.

Inflation and property

A booming housing market such as in the 1980s is normally associated with rising inflation. The government's anti-inflationary policy of higher interest rates caused a downturn in the housing market, leading to a fall in demand for housing and a fall in construction in the 1990s.

Traditionally in periods of high inflation investment in real property is attractive to institutional investors such as pension funds and insurance companies, as property offers rising rental income through periodic rent reviews and increasing capital values. When demand rises capital values rise and property yields fall, but demand will fall when the reverse occurs, i.e. when the government increases interest rates to constrain rising inflation, causing property yields to rise and capital values to fall.

The public-sector borrowing requirement (PSBR)

Part of recent government financial strategy has been to reduce the PSBR, which, as explained above, may affect the supply of money. Alternative means of financing the PSBR are either to reduce public expenditure or to increase taxation. Both options produce adverse public reaction for the government, which now relies more on interest rates as a means of controlling the money supply and as part of a policy of maintaining low inflation. When government believes that inflation or economic activity can be affected by changes in the amount of money in circulation or by the general level of interest rates, it will use the Bank of England as its main instrument in the money market to balance the supply of money with the demand for money in the market through the manipulation of short-term interest rates.

8.4 BANK OF ENGLAND METHODS OF CONTROL AND DIFFICULTIES

The Bank of England was first established under Royal Charter by King William and Queen Mary, who needed money to fight Louis XIV of France. A Scottish merchant, William Paterson, suggested forming a bank to lend money to the government. Within fifteen years it became the largest bank in the UK and was affectionately known as the Old Lady of Threadneedle Street. During the nineteenth century it became the lender of last resort, which helped to maintain public confidence and creditability within the banking system. It was nationalized under the

Attlee government in 1946 and is now answerable to the Treasury. It comprises a governor (Eddie George at the time of writing) and sixteen directors appointed by the Crown but recommended by the prime minister. In 1997 the government gave greater delegated powers to the Bank of England in respect of changes in the interest rate. While in the past any change in interest rate had to be ratified by the chancellor, the Bank of England, acting on advice, may now make such changes.

The Bank of England holds the accounts of clearing banks, discount houses, merchant banks, foreign banks, overseas banks, the International Monetary Fund (IMF) and some industrial companies, as well as the official reserves of certain countries. It has three main objectives: first, to maintain the value of the nation's money or restrain increases in the price level of goods and services through policy and market operations agreed with the government; second, to ensure the soundness of the financial system by supervision of the banks and some financial markets, e.g. the gold market and foreign-currency market; and third, to promote the efficiency and competitiveness of the financial system.

The Bank of England achieves the first objective through monetary policy by influencing the price of money, i.e. the rate of interest. The Bank of England is the banker to the government and other banks, and is therefore in a position to forecast the pattern of monetary flows between the government's account and the commercial banks' accounts. When more money flows from banks to the government, the banks will find themselves short of liquid funds. The Bank of England, as lender of last resort, relieves this shortage by buying commercial bills from discount houses and releasing more money into the market.

Bills of exchange

The familiar cheque is, in essence, a type of bill of exchange, which is a written IOU promising payment of a stated sum at a future date. Bills of exchange are negotiable, so the owner can sell them on to a buyer, who can claim payment at a future date. The original issuer of the bill or his/her bank will pay the amount on the due date. When the bill is issued a bank must accept it by signing the bill and agreeing to pay the full amount on the due date. Bills tend to be issued by large companies which wish to borrow money from banks.

Certificates of deposit (CDs)

Certificates of deposits (CDs) are issued by banks and financial institutions as proof that a deposit for a specific, normally short, time at a fixed rate of interest has been made. These are negotiable and can be sold on at any time. They usually have a life of between three months and five years, and are used by mainly large organizations as the smallest deposit is £50,000.

Discount houses borrow from day to day any surpluses of the commercial banks and invest them in short-term investments such as Treasury bills, commercial bills, gilt-edged stock maturing in less than five years, local-authority bills and undertake to repay the money when required. If the demands of the banks leave the discount houses short of cash they have access to the Bank of England to sell part of its bill portfolio. Bill transactions normally take place twice daily, at 12.15 p.m. and 2.15 p.m. If the Bank of England finds the rates offered by the discount houses too low it will refuse to buy and therefore fail to relieve the shortage of money, so pushing up interest rates. If the rates are too high it will accept additional bills at a lower rate, injecting more money into the money market and forcing interest rates down.

Thus, the Bank of England can provide cash by purchasing commercial or Treasury bills, short-term three- or six-month IOUs from the discount houses, who in turn supply cash to commercial banks in exchange for commercial bills. The bills are purchased by the Bank at a discount, which reflects the rate of interest the Bank has selected. This interest rate is passed through the financial system. When the Bank changes its dealing rate the commercial banks quickly react by deciding on a base rate; this influences the level of interest rates for the whole economy in the short term and will ultimately affect longer-term mortgage-interest rates. The Bank can also use this method to reduce or increase the money supply in the economy in order to facilitate the operation of monetary policy.

8.5 BANKS

Clearing banks, overseas and foreign banks.

These are the large clearing or retail banks such as Barclays, Midland, NatWest and Lloyds TSB plc, which have their headquarters in the City and operate about 13,500 branches in the UK. They include British overseas banks such as Standard Chartered and foreign-owned banks which have their head offices overseas and subsidiaries in London. UK clearing banks are institutions which are licensed and supervised by the Bank of England under the Banking Acts 1979 and 1987. Authorized banking institutions range from Barclays Bank to the financial subsidiary of Marks & Spencer.

Retail clearing banks offer services to the individual which include personal loans, budget accounts, formal overdraft facilities, and credit card facilities such as Visa or Access; they undertake foreign-exchange transactions and house-mortgage lending. They can also provide a range of financial services, including the arrangement of insurance policies and the sale of unit trusts and executor and trustee services.

These banks also offer a range of services to traders/businesses. They accept short- and long-term deposits in current and deposit accounts for individuals and businesses where money can be kept safe, receiving interest, yet payments or receipts can be made easily and quickly through cheques between banks. They are referred to as clearing banks as they use a cheque-clearing system to provide for the transfer of money. The cheques are paid into the automated clearing system, known as the Clearing House Automated Payment System (CHAPS), enabling individual institutions to pay net amounts to each other via accounts at the Bank of England. These banks will also offer overdraft facilities to traders/businesses, for example to finance stocks or works in progress.

Most of the large clearing banks are public limited companies listed on the Stock Exchange and therefore have an obligation to increase profits for the benefit of shareholders. Some banks have merged or taken over building societies. For example, Lloyds TSB Group plc was renamed after Lloyds Bank bought out the Cheltenham & Gloucester Building Society in August 1995 and merged with TSB in the December of the same year. It has now become a strong force in the market, having combined Lloyds' expertise in mortgage and small business lending with the TSB's recognized strength as a saving institution and its success in general insurance underwriting business. The privatized Girobank was originally part of the Post Office but is now owned by the Alliance & Leicester.

Merchant banks (accepting houses)

The big merchant banks include names such as Baring's, acquired by ING (a Dutch bank) in 1995 for £1 following the Nigel Leeson banking scandal, Rothschild's and Warburg's. Merchant banks traditional function was to finance overseas trade by guaranteeing or 'accepting' bills of exchange issued by merchants for a fee. They offer banking services to commerce, which include credit acceptance (i.e. they accept or guarantee bills of exchange on behalf of customers and sell them on to discount houses) and foreign-exchange business. An important area of work is giving financial advice to large corporations on raising finance, devising dividend policies, undertaking acquisitions and mergers, and initiating and defending takeover bids. Merchant banks will advise companies including property companies on the drawing up of prospectuses and the handling of new issues of debentures or shares to the public. They are also involved with the management of funds for pension funds, investment and unit trusts; their area is expanding due to the greater interest of private investors in the equity market and the growth of personal pensions providing more funds for the banks to manage. The merchant banks have a significant role to play in the commercial property market.

Since the 'Big Bang' in October 1986 some of the leading merchant banks have been taken over by clearing banks–for example the acquisition of Montagu Evans by the Midland Bank–but they have retained worldwide clients and undertake wholesale banking business for large industrial and wealthy private clients, institutions and the government due to their expertise in advising on complicated financial deals.

Rothschild merchant bank houses the London gold market and provides the daily chairman. In April 1988 the core members formed the London Bullion Market Association which is supervised by the Bank of England. Five members meet daily to 'fix' a price to satisfy buyers' and sellers' orders. The agreed price at each fixing is used in legal negotiations and by the world's central banks to value their reserves.

Discount houses

There are nine discount houses, including such names as City Union Discount, whose prime function is to borrow and lend spare money for short periods. They buy bills of exchange and short-term securities such as bank acceptances and certificates of deposit (CDs) at a discount, and sell them to other banks and investors such as the government or commercial borrowers who need liquid assets. The bills are repaid at their full face value at maturity, the discount being the interest earned by the discount house.

Discount houses provide industrial and commercial firms, financial institutions (banks, building societies, finance houses etc.) local authorities and the government with liquid assets. They sell bills of exchange which if drawn up between two industrial firms are called 'trade bills' (or commercial bills) and if accepted by a bank are known as 'bank bills'. The customer gives the supplier an IOU and the supplier sells it to a discount house, at a discount, in order to obtain the money in advance. The customer eventually pays in full to whoever holds the bill. A CD is a tradeable document which accrues interest but provides extra liquidity for the borrower – mainly banks. These were used to finance domestic trade but are used increasingly to finance foreign trade through the 'international bill on London'.

A growing number of industrial firms regularly use discount houses for their borrowing and lending facilities. Their lending is competitive with the traditional overdraft or fixed-term loan, as commercial money can be deposited overnight or longer at rates close to the inter-bank rate and yet is still secure and liquid.

Discount houses are used by the Bank of England to influence the economy via its monetary policy. The discount houses bid competitively for the money or Treasury bills which the Bank makes available until supply and demand balance at a rate acceptable to the Bank. This rate influences monetary policy and affects other interest rates, as described earlier in this chapter.

Building societies

Building societies started in the eighteenth century as friendly societies where members made regular payments to finance house-building in their locality. Members placed deposits but were not shareholders or owners in the traditional sense. This enabled them to be exempt from banking regulations. The concentrated growth of building societies in recent years, due to the increase in home ownership, has resulted in a few large building societies dominating the market but with an increasing number of branches. Initially they enabled individuals to deposit spare money in interest-bearing accounts and also provided individuals with finance for home purchase or improvements. Since the Building Societies Act in 1986, building societies have been able to diversify and compete with banks by providing individuals with a range of banking services including current accounts (with interest), cheque cards and credit cards, a cash-point service sometimes linked to banks ('LINK'), and to adopt a freer open-market approach to mortgage lending which has resulted in more frequent changes in interest rates.

The Building Societies Act also gave societies the power to become incorporated, i.e. to become a public limited company with shareholders rather than members. The Abbey National was the first building society to become a public company listed on the Stock Exchange. In the 1980s and 1990s several building societies have incorporated and many of the major building society names (Abbey National, Halifax, Woolwich, to name but three) have become banks. The act also established the Building Society Commission to supervise the conduct of societies to ensure they meet with the intentions of the Act.

8.6 THE NATURE OF INVESTMENT

People with surplus money to spend generally consider all the known available options before making their decision in order to achieve the best value for money. Investment is the use of 'spare' cash, over and above day-to-day expenditure, in the hope that it will provide returns for the future. Investment may be defined as the laying out of money now in order to receive a financial return in the form of a future income and/or a capital gain. The future income flow may be fixed or variable and may not be guaranteed. The expected size of the future financial return and the length of time the investment is held will determine how risky the investment is considered to be. Generally, the higher the risk of receiving a financial income, the higher the rate of return expected by the investor. Likewise, the longer the period of time the investor is laying out money before a return is achieved, the higher the rate of return required. It should be noted at this stage that different investments display many other additional qualities, which will be examined in detail in volume 2 of this series, Property Pricing: From Investment to Value. However, investors should generally attempt to select the investment whose qualities most suit their particular needs.

8.7 AN INTRODUCTION TO INVESTMENT MEDIA

A wide range of investment opportunities is available to the individual investor including cash assets such as building society and bank deposits; financial assets such as securities; and tangible assets including 'real' property such as land and buildings, and personal property such as antiques or paintings. However, individual investors are not the only investors in the market; financial institutions such as banks, insurance companies, pension funds, investment trusts and unit trusts also invest heavily in the investment media and offer financial investment assets in packages to suit the individual investor, such as life-assurance policies and pensions.

Cash assets are normally non-marketable investments which offer security in monetary terms, but no real capital growth, and earn interest which can be either fixed or variable. The original capital invested remains the same over time with no increase in monetary value. Growth is achieved only if the interest is not withdrawn and spent, but reinvested by adding it to the original capital sum invested. Thus the interest and capital both earn interest in future years and increase in value. This is known as compounding (see volume 2 for more detail). The investments may not be protected against the effects of inflation, and a period of notice of withdrawal may be required to prevent penalties in the form of loss of interest being imposed.

Examples of cash assets include building society and bank deposits which provide low but variable interest rates according to the prevailing levels, and the National Savings scheme, available from the Post Office and offered by the government as a method of funding its borrowing requirement. These comprise National Savings Certificates; National Savings Bonds; Indexed-linked Savings Certificates which overcome the effects of inflation by index-linking the value of the certificate to changes in the retail price index; capital bonds, where the gross interest is added back to the value of the investment; and the National Savings Bank investment account, which pays gross interest and is therefore suitable for the non-tax-payer.

Financial assets such as fixed interest stocks are securities issued by the government, a local authority or a company as a loan in return for fixed interest over a specified term until redemption date when the loan is repaid. The redemption date is the future date on which a security is due to be repaid by the issuer or borrower at its full face–value that is, the original amount on the date of issue. In financial papers the year of the redemption date of government securities is included within the title, e.g. Treasury 12 per cent 1998, and is the date of the last payment of interest. The government issues gilt-edged stocks in order to finance its PSBR and regulate the economy. The term 'gilt' is derived from the high-quality gilt-edged paper used for the certificates issued by the government in earlier times. Gilt-edged securities may be short-dated i.e. redemption is within five years; medium-dated, where redemption lies between five and fifteen years away; and long-dated, where their life exceeds fifteen years to redemption. They are readily and quickly marketed on the Stock Exchange, but the price will fluctuate depending on current market conditions. Their attraction relies on the fact that the government is unlikely to default on the payment of the interest or the redemption value on redemption day, which can be fixed or lie between two dates. Hence the income and capital are considered to be very secure in monetary terms. However, in times of rising inflation gilts become unattractive, as the income and capital are fixed and will lose their purchasing power, and they are not inflation proof. The government also issues index-linked gilts, where the repayment of capital and interest is guaranteed to move in line with inflation based on the retail price index. Although the coupons are low at 2 per cent–2.5 per cent, the return is above inflation.

Businesses too need to raise money to expand, and they can obtain loans on the stock market by issuing debentures and loan stock, which are tradeable either through the main Stock Exchange or, for less well-established companies, on the alternative investment market. A debenture is a loan raised by a company, paying a fixed rate of interest and normally secured on the assets of the company. A company can issue loan certificates which can be secured against specific company assets (fixed debentures), secured against the general assets of a company (a floating debenture), or unsecured (naked debenture). The debenture holder is entitled to a fixed annual rate of interest, usually paid half-yearly, over a specified term. Convertible loan stock are certificates which are convertible into ordinary shares on terms specified at the date of issue. Local-authority loans are similar to debentures but are advertised in the financial pages of national papers.

A share is a security giving part-ownership of a company to the shareholder and is another method of corporate funding, i.e. it enables companies to raise funds to expand business. A share is often known as an equity, as it is the residue of the company's assets after paying all its debts. There are a number of different shares, the main two being an ordinary share and a preference share. An ordinary share can be sold easily and quickly on the Stock Exchange, where the price will fluctuate depending on the demand for and supply of the company's shares and on how well the company is performing. The shareholder is entitled to a dividend, which is a share of the profits after all expenses, charges and interest have been met and is usually paid twice-yearly and net of the standard rate of income tax.

The size of the dividend will fluctuate from year to year, depending upon the amount of residual profit and the success of the company. A preference share is a security offered by a company which pays a fixed dividend, and it takes priority over ordinary shareholders' dividends.

Tangible assets are investments in real property or personal property, and include commodities such as antiques, works of art and paintings. Commodities will give the owner some pleasure and may provide a capital gain on resale if chosen wisely, but future value is unpredictable and they can easily make a loss. However, they do not provide an income but could make an annual loss as they may require high insurance premiums, and they may need to be placed in a safe environment and be protected from deterioration.

Investment in real property can be either direct or indirect, as illustrated in Figure 8.7. Direct property investment is the purchase of an interest, either a freehold or a leasehold interest in many different types of property. The acquisition of a freehold interest provides for perpetual ownership subject to covenants in the deed and local planning controls, while a leasehold interest is restricted to a specified term of years, and the leaseholder is, in addition, constrained in the use of the land and property by the terms of the lease. The various types of property investments are residential; retail, which comprises the high-street shop, superstore, retail warehouses, and in- and out-of-town shopping centres; office property, which range from purpose built-office blocks and business parks to converted houses and upper floors of a shop; factories, hi-tech and warehouses, leisure property, agricultural property and forested land. Direct investment in property generally requires a large amount of capital outlay and has the disadvantage of being illiquid, as property-buying is a costly and lengthy process, requiring the skills of several professionals, including solicitors, surveyors and estate agents. Property therefore tends to be a long-term investment which, in addition, requires maintenance and expert management. Security of the rental income will depend on the type of tenant. It is possible to make capital gains on resale.

Indirect property investment can take several forms and is ideal for the individual investor who wishes to benefit from the gains made on large property investments but who does not have the funds to purchase his/her own property or the necessary skill to manage and maintain it. The individual investor can acquire shares in a publicly quoted property company, units in an authorized unit trust, which can purchase interests in property and employ a professional to manage the property fund, or units in a life-assurance company's unitized property fund by acquiring a regular-premium policy or a single-premium insurance bond. To provide for an income on retirement an employer and employee make regular contributions to a pension fund which invests the proceeds in property and other financial assets. The income received from these investments is used to pay pensions on retirement.

8.8 INVESTMENT QUALITY

Many of the above-mentioned investment media will have different features which make them attractive or unattractive to different investors depending upon their requirements. Some of the most common and important qualities which should be

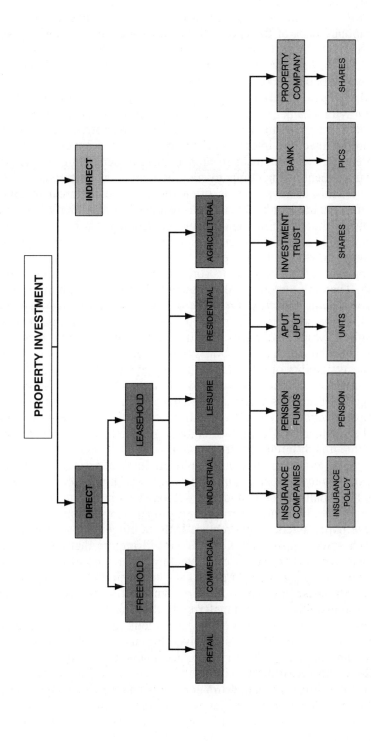

Figure 8.7 Property Investment
Notes:
APUT = authorized property unit trusts
UPUT = unauthorized property unit trusts
PICS = property income certificates

considered by the investor to enable him/her to select the most appropriate investment are briefly examined below.

Investors will want to know that their invested capital is **secure** and that they will get their money back at the end of the loan period. An additional desirable quality would be if the capital appreciated in value above the rate of inflation, i.e. achieved real growth. Investors will also require an **income**, such as interest from gilts, dividends from equities or rental income from property. An income will be more secure if it is paid regularly by a reliable borrower – such as interest on a deposit account with a bank or coupons paid by the government on gilts – who is unlikely to default on payment. The more reliable the borrower, the more secure the income and the lower the interest likely to be received. Conversely, dividends receivable on equities will fluctuate from year to year, depending on the performance and management of the company and the income is considered to be less secure. However, this disadvantage is often offset by real growth in dividend expectations. The security of rental income receivable on property investments will depend upon the reliability and financial standing of the tenant. Rental incomes are normally fixed for a period of years between rent reviews, which is when any income growth can be achieved.

Securities can be easily and quickly sold on the stock market and converted back into cash. They are therefore said to be very **liquid**, which may be a desirable quality for certain investors. Property, on the other hand, can take several months to sell, as the services of professionals such as surveyors, solicitors and agents are required, which also makes it costly and a comparatively illiquid investment. Another problem which affects liquidity is the efficiency of the market organization and the availability of information. The stock market is very efficient with full information on its products updated by the minute, allowing for exact and instant pricing, and securities can be liquidated within one week. The property market is comparatively inefficient, lacking full information on sales as it is spread across a number of local, regional and national geographical markets and every property investment is different (heterogenous).

Investments such as securities can be sold off in smaller lots if required by investors. Unfortunately, property normally requires a large capital outlay, often too large for the small investor, and can seldom be divided up on resale, so investors are unable to liquidate a part of their property investment.

Securities are paper assets which require **little management and no maintenance costs**. The ownership of units in a trust will require that an investor pay management fees for his/her expertise in selecting a portfolio of assets. Property also requires skilled management to collect the rent and ensure that tenants are complying with the lease covenants. Property will need expensive maintenance, although this responsibility can be transferred to the tenant.

Finally investors require a **return** on an investment, and this is a combination of income and capital gain. The risk involves the uncertainty of achieving the required return, and higher levels of risk are acceptable only with higher rates of return. **The life of an investment**, will also affect risk. The longer the life of an investment the more difficult it is to estimate returns and the riskier the investment is considered to be. The **tax** status of investors is another important quality to be considered, as it will affect the level of income and capital gains made, and therefore adversely affect return. Risk can, however, be reduced by building a fully

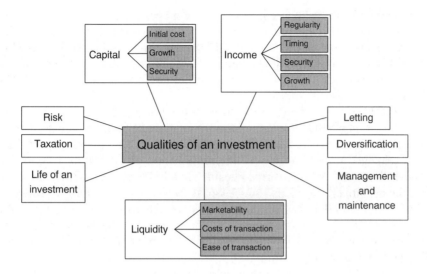

Figure 8.8 The qualities of an investment

diversified portfolio of assets comprising a wide range of different types of assets with different qualities. A diagram illustrating a summary of the key qualities of an investment can be seen in Figure 8.8.

8.9 INVESTOR'S CHOICE

The choice of investment will depend primarily on the level of risk the investor is prepared to accept for the level of return required for a particular type of investment. Individual investors will need to consider their personal circumstances: how much can they afford to invest? are they looking for income or growth in capital value? what is their personal tax position? how long is the investment to last? Do they want to take on the responsibility for selection and management or would they prefer to hand over the control to a professional manager? Individual investors' risk, will be dependent on their preferences for particular investments and those investments' respective qualities.

A portfolio of investments of financial institutions such as insurance companies, pension funds or trusts tends to comprise equities in the UK, overseas equities, government securities, property and cash to provide for liquidity. Their proportions may be decided by the managers, a board of trustees or directors. It is, however, up to the managers to select specific investments within their sector and to meet certain target rates of return laid down by the principals.

8.10 AN INTRODUCTION TO THE STOCK EXCHANGE AND THE FINANCIAL MARKETS

In 1553 the first joint-stock company was formed when a merchant, Sir Hugh Willoughby, needed to raise sufficient funds for three ships to sail to the Far East.

The public could subscribe to equal shares giving part ownership of the company. This set a pattern for the future to enable government and companies to raise funds. Trade grew quickly and by the 1760s 150 brokers had formed a club at Jonathan's coffee house, which later, after burning down, moved to New Jonathan's in Threadneedle Street. In 1773 the name was changed to the Stock Exchange.

In 1986 the Stock Exchange merged with the International Securities Regulatory Organization (ISRO) to become the International Stock Exchange of the UK and the Republic of Ireland Ltd, although it is still commonly referred to as the Stock Exchange. It became a private limited (non-profit-making) company in November 1986 and member firms became shareholders, each with a single vote. Under the Financial Services Act 1986 it became a Recognized Investment Exchange (RIE), and it has produced rules for the listing of securities and to ensure fairness in the marketplace. The Stock Exchange has a supervisory role, with the authority to lead investigations into criminal offences such as insider dealing and market manipulation.

The London Stock Exchange is a marketplace where securities can be traded efficiently, enabling investors with money to lend to contact borrowers who wish to raise money, such as the government and corporate companies in industry and commerce. Four main types of security are traded on the Stock Exchange, including UK equities, overseas equities, UK gilts and, lastly, bonds or fixed-interest stocks, issued normally by either companies or local authorities.

Market-makers can quote a two-way price for securities they deal in and will specialize in certain types of securities. Gilt-edged market-makers (GEMMs) deal with the Bank of England, which issues gilts on behalf of the government. Other market makers deal in equities and corporate bonds, specializing in different sectors of the market. The traditional method of dealing between members face to face on the market floor has been replaced by new technology which allows market-makers to trade by telephone from their own dealing rooms.

The primary market

The Stock Exchange is a primary market, where new securities are issued for cash and a secondary market, where existing securities can be traded between investors. To raise money on the primary market a company must first be listed.

Listing on the stock exchange

When a company reaches a certain size in terms of turnover it can seek a listing on the Stock Exchange (costs £400,000). The purpose of a listing is to enable the company to raise capital. A listing involves providing the exchange with historic record of the company's trading and finances, together with its management and business prospects. The company must then continue to give the exchange any information which may affect its share price. When a company is first listed the share issue is underwritten by merchant banks which, for example, will buy any shares not taken up. Shares are normally issued in blocks, and the hardest task is for the company and underwriters to seek a listing at a sensible price. If it is too low **stags** will subscribe in order to sell and make a quick profit. Once a company is listed market forces determine the share price. The shares of more successful companies are known as 'blue-chip'.

According to DTZ Debenham Thorpe (1996) research, the Bank of England and brokers reports, £1.2bn was raised by property companies in 1995/96 through the issue of equities and debentures on the primary market, a decrease on the £2bn raised in 1993 (see Figure 8.9). Examples of the major equity issuers are property companies such as Land Securities, British Land and Burford. The primary market also allows the government to raise capital through the issue of gilt-edged securities, and local authorities to do so by issuing negotiable bonds.

Trading of UK equities on the secondary market

Once the company is listed its ordinary shares can be traded on the secondary market through market-makers, who deal with brokers acting on behalf of clients or directly with institutional investors. The market-makers fees are the difference between the prices at which they offer to buy and sell the securities.

In a perfect marketplace the prices should accurately reflect the companies' prospects and allow for the accurate pricing of new issues. On the Stock Exchange companies are constantly being valued, and information concerning their performance is analysed and reflected in prices almost immediately. To enable the Stock Exchange to operate efficiently, a computerized network system has been developed called SEAQ (Stock Exchange Automated Quotation System), which provides all brokerage offices with a screen continuously displaying updated price quotations, reports on shares traded, with best prices offered and dealing can be carried out over the telephone. There is also a SEAQ International, which allows for the trading of international equities. To support SEAQ the Stock Exchange

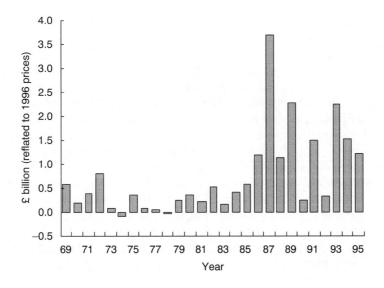

Figure 8.9 Net UK capital issues by property companies
Source: Bank of England; Broker's reports; DTZ Debenham Thorpe Research (1996)

introduced the Stock Exchange Alternative Trading Service in 1992 to provide, for example, more detailed information on companies, historic trading activity for stocks and quoted two-way prices.

The Stock Exchange has a five day account period. The settlement is operated by an electronic system called CREST, introduced in 1996. CREST allows for the electronic transfer of registered stock to minimize the movement of paper. However, the shareholder can still opt to keep his or her share certificate. It is also supported by SETS–an electronic trading service, introduced in 1997, which provides an electronic order-matching service dealing in FTSE 100 stocks.

By 1991 the Third Market had been abandoned due to lack of trade, leaving the Unlisted Securities Market, where shares of unlisted companies can be traded. The Unlisted Securities Market, however, was wound up by the end of 1996 and replaced by the Alternative Investment Market (AIM), which was launched in June 1995. AIM allows young, small, growing companies (plc) to raise capital. These companies do not need an operating record of over three years or minimum proportion of equity, but they do need a prospectus with details of director, shareholdings and working capital. AIM attracts start-up companies, management buy-outs and buy-ins. In 1996 there were 251 companies in AIM, with a collective worth of £5,298.5 million (London Stock Exchange 1997: 48).

International importance

The location of the Stock Exchange within the time zone allows it to deal with markets such as Tokyo in the Far East and New York in North America on the same day. More overseas companies are listed in London than on any other exchange; around 65 per cent of all shares traded outside their home country use the London Stock Exchange (London Stock Exchange 1993).

8.11 CONCLUSION

This chapter has examined the role of money and explained how changes in the supply of and demand for money will affect the interest rate. The reader should appreciate how the money market operates and why the government feels it necessary to control the supply, and hence interest rate levels, as part of its monetarist policy. It is important to understand that it is surplus funds that lenders wish to invest and that there are various alternative investment media to choose from–the lender's choice will depend on the qualities required from an investment.

The banking institutions play a vital role within the money market, enabling the government to control the economy and acting as financial intermediaries between lenders and borrowers. The capital market or stock market also allows borrowers such as the government and corporate companies to raise funds for expansion and to produce economic growth, which will hopefully raise living standards for individuals–the original lenders–to provide them with more surplus funds to invest and so the money goes round!

> 8.12 SUMMARY ● The money market and the stock market enable investors to lend surplus funds to borrowers such as banks, corporate bodies and the government.
> ● Changes in the supply of or demand for money will ultimately result in changes in price levels. If supply exceeds demand price levels will rise, i.e. inflation.
> ● The government uses the Bank of England and discount houses within the money market to control the supply of money by manipulating interest rates to pursue a policy of low inflation.
> ● The Bank of England, commercial banks, discount houses and merchant banks act as financial intermediaries between lenders (investors who deposit money) and borrowers (government and corporate companies, including banks).
> ● Investors invest surplus money in exchange for a return (interest and/or capital). They select investments – such as equities, fixed-interest investments, including gilts, property or cash – which display qualities most suited to their needs.
> ● The Stock Exchange enables the borrower to raise capital to fund projects, expenditure and expansion on the primary market, and allows investors to trade investments on the secondary market.

FURTHER READING

Goff, T. G. (1986) *Theory and Practice of Investment*, 5th edn, London: Heinemann.

Gough, L. (1995) *The Investor's Guide to How the Stock Market Really Works*, London: Pitman.

Howells, P. G. A. and Bain, K. (1994) *Financial Markets and Institutions*, 2nd edn, London and New York: Longman.

Kerridge, D. S. (1988) *Investment: A Practical Approach*, M & E Handbook Series, London: Pitman.

London Stock Exchange (1993) *Introduction to the London: Stock Exchange*, London: International Stock Exchange of the United Kingdom and the Republic of Ireland Ltd.

Manser, J. E. (1994) *Economics: A Foundation Course for the Built Environment*, London: E. & F. N. Spon Ltd.

Molyneux, P. (1991) *Banking: An Introductory Text*, London: Macmillan.

EXAMPLE QUESTIONS

Below are questions relating to this chapter. For each chapter, model answers have been prepared for some of the questions set; these are found in the Appendix.

8.1 An investor has recently won the lottery and wishes to invest £2,500,000 in property (direct and indirect). Explain the options available and how you might advise him/her to invest the funds.

8.2 a) What are the main objectives of the Bank of England? Explain in particular how it serves the government.

b) Explain the role of the various banks as financial intermediaries within the money market.

8.3 Explain the role of money. How and why does the government attempt to control the supply of money in the money market?

8.4 Distinguish between a commercial bank and a merchant bank. Explain how each might advise a property company on how to raise funds.

8.5 a) What are the ideal qualities of an investment?

b) Compare and contrast the investment characteristics of equities, gilts and property.

Financial intermediaries $\boxed{9}$

OBJECTIVES

The objectives of this chapter are to:

- introduce the important role that non-bank financial intermediaries play in the City;
- examine the purpose, structure and investment of funds by the two main types of financial institutions, namely insurance companies and pension funds;
- compare the roles, as financial intermediaries, of unit trusts and investment trusts within the investment markets;
- describe the types of property company and how they raise finance, highlighting the important role of banks as lenders to property companies;
- examine the composition of the typical institutional portfolio and explain the logic behind the different weighting in each asset class;
- emphasize the need for, structure of and success, or otherwise, of the regulation of financial institutions under the Financial Services Act 1986, with brief reference to some city scandals.

9.1 INTRODUCTION

Chapter 8 looked at the role of banking institutions within the City and how they act as intermediaries between the savers who have surplus money to invest and borrowers who wish to borrow money. It is clear why the banks exert such an influence on property and construction, but the role of the financial intermediaries perhaps requires a note of introduction. Their growth, as described below, has been both rapid and large. It also coincided with a period of expansion of demand for new commercial property following the Second World War. During the period since the late 1960s the financial institutions have become major participants in development, both as funders and as owners. Their participation has affected construction and property both in form and in financial structure. This chapter now examines the role of financial intermediaries, and in particular other non-banking institutions such as insurance companies and pension funds, in more detail. It will describe their structure and how they raise funds through the financial packages they offer to individual investors. How the institutions invest their funds and what constitutes a typical institutional portfolio will be examined, and, where appropriate, their impact on the property market.

Financial institutions have experienced tremendous growth since the late 1960s, resulting in a greater turnover in the stock market in particular. As a consequence there is an increasing need to protect the investor from fraud and malpractice. This has been achieved, successfully or otherwise, by a system of regulation of the financial institutions and markets in the City, which is briefly explained in the final part of this chapter.

9.2 FINANCIAL INSTITUTIONS AND THE ROLE OF THE CITY

Financial institutions can be classified into deposit-taking institutions and non-deposit taking institutions. Deposit-taking institutions include the Bank of England, commercial high-street banks, merchant banks, discount houses, building societies and overseas banks. They tend to specialize in debt investments with short-term horizons (and were discussed in Chapter 8). Non-deposit taking institutions are insurance companies, pension funds, unit trusts and investment trusts, which have longer-term obligations and specialize more in equity-type investments.

The non-deposit-taking institutions are financial intermediaries which act as go-betweens between savers or lenders, i.e. those who want to put aside money for future retirement or have spare cash to invest, and borrowers – companies which raise capital by issuing debentures or shares in order to, for example, expand their business. The government, which tends to spend more than it can raise in taxes, raises money by issuing gilts. Financial institutions do this by providing assets for savers, e.g. life insurance policies and pensions and liabilities for borrowers, e.g. shares and gilts. The financial institutions also take on the management of risk for individual savers as their ability to manage investments collectively makes it theoretically more effective and cheaper than for an individual.

Financial institutions play a very important role in the investment of individuals' funds. They act as intermediaries, channelling the savings of investors into the hands of borrowers who need the capital to keep industry and commerce efficient and competitive in national and international markets. For example, an investor may invest cash in a bank deposit account in return for interest and the ability to withdraw cash easily and quickly. The bank will lend these savings at a higher rate of interest to a borrower, such as a company which needs a mortgage or term loan to purchase premises or machinery and plant to expand its business.

Financial institutions such as insurance companies can offer financial packages to individual investors. For example, an individual investor may take out a life endowment assurance policy with an insurance company, which may invest the regular premiums paid by the investor on the Stock Exchange to buy shares in a company, which allows the company to expand its business, or it may invest in government securities or the acquisition of an interest in property. The dividends the insurance company receives from the shares, coupons on the gilts or rental income and any profits on sale are used by it to pay the individual investor any profits on maturity of the life policy or a death claim.

The financial institutions have grown since the late 1960s as living standards have risen and individuals have been able to save through investment of their funds into the institutions. They, in turn, use the funds to finance economic activity. The insurance companies and pension funds have tended to dominate the property investment market since the late 1970s.

The term 'the City of London' is often used to describe the financial institutions and markets located within the Square Mile in the Corporation of London. In fact only the headquarters of most financial institutions are located in the City, yet it is the financial centre which enables funds to be channelled from lenders to borrowers, and attracts funds for investment from all over the UK, Europe, and international cities such as Hong Kong and New York.

The City houses markets which enable financial institutions to carry out their investment transactions. For example, banks act as financial intermediaries in the money market, the capital market provides for the purchase and sale of stocks and shares through the stock exchange, and the foreign-exchange market allows for the transfer of funds abroad for foreign investment. There is also a growing international capital market, which enables individuals, companies and government to borrow and lend across national boundaries through the use of the Eurocurrency market.

There are also firms providing professional back-up and this is where property advisers are involved. Surveyors and estate agents will be involved in the valuation of company properties and arrange finance for the development of properties. They will also manage property investment portfolios in the investment and letting market. Accountants audit company accounts and prepare prospectuses for the marketing of new shares and wind-up companies. Consulting actuaries analyse and advise on the performance of pension funds, while commercial lawyers prepare legal documents for most types of commercial work.

9.3 FINANCIAL INTERMEDIARIES

For the purposes of this text the non-deposit-taking financial intermediaries are divided into insurance companies, pension funds, unit trusts and investment trusts. Other investors in property that will be referred to include property companies, overseas investors, charities and owner-occupiers. Pension funds, unit trusts and insurance companies are often termed 'funds', and it can be difficult to distinguish between them, although their structure and characteristics are very different.

9.4 INSURANCE COMPANIES

There are two main categories of insurance business (see also Dubben and Sayce 1991): general insurance and long-term or life insurance. Companies may specialize in one area only or may deal in both. In general it is the larger insurance companies such as Commercial Union and General Accident which are both general and life insurers. Both general and life insurers operate on the basis that the insurer gives the insured or policy holder a policy, agreeing to pay a sum if or when an event takes place in exchange for a regular payment (premium), which is pooled to pay claims. Any excess of premium contributions over claims is invested by the insurer to provide a further source of income. In the case of long-term insurance the reinvestment of premiums provides the opportunity to offer the investor positive returns.

General insurance

General insurance companies (e.g. Eagle Star, Guardian Royal Exchange) provide insurance cover for motor, fire, marine, aviation, theft or damage to property, and personal accident. Thus individuals can carry on with their day-to-day living and companies can concentrate on their business knowing they have financial protection against loss, theft or fire, etc. Some risks are so large (e.g. the possibility of a ship sinking, a jumbo jet crashing or terrorist activity) that the insurer will share the risk with other insurance companies by a process known as reinsurance. The general funds set annual premiums at levels estimated to meet likely claims from policy-holders in the short term. Contracts are usually annual and the premium is reviewed on renewal each year. In recent years many companies have made large losses, partly resulting from natural catastrophes but also due to oil-rig disasters and terrorism, where payments have been well in excess of premiums. As payout is so unpredictable, this can lead to risks becoming uninsurable. General insurance funds can only invest the premium received in short-life or easily transferable investments and have a greater need for liquid and short-dated stock. They are not therefore regarded as major investors in the property investment market.

Long-term funds

Whereas people and companies take out general insurance policies for reasons of protection and security exclusively, the same is not true of long-term funds. Long-term or life-assurance companies such as the Prudential, Pearl, Norwich Union and Legal & General provide insurance cover for life, pensions and permanent health insurance which provides protection against disability from sickness or accident during a person's working life. Most life insurance therefore relates to protection and savings over periods of between ten and thirty years. These long-term insurance companies provide substantial funds for investment in the investment market in general and the property market in particular. Some insurance companies are public limited companies listed on the Stock Exchange. This enables them to raise capital from equity markets. Mutual insurance companies such as Scottish Widows are owned by the policy holders and are known as friendly societies. Many mutuals are incorporated into limited companies due to the advantage of raising capital on the equity market.

Life-assurance policies can take several different forms but are long-term contracts where the policy holder usually pays a regular premium, either monthly or quarterly. A **term policy** is where an agreed sum is paid to the next of kin if a policy holder dies within a specified time. A **whole-life policy** is similar to the term policy but has no term limit. An **endowment policy** can be with or without profits, where a sum is paid at the end of an agreed period or on death if it occurs earlier. An annuity policy holder receives an income at regular intervals, having paid a lump sum to the insurer.

Long-term insurance requires a payment of regular premiums over many years until the policy matures, when the benefits are received. Life funds are able to predict their payment liabilities by using actuarial tables, so there is a greater certainty in the timing and amount of their long-term liabilities than in general insurance. If premiums are paid periodically their cash flow is known and long-term investments can be made to match their long-term liabilities. So, for example, any fixed-sum life-assurance policy can be matched by investing in a gilt or bond which matures in the same year. A with-profits policy is more likely to be matched with equity investments such as ordinary shares.

Taxation

Insurance companies are subject to corporation tax on incomes which have not already been taxed, such as income received from overseas companies, some interest payments and gilts. Dividends from UK companies are tax free as corporation tax has already been paid by the company. Any capital gains made on investments by an insurance company are subject to capital gains tax. An insurance company must therefore make provision for any future tax liabilities out of profits.

Investment of funds

Long-term insurance companies will invest their funds in a portfolio of investments which can be classified primarily into **UK equities**; **overseas equities**; **fixed-interest** investments such as gilts, debentures, loans and mortgages; **property** assets; and **cash**, including short-term liquid assets. Figure 9.1 illustrates the growth of monies committed to and invested by life companies since 1966.

Most insurance companies have in-house expertise in property investment and take responsibility for decisions on property acquisitions, disposal and development. Property holdings account for an average 7 per cent of an insurance company's portfolio, although larger companies tend to have a larger weighting, with Scottish Amicable reported to hold 14 per cent of its portfolio in property in 1993. (DTZ Debenham Thorpe Research 1994).

Until the 1960s insurance companies invested most of their funds in gilts, but

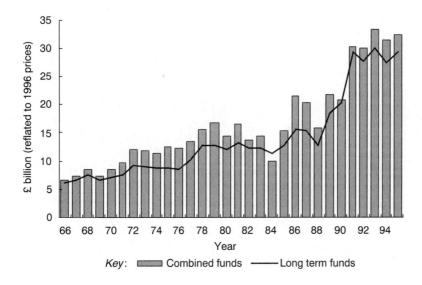

Figure 9.1 Net investment by insurance companies
Source: Office for National Statistics

when inflation started to rise and erode the value of their fixed-income investments they looked to growth-type investments, notably equities and property. Insurance companies have a history of investing in property since the 1960s and early 1970s, when inflation was high and property was regarded as an equity-type investment providing a 'good hedge against inflation' with high rental growth. The property market was very active during this time, with insurance companies lending money to property companies for development. Following the crash of the property market in 1974 and the collapse of many property companies, insurance companies and pension funds emerged as a major force in property investment and funding. In the 1980s institutions became disillusioned with property due to its poor performance in the short term as the government pursued a policy of restraining inflation. Wider investment opportunities such as overseas investment became available, and property was considered to be management-intensive with high transaction costs. As a result, average property holdings for insurance companies were reduced from 20 per cent to 9 per cent (DTZ Debenham Thorpe Research 1994). However, it is interesting to note that investment into property by insurance companies has dramatically increased in monetary terms since the late 1960s, as illustrated in Figure 9.2. In real terms the notable increase occurred in 1989 and 1994 (when equities and gilts showed poor performance compared to property returns). Despite the substantial fall in investment into property in the early 1990s, the average between 1990 and 1995 was consistent with the 1980s.

Regulation of insurance companies

The Insurance Companies Act 1982 is the main legislation affecting insurance companies, and requires authorization for anyone conducting insurance business. It monitors the performance of insurance companies and imposes regulations for

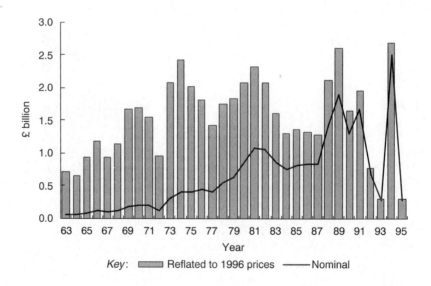

Figure 9.2 Investment into property by insurance companies
Source: DTZ Debenham Thorpe Research

the marketing of insurance products, but it does not directly influence the way in which an insurance company may invest its funds. Additionally, insurance companies and their employees involved in the marketing of life-assurance products must be authorized by the Personal Investment Authority (PIA) under the Financial Services Act 1986 (see the section on 'City regulation' later in this chapter).

Lloyd's of London

Lloyd's of London is mentioned here as it forms part of the insurance business, although its structure is unique. It is also self-regulating and exempt from the Financial Services Act 1986.

Lloyd's originated from a coffee shop in Tower Street in London, where a group of insurance brokers met to carry out their business. Lloyds has about 7,000 members, called 'names', forming about 155 syndicates, whose insurance market extends from marine business, aviation, space technology, offshore oil and gas exploration to filmstar's legs and political risk covering books and magazines. Syndicates are the original insurers (and underwriters) and they use a Lloyd's professional working underwriter to estimate and charge a premium commensurate with the risk undertaken in the expectation that the premiums received exceed the claims, resulting in an underwriting profit. The professional can also invest the premium to earn income, which can be used to offset losses. Names are normally rich individuals who invest clients' premiums and accept unlimited liability for claims – this makes Lloyd's unique. If the claims are greater than the premiums the names will pay a proportionate share out of their personal wealth.

During the late 1980s and early 1990s there were some very large insurance claims following exceptional natural catastrophes such as Hurricane Hugo, the San Francisco earthquake, European storms and the Piper Alpha explosion. Several syndicates experienced large losses potentially disastrous to the finances of the 'names' involved.

9.5 PENSION FUNDS

There are two types of pension fund, the funded and the non-funded. A funded pension fund exists to invest the regular contributions made by the employee and employer, rather like premiums on an endowment policy, so that the invested funds accumulate to a sufficient capital sum to provide the retired employees with annuities or pensions for the rest of their lives. The revenue is based on the pooling of regular contributions from occupational pension schemes. In unfunded pension schemes the contributions are not invested (such as the civil-service scheme); the government treats the contributions as part of its total revenue and pensions are paid out of its current expenditure. It is interesting to note that most of Europe operates non-funded schemes. However, only the funded pension funds act as important financial intermediaries within the investment market.

There are two main types of pensions. The first type is an occupational pension set up by an employer for its employees, where the benefits relate to an employee's salary, called the 'defined-benefit scheme'. These may be known, for example, as executive pension plans, company pension schemes or superannuation funds. The employers offer a pension benefit which relates to the member's final salary and the pension fund trustees will be responsible for determining a policy where funds are invested over the long term to meet future liabilities. The policy will set objectives, which are reviewed regularly. Any shortfall between the invested funds and the liabilities is met by the employing body. This type of scheme is very common in the UK.

The second type of pension scheme is where the employer and employee or the self-employed may contribute to a personal pension scheme in which benefits are related to contributions paid, i.e. a 'defined-contribution scheme'. The members' contributions are invested and the benefit determined by the performance of the investments selected. This scheme is more flexible as investments can be switched and the member can choose the investment strategy, e.g. those close to retirement age may be offered a fixed-interest investment. These are relatively new but are expanding.

The benefits from most pension schemes relate to final salary levels so the employers' contribution is expressed as a percentage of total pensionable salaries of employees, known as the funding rate. This is calculated after making certain assumptions on, for example, a constant salary growth rate, e.g. 8 per cent, a net yield on the fund, say 9 per cent, mortality rates, a constant ratio of male:female staff, and/or a constant age/salary profile of the group of employees. These assumptions are checked against the performance of the fund and the funding rate is adjusted if necessary. In recent years pension funds have created surpluses, largely due to the growth rate of the pension-fund investments exceeding the growth in earnings and the profit pension funds have made from early leavers. The surplus in pension funds resulted in 'contribution holidays' following the March 1986 budget, which limited pension-fund surpluses to 5 per cent. Surpluses in excess of 5 per cent must be offered to contributing members in the form of improved benefits or reduced contributions.

The collapse of the Robert Maxwell empire led to the Pension Fund Act 1995, which requires pension funds to have liquidity to safeguard funds as pension funds reach maturity. By April 1997 pension funds were required to show that they had enough assets to meet their liabilities as indicated by the minimum funding rate (MFR). The implications for the property market are not yet known, although it is considered that investment in gilts could increase.

Pension funds are trust funds bound by legal restraints imposed by their trust deed. The board of trustees decides on the fund's investment policy, which is usually geared to maximizing returns. The board takes investment advice from a bank or professional adviser and the fund is managed by either an in-house investment manager or a professional management company such as a merchant bank.

Some of the largest funds are those of the big corporations such as British Airways, Unilever, Electricity Supply and British Gas plc. Local authorities, too, have pension fund schemes. While large pension funds have their own teams of investment managers, including property specialists, many of the smaller funds are managed by external advisers. Figure 9.3 illustrates the growth in the monies committed to pension funds since 1974.

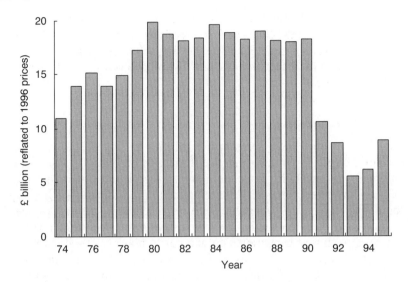

Figure 9.3   Net investment by pension funds
Source: Office for National Statistics

Maturity

An immature pension fund is a new scheme with no pensioners and one where contributions exceed liabilities. For these funds the objectives may be to achieve real growth in their investments over the long term, with any short-term losses off-set by long-term gains. Funds will increase in maturity, resulting in a reduced cash flow as some benefits are paid. Conversely, a mature fund has a high ratio of pensioners to members and therefore has a high proportion of its liabilities related to those receiving a pension. These liabilities are more likely to be fixed, and investments may have a shorter horizon. Investments may need to be sold to pay pensions, so liquidity and marketability of investments become important (*Property Investment for UK Pension Funds*). In recent years the increasing age profile of the UK population due to changing demographic trends, combined with changing employment patterns, has resulted in a significant increase in the number of pension funds approaching maturity (DTZ Debenham Thorpe Research 1995). A closed fund receives no contributions, but the assets need to match liabilities and investments need to be marketable.

Tax

Both occupational pension plans and personal pension schemes are entitled to tax concessions provided they are approved by the Pension Schemes Office (PSO), a branch of the Inland Revenue. Contributions paid by the employer and employee are tax-deductible. Any lump-sum payments taken from the pension are tax-free, although the pension is treated as earned income. The fund itself is also exempt from capital gains tax on gains made on the disposal of investments but is now liable to income tax on earnings from investments and deposits.

The PSO requires that a fund meet certain conditions before approval is given for the scheme to receive the tax concessions. The scheme must be established under a trust to ensure that the funds and assets of the pension fund are legally separate from the employer's assets. For large pension schemes the trust can be set up under a formal deed which appoints trustees, who have power of investment and must adopt certain rules.

Pension fund investment

Funded pension schemes have long-term liabilities to pay pensions, which are linked to future, currently undetermined, salaries. In order to be able to do this, investment managers need to place the funds in growth investments. For this reason they have invested a majority of their funds in investments such as equities in UK companies. They also invest in equity markets overseas to provide for a diversified portfolio. Pension funds' portfolios have a relatively low need for liquidity compared to those of insurance companies, with only 10 per cent invested in fixed-interest investments such as high-income-yielding bonds and gilts, and 7 per cent invested in cash and short-term assets such as commercial bills. Many funded pension schemes also invest in property, both in the UK and overseas. As pension funds become mature, with an increasing ratio of expenditure to income, greater emphasis is placed on income return, implying a possible switch to non-growth investments such as gilts.

Growth of pension funds

Investment into property by the pension funds grew from £0.4bn pa in the early 1960s to £2.6bn pa by the 1980s. This phenomenal growth was due to a number of factors such as a growth in people's real incomes, which left a surplus for investment; pay-restraint policies in the 1970s, which encouraged employers to give 'hidden' pay rises in the form of improved pensions rather than increases in the pay packet; inflation, which meant that people could no longer rely on personal savings as an adequate means of providing for their old age; and favourable tax concessions, which also made them an efficient investment intermediary.

In the early years of the growth, property was a favoured medium for investment (Dubben and Sayce 1991) but the institutions became disillusioned with property investment in the 1980s because of the government's policy of maintaining low inflation and the introduction of wider investment opportunities such as overseas equities. The high management and transaction costs of property were seen as a disadvantage, while poor performance in the short term meant that property compared unfavourably with equities.

As a result, investment in property by pension funds was reduced from 15 per cent at the start of the 1980s to 4.2 per cent at the start of 1996, while larger pension funds have slightly larger weightings (DTZ Debenham Thorpe Research 1997: 5). It is clear from Figure 9.4 that, in real terms, pension funds have dramatically decreased their investment into property, from the peaks in 1974 and 1980 to disinvestment in 1990 and 1994, with more sales than purchases. Equities have now become their dominant investment choice.

9.6 OTHER INSTITUTIONAL INVESTORS: A GENERAL INTRODUCTION

Unit trusts and investment trusts are movements which have grown up in response to demand from small investors as a means of alternative investment of funds. However, although their primary role is an investment route for small investors and hence the source of funds for investment in equities, gilts and property (via property unit trusts (PUTS) and authorized property unit trusts (APUTS), they also play a role as a destination for pension-fund money. Thus the saver's money – i.e. the contribution from the employer and employee deducted from the salary and paid into a pension scheme – is handled twice before it starts to produce a return. This additional intermediary stage can mean lower returns as two sets of fund mangers must receive payment, and the 'double investment' has taxation implications. However, many insurance companies and pension funds have set up their own managed funds for occupational pension schemes, which benefit from the tax-exempt status of pension funds and offer the individual investor a flexible 'pick-and-mix' range of investments in a choice of funds.

9.7 INVESTMENT TRUSTS

An investment trust such as TR Property Investment Trust is, in fact, not a trust as there is no trust deed, but, rather, the company is a limited company managed by a professional investment trust manager. Each trust has a board of directors which is responsible for laying down the investment policy, while the day-to-day management is carried out by a professional management company. An investment trust is quoted on the Stock Exchange, where shares in the trust can be purchased, and the dividend income is regularly distributed among the investment

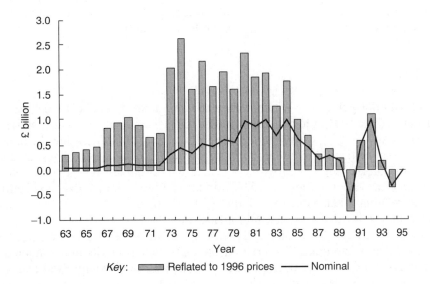

Figure 9.4 Investment into property by pension funds
Source: Office for National Statistics; DTZ Debenham Thorpe Research

trust's shareholders. As with a limited company, the share capital of an investment trust is fixed but it can borrow a term loan to buy more shares, a form of gearing, which means that the shareholder can benefit from the income appreciation and get higher returns than from unit trusts. However, when markets fall losses can be incurred. New investors can buy shares in an investment trust only from other shareholders on the Stock Exchange, as the trust's share issue is fixed. Thus an excess of demand will result in an increase in the market price of the trust's share. Shares of a trust normally trade at a discount to their net asset value. Although small investors have the benefit of the trust's professional manager's skill in selecting a range of assets, they have to pay management fees and corporation tax on trust income, which reduces the income to below what they would have received had they held the assets directly. This disadvantage reduces the market price of each trust share to below its net asset value.

An investment trust will receive income from dividends and interest from its assets, plus any capital gains. After allowing for the deduction of operating costs and payments to its shareholders, the balance left, i.e. the reserve funds, can be used to acquire new assets. An investment trust is not liable to capital gains tax within the fund provided it is approved by the Inland Revenue.

Investment trusts enable the small investor to invest funds in a wide variety of shares – to spread the risk – under expert advice and to enjoy the dividend income. The choice of a good investment manager is crucial to the success of the investment trust.

Although the first trust was established in 1868, their growth in comparison with insurance companies and pension funds was slow until the 1980s, when their assets doubled in value and their weighting in overseas equities increased dramatically. At the end of 1991 there were almost 150 investment trusts, managing £23 billion of investment funds. Investment trusts are bound by legal requirements not to invest more than 15 per cent in one holding. This ensures that monies in their control are invested in a spread of assets. Investment trusts can invest in equities and property, which can result in higher risk but higher returns.

9.8 UNIT TRUSTS

A unit trust is a legal trust in which money and investments are held by the trustees on behalf of the unit holders. There is usually a managing company which is responsible for the day-to-day management of the trust by rearranging the portfolio to achieve the maximum return. A trustee, which may be a specialist subsidiary of a major bank, ensures the trust is managed within the terms of the trust deed. An investor can buy units advertised by a unit trust fund at a price fixed by the trust manager relating to the value of underlying assets plus management costs. Money invested in a unit trust is pooled into a trust fund which invests it in stocks and shares. As the price of the underlying assets, i.e. stocks and shares changes, so does the value of the units. The price of the units changes daily and is quoted in the financial press. The income produced by the assets is accumulated and then distributed at intervals to each unit holder. Unit trusts are open-ended as their size will increase with demand, so new savers or existing holders can apply for more units at any time. The units themselves are tradeable through the unit trust manager. A comparison of the characteristics of investment trusts and unit trusts can be seen in Table 9.1.

Purpose

A unit trust enables the small investor to invest in a medium, i.e. units, which spreads investment risk by creating a diversified portfolio of assets. The minimum investment in a unit trust is usually £500 lump sum or £20 regular monthly contribution. It can also offer the small investor a unit-linked package with life assurance and certain tax advantages. Units can quickly be liquidated by completing a renunciation form on the reverse of the certificate, where the number of units held is stated. This is sent back to the trust manager, who pays the current market value to the seller within fourteen days.

Specialization

Some unit trusts will specialize in different classes of investment to suit different types of investor, such as high-capital-growth stocks and shares, income-only stocks and shares, certain countries such as the Far East, or certain industries such as high technology or property.

Disadvantages

Fees have to be paid to both the managing company and the trustee company for their services. The management company's fees are funded from two sources: first, the difference between their unit offer price (selling price) and their bid (buying price), which is around 6–7 per cent of the underlying asset value and is known as the spread; second, an annual management fee of 0.5–1 per cent of net asset value plus a percentage fee for the trustee company, both of which are normally

Table 9.1 Comparison of the characteristics of investment trusts and unit trusts

Investment trusts	Unit trusts
Listed company quoted on the Stock Exchange	Legal trust not quoted on the stock market
Investors buy shares on the stock market	Investors buy units from the trust manager
Sale of shares cannot be advertised	Sale of units can be advertised
Shares are priced on supply and demand and normally sell at a discount to the asset value	Units are priced by the manager and relate directly to the value of assets
Closed-ended fund as the share capital is fixed	Open-ended fund as the number of units can be increased or decreased according to demand by investors
Can borrow additional funds to achieve gearing	Cannot borrow additional funds
Annual management charge of 0.5–0.75%	Annual management charge of 1–1.5%
Investor pays broker's commission of 1.5–2.5% plus 0.5% stamp duty plus market buy–sell spread	Investor pays 5–6% initial fees, included in bid–offer spread

deducted from the dividend income. These high fees limit the marketability of unit trusts and make them unattractive as short-term investments as the management costs adversely affect returns. Specialization, mentioned above, may defeat the object of diversification and returns are often very volatile, varying from year to year and from fund to fund.

Authorized and unauthorized property unit trusts

With respect to property investment there are unauthorized property unit trusts (UPUTs) and authorized property unit trusts (APUTs). UPUTs have existed since the 1960s but are tax-inefficient as they are liable for capital gains tax and corporation tax on income. However, an UPUT can be tax-exempt if all the investors are exempt, and is therefore attractive to exempt funds such as pension funds, superannuation funds and charities. They are also not subject to investment restrictions and requirements like authorized unit trusts.

APUTs came into being in July 1991 and aim to provide liquidity to a generally illiquid property investment market. So far Norwich Union and Barclays Unicorn are the only two established. Certain rules were laid down as to how an APUT may invest its funds. These include, first, less than 80 per cent in freehold or leasehold property in the UK, EC countries, Australia, Austria, Canada, Finland, Japan, New Zealand, Norway, Sweden, Switzerland, the USA – in residential, commercial, industrial or agricultural property; second, less than 10 per cent in leases shorter than sixty years; third, less than 25 per cent in development properties as these are considered to be too risky; and, fourth, up to 80 per cent in property-related transferable securities, e.g. shares in property companies. These may include up to 35 per cent in government securities to maintain liquidity. However, a fund must achieve a value of £5m within twenty-one days.

However, investment restrictions were also imposed; for example no single investor can hold more than 10 per cent and no more than 15 per cent can be invested in one property. A manager can withhold trading for up to twenty-eight days if he/she thinks, at a particular time, that too many unit holders are redeeming their units in a falling market.

The Stock Exchange has published a consultative paper proposing changes to the listing rules which will enable an APUT to be listed.

Valuation and taxation

Each APUT must have an independently qualified valuer, and properties must be valued to open-market value as prescribed by the RICS once a year and an 'armchair valuation' must be made once a month. Valuation and pricing of units are to be carried out on a monthly basis to encourage short-term investors. One concern is that the pricing of units will vary with the equity market, and will therefore be volatile and will not reflect growth in property capital values. APUTs are exempt from UK capital gains tax on disposal of property but are liable to corporation tax at basic income-tax rate on income profits.

9.9 MANAGED FUNDS

A managed fund is unitized but managed by either insurance companies or pension funds specifically for occupational pension schemes. There is usually a group of funds covering the main investment sectors, comprising equities, bonds and gilts. The fund manager will determine the sector split within the fund. The client can invest directly in his/her chosen fund and has flexibility by being able to switch investments between funds to gain maximum performance. The performance of the pension scheme for the individual investor will be determined by the assets of the fund.

The smaller managed funds tend to invest indirectly in property through property shares and APUTs, while the larger managed funds are able to invest directly in the property market. Pension fund status enables the managed fund to be tax-efficient, i.e. no capital gains and reduced income tax liability for the fund or its investors. The unit holder's investment is protected by company law.

9.10 PROPERTY COMPANIES

There are two main types of property company: a property investment company, which acquires rent-producing buildings or development sites and has a long-term interest in property; and property development companies, which acquire development sites or buildings for redevelopment or refurbishment and then let or sell the completed development to a long-term investor. Many development companies are subsidiaries of larger property investment companies and retain their developments within their parent company's portfolio. Some building contractors, such as John Laing and Taylor Woodrow, have set up property development and investment companies. There are also dealers who make short-term profits by trading in properties.

Property companies have property expertise and will often initiate a development, which might be funded by forming a partnership with a financial institution such as an insurance company or bank. In the early 1990s money lent by the commercial banking sector to property companies reached a peak in excess of £40bn. Property companies tend to operate with a high proportion of borrowed funds and are therefore vulnerable to rising interest rates. When a substantial rise in interest rates coincides with a downturn in the property market and a reduced demand for the completed development, property companies run into cash-flow problems arising from unrealized expectations in the market, and many property companies collapse (e.g. Speyhawk and Mountleigh). More recently many of the larger property companies – for example Land Securities plc and Hammersons plc, which are public quoted companies listed on the Stock Exchange – have successfully raised funds by rights issues on the stock market and have been able to repay their debt and reduce their gearing. The Stock Exchange is proposing new rules for listing which enable property investment companies to be listed without satisfying a three-year trading requirement, provided they fulfil new rules such as having minimum net assets of £30m, borrowings not exceeding 50 per cent of their gross asset value, and no single property consisting of more than 15 per cent of gross assets.

9.11 BANKS AND THE PROPERTY INVESTMENT MARKET

Clearing banks (described earlier, in Chapter 8) contribute the largest proportion of loans to property companies due to their wide geographical base and the wide range of services they offer. Their high-street presence means that they dominate the domestic banking market. Merchant banks are more enterprising and arrange financing packages for property companies.

In the second half of the 1980s pension funds and insurance companies reduced their commitment to providing finance for property investment, and the banking sector became the main supplier of funds for investment and development. The main banks have been the large British banks and finance houses (e.g. Warburg Securities) and some of the overseas banks, particularly Japanese and Swedish, but more recently German and French.

Their basic business is to back enterprise and initiative, although their aim is to obtain the highest return possible, but at acceptable levels of risk. Their decisions to invest often depend on the track record of the individual or company seeking funds. The better the track record, the more likely the company is to obtain funds as the risk is considered to be less. New businesses are often forced to obtain funds from syndicates of bankers working together to share the risk and commitment. Banks tend to lend short to medium term, and to lend to the developer with a charge (mortgage) against the property or other assets of the company. In times of high demand for bank monies the banks will sometimes lend money not secured against any property assets.

Commercial and merchant banks made excessive lending to property in the late 1980s, particularly development, leading to an oversupply of new property on the market. Rising interest rates and a reduced demand resulted in a fall in rental values and an increase in letting voids. The property companies were subsequently unable to sell their completed developments and were faced with rising debt payments. The Bank of England revealed in May 1991 that lending to property companies had breached the £41bn mark for the first time and property lending stood at about 12 per cent of all UK bank lending. The dramatic increase in bank lending to the property sector since 1985 is clearly shown in Figure 9.5.

If a property company borrows and is unable to pay the agreed interest it puts the bank into a position of risk. The bank has either to force a sale or extend/restrict loans to the property company. If the security covered on the loan was not adequate, as capital values fall due to poor property performance the banks could force the selling of property even in a weak market. This has a further dampening effect on prices. The result of such a chain of events, in both property recessions of recent years, was that debt to the banks by property companies was a major worry to the industry.

For example, property-company debt was reduced to £36bn by mid-1993 but stood at 11 per cent of the banking sector's commercial-loan portfolio – one of the highest exposures recorded. Interest payments quoted by many property companies were as much as 80 per cent of their investment and rental income, but this was reduced as interest rates fell in 1992 and further lettings of empty space boosted net income. The debt was further reduced to £33.5bn at the end of March 1994, representing 10 per cent of all commercial lending. Merchant banks and American banks in particular have reduced their lending since 1991, while UK

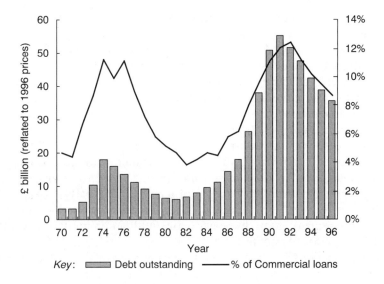

Figure 9.5 Bank debt outstanding to property companies
Source: DTZ Debenham Thorpe Research

clearers and other overseas banks have an exposure between 10 per cent and 12 per cent. Until 1986 bank lending to the property sector was short term.

In 1994 repayments of outstanding debt rose as companies were successful in rights issues, generating a substantial source of income to repay loans. Improvements in the property market – such as a fall in the number of vacant properties to let (often referred to as voids) and increased sales – led to some speculative developments financed through bank loans. Banks are now concerned with the funding of income-producing buildings and are looking more at risks involving the length of the lease, the cash flow and the quality of asset.

German banks are considered to be the most active overseas bank, followed by Middle Eastern and Far Eastern banks, particularly for secured lending. UK clearing banks put greater emphasis on relationship banking and are more willing to lend to property companies, although the proportion of values the banks are willing to lend has been cut back to 70–75 per cent and development funding is still seen as too risky.

9.12 OVERSEAS INVESTORS

Mention should be made of overseas investors, who have played an increasingly important role within the property investment market since 1987. During the peak years, 1988–90, the main source of funds came from Sweden and Japan, and were concentrated mainly on the office market within central London. However, their investments suffered from the downturn in the UK property market. Worsening conditions in the Swedish economy and high Japanese interest rates and restrictions on lending to finance property transactions resulted in a dramatic fall in their overseas investment.

The Germans are major overseas investors and in 1996 accounted for nearly half of total overseas investment (DTZ Debenham Thorpe Research 1997: 25); they are followed by the Middle East (many are wealthy individuals who buy through nominees as they seek anonymity). Other overseas investors include Japan, Scandinavian countries, Hong Kong and China. Favourable conditions for investment in the UK, combined with uncertainties over the future of Hong Kong because of the impending transfer of the colony to the republic of China, fuelled investment demand in the UK by Hong Kong organizations.

The typical UK **lease structure** of twenty-five years with a five-year rent-review pattern on full-repairing insurance terms is unique to the UK and provides security of tenure for the long term with upward-only provisions on the rent. However, the strong negotiating position of tenants in the early 1990s in the UK has resulted in a reduced lease length of fifteen or ten years and a greater variety of lease terms. Germany offers five-year leases with an option to renew after five years, and the landlord is liable for external repairs. Prior to 1995 the privity of contract clause in the UK lease ensured that the previous tenant was liable for any rent or repair liabilities if the current tenant defaulted. Abroad there is no privity of contract, and therefore no recourse if the tenant assigns his interest. However, in the UK the privity of contract clause was abolished on new leases under the Landlord and Tenant (Covenants) Act 1995 and is no longer an attraction to overseas or UK investors on new leases.

Taxation is another attraction. Overseas investors in UK property are liable for 25 per cent income tax on rentals and no capital gains tax. They can also obtain double tax relief on the rent if it is used to pay off interest. **Purchasing costs** of around 4 per cent in the UK are the lowest in Europe; in Germany the costs of a transaction are in the region of 5–8 per cent. **Fees** of 1–2 per cent in the UK are the lowest in Europe; in Germany fees can amount to 2–3 per cent for large transactions and 5–6 per cent for smaller ones. Also the UK offers high **professionalism**, with its members attached to and regulated by the RICS, and clients can sue for negligence. In the UK there is a **transparency** of transaction details arising from the free flow of information between chartered surveyors and owners, compared with other countries where it is difficult to obtain market evidence. In the UK, particularly in 1992/93, there was limited competition from institutions and so overseas investors were able to negotiate favourable terms.

In the early 1990s UK property was able to offer overseas buyers quality buildings let to some of the largest international companies on high yields with long-term security of income, upward-only rent reviews with privity of contract. UK interest rates were low and the timing of economic cycles was favourable. Germany, Spain, France and other European countries entered an economic recession, while the UK resumed recovery, with low interest rates encouraging foreign buyers. Overseas buyers maintained liquidity in the property market during the recession by investing in the larger lots of over £50 million. They tended to invest mainly in offices in the City and West End of London in 1989 and 1990, but in 1993 were investing outside London and spreading into retail warehouse and industrial. This is partly due to their increasing understanding of the regional market dynamics and to lack of choice of quality investments within London.

9.13 OTHER INVESTORS

These include **business occupiers**, who can invest in property while trading from
it; for example, department stores can participate in profits from a development
scheme while remaining anchor tenants (e.g. Bentalls at Kingston). Freehold
ownership of dwelling houses has enabled some **individuals** to participate in real-
izing gains. Many **charities** are small and are not allowed by the rules of their constitution to invest in property, while others, such as educational bodies (e.g.
Oxford and Cambridge colleges), have large and valuable property portfolios. The
Church too is a major landowner, with the Church Commissioners controlling
many valuable assets, including a large London estate. The charities have a
favourable tax position and this combined with their lack of borrowings, against
their ownerships, enables them to take longer-term views of their property.

9.14 THE INSTITUTIONAL PORTFOLIO

An institution will aim to have a balanced portfolio of assets to reduce risk but
maximize the return. The structure of an institutional portfolio will always be
changing, according to economic and market trends. However, according to Fraser
(1993:292), institutions are influenced by three main objectives when deciding to
invest new funds:

● **To reduce risk by matching assets with liabilities**. Short-term liabilities will
  be matched by short-term liquid investments, while long-term liabilities linked
  with inflation can be matched with growth investments such as equities or
  property.
● **To reduce risk by investing across a wide range of investments**, i.e. diversi-
  fying into UK and overseas equities, fixed-interest investments, property and
  liquid cash deposits. Property, by its nature, provides great diversification
  benefits within a portfolio – with regard to different sector types such as retail,
  commercial and industrial property, individuality of each asset and geographical location.
● **To maximize return by investing in assets which are expected to produce
  high returns after tax**. In the 1980s institutions significantly increased their
  weighting in favour of UK equities as they outperformed other assets. A more
  recent trend is to invest in overseas equities.

The mix of assets within a portfolio will change even if the assets themselves
remain the same; their underlying value will alter with market movements which
will change the weighting of a sector within the portfolio.

Figure 9.6 shows a typical weighting of assets within an institutional portfolio,
which comprises the following assets:

● **Cash**: Cash reserves in bank deposits tend to accumulate in the early years of a
  recession when interest rates are high (e.g. 1990), but will fall when interest
  rates are low as the economy starts to grow and long-term investments begin to
  perform.
● **Property**: property provides for diversification within a portfolio but has fallen
  out of favour with institutions due to poor performance, and its weighting has

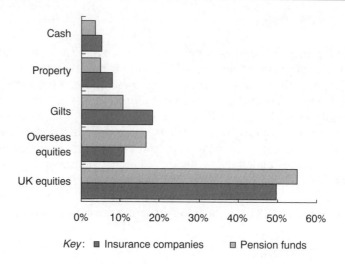

Figure 9.6 Typical institutional portfolio mix
Source: DTZ Debenham Thorpe Research

fallen from a typical 15 per cent in the early 1980s to around 6 per cent in the 1990s. However, some of the larger pension funds and insurance companies have maintained a higher weighting.

● **Equities**: UK and overseas equities dominated most institutional portfolios in the late 1980s and 1990s.

● **Gilts**: In the 1980s there was a decline in investment in gilts by institutions. This was partly due to a lack of supply as the government had repaid much of its debt, resulting in a negative PSBR in the late 1980s. However, following the recession in the early 1990s a positive PSBR returned, and since 1991 more gilts have been issued by the government.

9.15 CITY REGULATION

Financial markets should be able to operate efficiently while protecting the investor from fraud and malpractice. In the early days of the insurance and stock markets 'a nod and a wink' were considered sufficient to keep the City under reasonable control. However, a number of scandals breaching the City code on takeovers, mergers and insider dealing (acting on confidential information) emphasized the need for regulation. The Financial Services Act 1986 came into force on 29 April 1988. The act required any organization or person carrying out investment business to be authorized. Failure to be authorized while carrying out investment business results in a maximum penalty of a two-year jail sentence and/or an unlimited fine and seven years for giving false and misleading information. Inspectors can also be appointed to investigate insider dealing. This was a very important act affecting any person and organization giving investment advice, even if their main business was not investment-related but part of their client service included some investment advice. This act therefore affected members of the stock and commodity exchanges, unit trusts and investment trusts, pension funds, insurance companies, which advise on the retail personal market and manage investment schemes, and members of professional bodies such as accountants, solicitors and insurance brokers.

The act provided for a structured framework within which self-regulation could operate. It established the Securities and Investment Board (SIB), which is answerable to the Treasury and reports annually to the chancellor of the exchequer. The SIB is a private limited company financed by the City institutions, and has regulatory powers over three self-regulating organizations (SROs), recognized clearing houses, recognized investment exchanges (its members still have to be authorized under the Securities & Futures Authority (SFA)) and recognized professional bodies (see Figure 9.7, which illustrates the framework for City regulation of investment business). It can also take offenders to court and carry out criminal prosecutions.

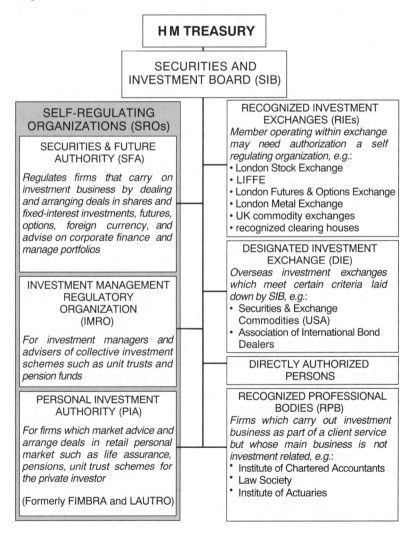

Figure 9.7 Framework for City regulation of investment business

To achieve investor protection, prevent malpractice and raise standards in the conduct of investment business, the SIB has written core rules which are central to each of the SRO's rulebooks. The SIB must approve each SRO's rule book, whose rules must be observed by the SRO's members. In essence, members must maintain high standards of integrity and fair dealing; act with due skill, care and diligence; put clients' interests first; act fairly between clients; and have due regard to clients' circumstances.

Outside of the SIB's jurisdiction lie the Bank of England, which has supervisory power over the money market – which includes banks, the gold market and foreign exchange – and Lloyd's of London, which is self-regulating. The building societies are regulated by the Financial Services Act when they carry out investment business, but otherwise fall under the control of the Building Societies Commission.

Since the implementation of the Financial Services Act a number of problems have arisen. The cost to the City has been very high. There are also concerns about the overlap of the work of several SROs, leading, first, to competitiveness among the SROs for members, with the implication that authorities which wish to maximize membership by reducing costs may lose out on maintaining standards, and, second, to the amalgamation of some SROs – e.g. the SFA arose from the merger of the Securities Association and the Association of Futures Brokers and Dealers, and the Financial Institute of Managers and Brokers Association (FIMBRA) and the Life Assurance and Unit Trust Organization (LAUTRO) were amalgamated into the Personal Investment Association (PIA). The system is too complicated, with rigid rules, and too much fraud is going unpunished. The regulators, such as the Serious Fraud Office (SFO), are experiencing difficulties obtaining convictions, with a number of embarrassing failures. In spite of this regulatory system there has been a glut of scandals in the City, as listed in Table 9.2.

The dissatisfaction with the regularity system led the chancellor of the exchequer to commission a report by Andrew Large, the SIB's Chairman. The report was published in May 1993, with a number of criticisms but still defending the existing self-regulating system.

The present two-tier system is considered to be inefficient and confusing, lacking clear identification of responsibilities. The chancellor of the exchequer expressed the need for reform to provide a simpler system which increased public confidence in the regulatory system and reduced member costs. In July 1997 the SIB, in conjunction with eight other organizations, including the Personal Investment Authority (PIA) and the Investment Management Regulatory Organization (IMRO), produced a report recommending the establishment of one single regulator, the Financial Services Authority (FSA; the SIB renamed). The FSA would take on the responsibility for the authorization and supervision of banks from the Bank of England and would acquire regulatory and registration functions from the self-regulating organizations (SROs), the DTI Insurance Directorate, the Building Society Commission, the Friendly Society Commission and the registry of Friendly Societies. It would also authorize firms carrying out investment business as recognized Professional Bodies (RPB) and supervise the Recognized Investment Exchanges (RIEs) and RCH. The three main aims of the FSA are to protect consumers of financial services, to promote clean and orderly markets, and to maintain confidence in the financial system (Financial Services Authority 1997).

Table 9.2 City scandals

- The collapse of the Bank of Credit and Commerce International (BCCI).
- The substantial losses made at Lloyd's of London and the subsequent effect of the huge claims made on Lloyd's 'names', resulting in some syndicates suing Lloyd's.
- The failure of the new property future exchange when it was evident that employees engaged in improper conduct in order to create an illusion of activity.
- Poor advice by insurance companies to encourage individuals to switch their pension funds from a sound occupational pension scheme to an inappropriate personal pension plan. Many individuals are now claiming compensation.
- The theft of large sums of pension-fund money by Robert Maxwell from various companies under his control.
- The collapse of Baring's, one of the oldest established merchant banks in the City, when an employee, in Singapore, Nick Leeson, acting as both supervisor and trader, invested huge sums of money in risky options. Nick Leeson was unable to recoup his large losses when the market fell, resulting in the subsequent forced sale of Barings to a Dutch bank, ING, for £1, plus large debts.
- The investigation by IMRO in Morgan and Grenfell European Trusts and the suspension of the trust manager, Peter Young, who invested nearly 30% of the funds money into unquoted companies and breached a number of SIB regulations. The trustees, General Accident, were concerned that a fund holding more than 10% in unlisted securities was breaching City unit trust rules and putting investors' funds at an unacceptably high level of risk. Unlisted securities are difficult to resell and to value accurately.

The FSA board was appointed in 1997 by the Treasury and the Governor of the Bank of England. The new regime is timetabled to be fully operational by Autumn 1999.

9.16 CONCLUSION

This chapter initially highlighted the role of the financial institutions within the City as intermediaries who invest the surplus funds of individual investors in exchange for financial packages such as pensions, insurance policies, shares or units. Figure 9.8 illustrates diagrammatically the flow of funds from lenders through financial institutions to borrowers. The structure and purpose of the main non-deposit-taking financial institutions in the UK were examined, with particular emphasis on the role that each plays in the property investment market. It is clear that there is a strong overlap between the institutions, as insurance companies and pension funds invest directly in unit trusts and investment trusts, and also set up their own managed funds. As the City becomes more deregulated, the distinction between the different institutions becomes less clear. Other investors, such as property companies, were briefly described and their dependence on the banking institutions for funding over the decades was highlighted. Overseas investors are more recent players in the property investment market but play an increasingly important role, as investment now spreads across the world on an international basis, and changes in foreign economies and the exchange rates have a great effect on the returns investors achieve. The Crown, the Church Commission, owner-occupiers and charities were referred to as they also play a part, although some-what smaller, in the property market.

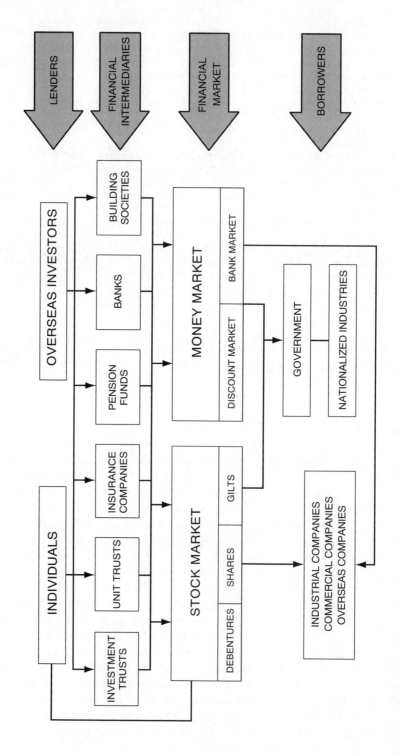

Figure 9.8   Financial intermediaries and the flow of funds

Finally, as the institutions and markets within the City became more deregulated and market-led the need for some form of regulation to protect the individual investor was provided by the Financial Services Act 1986. The cost of implementing it is high and convictions have been difficult to obtain; it is still somewhat controversial as scandals continue to prevail within the boundaries of the City of London. The success or otherwise of the new financial regulatory system under the FSA remains to be seen.

9.17 SUMMARY
- Non-bank financial institutions offer investors assets such as life policies and pensions in exchange for funds which are managed and invested by the institutions on the money, capital and property markets.
- Life-insurance companies and pension funds are the two main financial institutions dominating the investment market. Both offer pensions but life companies also offer life and health insurance. Their investment in property has declined since the mid-1980s.
- Unit trusts and investment trusts both offer the smaller investor a managed investment using in-house expertise to select investments, but they have high management costs.
- Property companies are entrepreneurs involved in the development and management of real property. They raise funds on the stock market and borrow from commercial and merchant banks.
- The typical institutional portfolio comprises equities, overseas equities, gilts, fixed-interest investments, property and cash.
- Members of investing institutions and anyone carrying out investment business must be authorized under the Financial Services Act 1986. Despite the enforcement of the Act, scandals are still prevalent in the City.

FURTHER READING

Brett, M. (1997) *How to Read the Financial Pages*, 2nd edn, London: Century Business.
Clarke, W. E. (1995) *How the City of London Works*, 4th edn, London: Waterlow Publishers.
Dubben, N. and Sayce, S. (1991) *Property Portfolio Management: An Introduction*, London: Routledge.
Fraser, W. D. (1993) *Principles of Property Investment and Pricing*, 2nd edn, Basingstoke: MacMillan
Howells, P. G. A. and Bain, K. (1994) *Financial Markets and Institutions*, 2nd edn, London and New York: Longman.
Isaac, D. (1998) *Property Investment*, London: Macmillan.

EXAMPLE QUESTIONS

Below are questions relating to this chapter. For each chapter, model answers have been prepared for some of the questions set; these are found in the Appendix.

9.1 a) Explain how pension funds and insurance companies obtain their funds and how they might invest them.

   b) Consider the role that both of the above institutions play in serving industry and the individual.

9.2   a) Describe the main types of property companies, giving examples, and the ways in which they can obtain finance.

       b) Explain why property companies are considered to be high risk, with many facing financial difficulties in a property recession.

9.3   a) Distinguish between investment trusts and unit trusts.

       b) What is an APUT and how does it overcome the disadvantages of investing directly in property?

9.4   Pension funds and insurance companies dominated the UK property investment market in the 1980s. How and why has their role changed? Who do you consider to be the major players in the UK property investment market today?

9.5   Critically discuss the role that banking institutions play in the property investment market and whether you think the Bank of England should intervene in bank lending to the property sector.

9.6   What role do overseas investors play in the property market and what qualities do they find attractive in property investments in the UK?

9.7   Briefly describe the main investing institutions and outline the role that one of these institutions has played since the 1960s in the property investment market.

9.8   Describe the composition of a typical institutional portfolio, providing justification for the percentage allocation of funds to each asset class. Why have institutions decreased their investment in property since the early 1980s?

9.9   What was the purpose of the Financial Services Act 1986 and how did it provide for the supervision of City institutions? In the light of continuing scandals since the late 1980s, discuss how successful you consider the act to have been.

Modelling property and construction economics **10**

OBJECTIVES

The objectives of this chapter are to:

- attempt a synthesis of all that has been said;
- illustrate simply the economics of a building and of the industry;
- show the place of the industry in the national economy;
- attempt to develop in the reader an understanding of the operation of the property markets and the development cycle;
- provide models to show the interrelationships between property, construction and the wider economy.

10.1 ECONOMICS AND THE DEVELOPMENT OF A BUILDING

A property does not simply exist; it is the result of a number of decisions by entrepreneurs and professionals within a particular prevailing environmental context. This context and these decisions are the economics of building and construction, which, within a capitalist market economy, ultimately seek to supply a need for profit.

If the model of a perfectly free market were taken to exist, then development would take place as a spontaneous reaction to demand-led factors and the built environment stock would reflect:

- the prevailing 'fashions' in terms of consumer preference for aesthetic design etc.;
- profitability of use to which buildings could be put, including technological change and physical deterioration;
- patterns of social change.

Figure 10.1 attempts to develop a model of how, in such a perfect market, environment adjustments to the nature of the building stock and the level of supply would come about. This model obviously does not hold up in the real world, however, and we must therefore examine the validity of each assumed reaction to the originally identified change in demand.

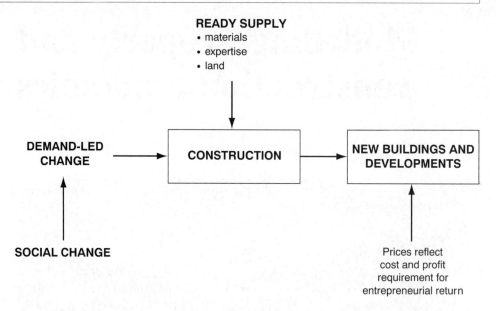

Figure 10.1 The unfettered development process: assuming a perfect market

Stage 1

The first stage of the development process is the decision to initiate new building works, or to carry out works of alteration or refurbishment. Our understanding of who takes these decisions, and what prompts the decisions is, even today, not well understood. The 'textbook' approach is that normally it is the developer who will decide, in the light of market research that he/she has undertaken, for speculative developments, and the 'end-user' who will decide when the building is to be owner-occupied either in the private or public sector. In reality it is not that simple, and the decision to commit capital monies to a building project depends on a variety of factors, social, fiscal, legislative and technological; some of these we explore below.

(a) Shifts in demand

The nature of the way people use buildings will change over time. While it is very easy to say that change will always occur, in reality it is extremely difficult to anticipate change in relation to:

● its nature;
● its timing;
● the scale of change.

In recent years the need to be able to predict change before it occurs to enhance decisions regarding investment and disinvestment has led to the growth of various forecasting services using econometric models. Basically, these models seek to input data on population, social trends and economic performance to build up predictions of levels of demand in the future on national, regional or local levels.

While greater sophistication in quantitative analyses has been applied since the late 1970s, all models seek to use past actual data as a basis from which to interpret the future. But what has happened in the past is not always a good indicator of the future, and no forecasting techniques have been developed which have been able accurately to predict demand. It is a characteristic of the property market that we have already noted that supply of new buildings often lags behind demand. If forecasting techniques were accurate such lags in production could be built into the predictions to ensure that supply came on stream at a time coincidental with demand change. The enormous mismatch of office-demand increase in the mid-1980s, which was not met by increased supply until some years later and then became oversupply (for a detailed analysis of this occurrence, readers are directed to Fraser 1993), stands as a testament to this phenomenon.

So, if forecasters cannot provide us with full information, what can we say about changes in demand?

The *nature* of changes in demand will be determined by many things. **Social change** is perhaps the greatest underlying factor. For example, with the change in family size, and in particular the breakdown of many marriages, the type of dwellings people require has changed. People no longer need large houses to accommodate ten or more children; the demand is for small units which are designed for modern lifestyles dependent on cars, and for use by people with little time or energy for maintenance and gardening.

Similarly, within work environments the design now required is for offices which enable computer equipment to be used and for workspace to be occupied flexibly. The cellular designs popular in the 1960s are now too inflexible to meet the demands of the late 1990s.

Perhaps the greatest of demand-led social changes have come about in the area of retailing, where the daily shop by a housewife who did not work outside the home has, in one generation, been replaced by the weekly or monthly shop undertaken by a car-borne shopper, often in the evening or at the weekend. So the high-street range of small food outlets is now very largely replaced by the edge-of-town or out-of-town superstore, which is open seven days a week and in the evenings. With the advent of computerized shopping the reduced need to shop physically may also affect change.

It is difficult to differentiate social change from **technological change**; the two are interlinked. Technological change revolutionized life in the nineteenth century with the coming of the railways; in the twentieth the development of road and air transport, of media and personal communications by telephone, fax and e-mail, has changed the ways in which it is possible to live and work. The notion of 'good' location also changes as aspects, such as accessibility, take on new meanings. Technological change has had other, less obvious, impacts on the requirements for buildings and the notion of location. Within retailing the development of computerized ordering means that the stock levels required in-store have been reduced; as a customer purchases an item, the till action automatically places an order to replace the item as stock. This has led to reduction in the size of retail unit required in expensive high-street locations and to a growth in demand for distribution warehouses, located in areas of good accessibility to transport systems, from where goods can be delivered on a daily basis. For the retailer, the saving on rental costs outweighs the costs of increased numbers of deliveries – but this of course increases the pressure on the road transport system, and the costs to the community, using the 'tragedy of the commons' argument, may be very high.

Changes in demand can also arise as a result of the action of the state, as we saw in Chapter 7. The action of the state is primarily twofold: fiscal and legislative. The decision to alter **fiscal measures** by taxation structures will have an impact on decisions; for example, the reduction of mortgage tax relief has altered the economics of buying and renting, and the imposition of extra taxes on petrol would affect the amount people are prepared to travel. In trying to establish the impact of demand-changes consequent on any such action, the government will assess the level of elasticity of demand. In practice, because people wish to use cars for lifestyle reasons, and a change in home or work location takes time to effect, price elasticity of petrol is low. While this may help the government to raise money quickly, it is proving to be a barrier to restructuring transport modes in the UK – and traffic congestion, long seen as an economic and social problem, becomes ever worse.

Other examples of fiscal measures taken by the government that can change demand for property are alterations to the money supply (see Chapter 8). These affect peoples' ability to raise funds for purchase or occupation.

Legislative measures, other than taxation and money supply, that affect the demand for property are many and varied. Changes in legislation regarding health and safety may prompt the requirement to upgrade buildings and hence *reduce* the demand for buildings which no longer comply. For example, changes to legislation to ensure access to buildings for disabled people reduce the occupier attractiveness of buildings which require capital injection for compliance. The right-to-buy scheme for council-owned housing introduced in the Housing Act 1980 has brought about great changes in economic demand patterns in many residential areas, with some previous council estates becoming 'gentrified'. Similarly, the expectation of changes in legislation may stimulate short-term demand; so the prospects of further control over 'greenfield' site developments and the channelling of new ventures into 'brownfield' sites, which are more expensive to develop, will shift demand patterns.

The timing of changes in demand can affect the decision to develop or alter property in a critical way. Some changes of demand occur very slowly over time. For example, changes triggered by the demographic changes in society have long-been recognized and thus there is time for the market-makers to react by making changes to the nature of stock – for it must always be recognized that the property market is dominated by second-hand stock. However, changes in the level of demand (rather than the nature of demand) can be very sudden.

So, for example, the introduction of 24-hour stock-market trading in 1986 (the so-called 'Big Bang') produced, over a comparatively short space of time, an enormously increased level of demand for office space as international banks sought representation in the City of London. In this case, as the period of time taken to generate new stock (including land purchase, building design, planning consent and construction) within an already heavily developed and complex environment can often take up to five years, the increase in supply followed some time *after* demand had increased. In the short term, therefore, rents were pushed up because of the situation of disequilibrium and this attracted more development. Not surprisingly (in retrospect), an oversupply had occurred by 1990 and this was associated with a decrease in rents to levels only 50 per cent of those obtainable three years earlier.

Another example of a rapid change in demand for property occurred as a result of fiscal change in 1988. In that year the chancellor of the exchequer announced at short notice a change to the provisions for income-tax relief for joint mortgages (normally either married couples or co-habitees) preventing any couple purchasing after August 1988 from benefiting from a long-standing tax loophole. The result was a surge in demand for the purchase of 'first-time buyer' homes, followed by a near collapse of the housing market.

Thus the timing of changes in demand is critical to whether the property market will remain in equilibrium as the nature of demand changes.

The scale of change will also affect the decision to initiate development. The difficulty facing decision-makers is to establish whether observed, or forecasted, changes in demand are significant in scale or structural in nature, for change does not in itself indicate that a structural change has occurred. Research has shown that changes in the level of demand for most types of property will take place over time, and it has been shown that property markets display cyclical change consequent on cyclical change in the wider economy (Key *et al.* 1994). These changes are independent of other structural changes in the nature of demand. If it is decided by the decision-maker that a change in demand is structural and not merely temporary, new development or new forms of development may be indicated. However, even if the nature of the change can be calculated, and it has already been indicated that this is far from easy, the scale of change which can be influenced by a whole range of externalities, is very hard to predict – yet it is the scale of change which is critical in determining whether new types of development may be financially viable.

(b) Shifts in need

Neoclassical economics is concerned primarily with the theory of the market. Under this theoretical model, production is a response to economic demand (see Chapter 4). If demand exists and people are prepared to pay for a particular good or service, then 'the market' will respond. We have already demonstrated that in relation to the provision of buildings and infrastructure the market produces distortions due to various factors, including the structure of the construction industry and the 'lag' in supply response. However, for reasons known as 'market failure' some goods and services – and in our cases buildings–will not be provided by the market, because the potential user group may have a requirement but lack the financial means to demand the product. Thus, even in an economy which espouses market principles, the provision of some buildings is made for reasons of need, not demand. Traditionally, this role has been undertaken by the public sector, in the support of welfare (such as hospitals and council housing) education (schools, colleges and universities) and 'merit' provision (such as sport and recreation). In these cases the decision to provide has been taken for reasons of political expediency, altruism, prestige (such as town halls) and the nebulous concept of social good.

However, over time and due in part to other external factors, attitudes towards 'needs' provision will change. Also, the nature of economic demand may change.

Something previously not deemed to have market demand–and thus a legitimate object for social provision–may experience rising demand such that it is capable of being produced by the private sector under the usual pricing model. A good example of this has occurred in recent years in the leisure property market. Due to the political decision by the government to promote 'Sport for All' and in the interests of improving local facilities, over the period of the 1970s and 1980s most local authorities provided 'leisure centres', often developments of old public swimming pools. These have operated with pricing policies dictated on a needs basis and, accordingly, have run at operating losses, with little attention paid to maximizing income. However, the growth of leisure as an economic sector of activity has caused a change, with local authorities devolving the management of existing centres to the private sector in moves towards greater economic efficiency and with the development by commercial operators of facilities which replicate those traditionally publicly provided.

Similarly, as we observed in Chapter 2, the adoption of initiatives such as the Private Finance Initiative (PFI) have reduced the previously clear distinction between public and private incentives for the supply of new properties – and the concepts of need and demand have become intertwined.

Thus, in summary, the model's expectation that demand is capable of easy interpretation such that it can be instantly satisfied by supply is flawed.

Stage 2

(a) New development of the type now in demand becomes viable

Whether or not new development will become viable is a function of many things, some of which are outside the scope of this book. However, at the level of first principles, development is viable only if the **gross development value**, by which we mean the net amount for which the finished units can be sold in total, exceeds the **total of all the costs involved in development**, including:

● construction costs;
● land costs;
● costs of land purchase and eventual sale;
● rolled-up finance costs over the period of the development;
● payment of an amount to represent the opportunity cost of undertaking the development (i.e. the interest foregone on the money involved); and
● developer's profit for risk-taking and entrepreneurial skill.

In reality, although the fundamentals may exist for demand to increase, this will not always translate into an actual increase in demand resulting in higher prices or rental bids. This is because other factors will affect the model that we have developed and 'peg' any increased ability to pay. In the case of the residential land and property markets these factors are outlined below:

1. People's ability to borrow money to finance the purchase, which may be restricted by, for example:

   ● the attitudes of lenders – and what returns they can achieve by other business;
   ● salary levels;

- interest rates;
- their ability to sell their existing (now unsuitable) stock.

2. People's attitudes towards whether such units will be saleable in the future.
3. Attitudes towards renting as against buying, which are affected by social and cultural conditioning as well as economic issues.
4. Fiscal measures such as mortgage relief to encourage home ownership, which historically increased the ability to pay.

The costs now have to be examined closely:

1. **Construction costs** relate to:

   - wages in the wider economy;
   - costs of materials, which may come from other than the domestic market;
   - ground and site conditions;
   - the availability of suitable labour.

2. **Land costs** will be affected by:

   - the reluctance or willingness of landowners to bring forward land for development;
   - whether land tax exists or might be introduced;
   - prospects for greater prices for land in the future, which can make owners reluctant to bring land forward;
   - the planning situation and whether or not consent is forthcoming to allow land to be developed for this use.

3. **Costs of land purchase and eventual sale** are affected by:

   - levels of taxation (for example stamp duty, which is payable on all land and property purchases);
   - professional codes affecting the charges that can be made by lawyers and other professionals (such as chartered surveyors) involved with the sales and purchase processes.

4. **Financial Costs including interest costs and opportunity costs** will be influenced by:

   - the prevailing level of interest rates;
   - the length of time that the development takes to complete;
   - the length of time that the development takes to produce income or sell.

5. **The developer's profit for risk-taking and entrepreneurial skill** is an item included in most appraisals of land. The three factors of production are land, labour and capital; included within the costs of labour are the skill costs of the developer in recognizing the opportunity. If many people simultaneously see the same opportunity the reward to the developer will, in theory, be driven down by the forces of competition towards zero, whereas if only one or two developers identify the shift in demand abnormal profits may be available in the short term. In practice, an allowance of say 20–25 per cent return on costs is typically taken, although some appraisers seek to relate the developer's profit to a percentage of the gross development value.

(b) New developers enter the market

Under perfect competition, if a profitable enterprise is available due to a new demand, then new players (in this case developers) will move into the market-place. In our scenario it is possible that this might happen. However, we have already drawn attention to the flaw in this argument earlier in the book. New entrants to the market are restricted by the following factors:

● **lack of suitable expertise**. A development company needs to be backed up by professional teams and it takes time to develop groups of individuals with the skills to enter any new market. Thus, there is plenty of evidence of new types of developments emerging which in the first few years produced inappropriately designed or located units due to a misreading of consumer (or occupier) demand.

● **lack of finance**. While the well-established 'players' will be able to win the confidence of financiers and the institutions to back their schemes (if they do not choose to pursue a corporate financing policy), for new companies the lack of a 'track record' makes them either unable to borrow money or able to borrow it only at high cost, thus reducing their ability to compete.

(c) The availability of land

The availability of land will depend on various factors, as noted above. In practice, the major constraints on the availability of land are planning and taxation, both governmental measures. Planning is not primarily an economic measure, despite its vital economic implications. In the UK all land brought forward for development can be developed only if planning permission has been granted. In many locations residential development is resisted on the grounds of amenity to existing land, lack of infrastructure to support new development, and the need to channel development into certain areas for political or social reasons. More recently a consideration of environmental issues, including the desire to see the regeneration of existing urban areas and to control traffic generation, has reduced the availability of so-called 'greenfield' sites, which are commonly the cheapest to develop as they involve no clean-up' costs or demolition of old buildings and result in the most pleasant ambience for living. Supply and demand of such sites is unlikely to result in a stable equilibrium.

Figure 10.2 demonstrates the development process and its constraints. One item that should be emphasized is the impact of timing – and in particular the time it takes for supply to respond to changes in demand. Not only is the actual construction process frequently a lengthy one, but the difficulties inherent in site assembly, the obtaining of planning and other consents, together with the establishment of funding result in delay in achieving new supply.

Stage 3

Once development has taken place there will be an effect on the remaining stock and potentially a situation of oversupply will occur. Thus it can be expected that if the model is truly representative the developer will be able to take his/her profit from the scheme and the new supply will be absorbed, leading to a price fall of the

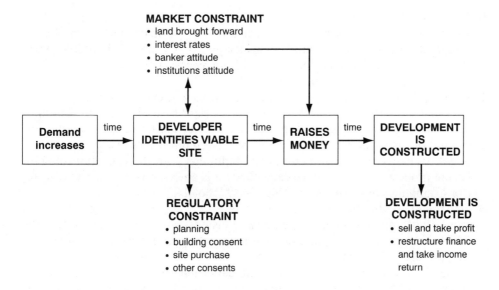

Figure 10.2   The developer in the real world

(now) less attractive older stock. However, events do not always follow this model example, as detailed below:

- **Change in prices of existing stock**. One of the characteristics already noted is the comparatively small size of the new stock each year compared to the size of the existing stock; hence prices are overwhelmingly the product of the interaction of supply and demand in the market for existing units of that particular type, rather than the prices required by developers of any new units. Thus the pricing of new units must follow that of the existing stock and not the other way around.
- **Transaction costs**. The costs of transfer, which in a perfect market are assumed to be zero or negligible, are considerable with property. This in turn produces an inertia in the market and reduces the transaction level. The purchase of property for occupation is, for most people, a major decision and, once undertaken, even if a more suitable or advantageous unit becomes available, there is a natural reluctance to move due to cost, the energy required, and the often high levels of stress involved in buying one house and selling another. So, although as new buyers–either first timers, up-traders or movers of necessity–move into the market a price adjustment to reflect actuality will take place, this is neither swift nor accurate in its impact on pricing.
- **Product differentiation**. When creating a new development a speculative developer will seek to represent his/her development as something new and different – not a replication of already-existing provision. This is known in marketing terms as product differentiation, and is a means by which the pricing levels achieved may be isolated from the prevailing levels and 'drivers' in existing stocks. How far product differentiation of new building stock can be achieved depends partly on the ability of the developer to recognize the fragmentation of purchaser demand and partly on the skill of the marketing departments.

- **Location**. Related to product differentiation is location. It has already been argued that the property market is not one market but many. One of the factors leading to fragmentation of markets is location. If new stock is built in one part of the country, the change in stock will not necessarily have any impact on property markets in different locations.
- **Heritage**. The presence of new residential stock will not necessarily adversely affect the pricing structure of nearby old stock, where elements of 'heritage' value occur, as such properties, particularly if they are listed as being of architectural or historic interest, may command premium values. This phenomenon is not generally present in commercial buildings with the exception of some leisure properties where the heritage element is an essential ingredient of value (for example stately homes and 'olde-world' hotels).
- **Sentiment**. Within the residential markets, although buyers will seek value for money·when making an initial purchase decision – and, indeed, if they are relying on borrowed funds cannot purchase other than on this basis – thereafter an 'inertia' factor may set in as owners customize their property from a house to a home. The decision to stay or move thereafter may become one based not on economic reasoning, but on sentiment and emotional reactions, as well as on social convenience or expediency. This natural inertia factor will reduce the ability of new housing stock to influence pricing.

Stage 4

Once demand for existing stock declines, in theory occupiers will move to other premises, thus freeing up the stock to be redeveloped or refurbished to bring it back into a use for which demand exists. However, once more there are practical reasons why this does not always happen in accordance with theory. Some of the main reasons can be summarized as follows:

- **Decline in demand** may be too small to overcome the inertia identified above.
- **Planning restrictions** may not permit the economic re-use.
- **Legal impediments** may exist, including the 'listing' of buildings for architectural or historical reasons, which restricts the ability of the owner to carry out physical alterations; the presence of occupiers with rights to remain in occupation on preferential terms, either through the operation of contract or statute law; and restrictions on the title of the property preventing development.

So much for the ability of our simple free-market cause-and-effect model to provide an explanation of the economic re-use of land to ensure that conditions of economic efficiency, beloved of the neo-classical economists, prevail. Even taking the simple scenario of a slight demand change as a result of changes in demographic and other social phenomenon, the model fails to accommodate the complex interactions which have an impact. Clearly the model needs to be adjusted at this stage to take account of:

- government interference (planning, taxation);
- skill and expertise (inability to enter new markets);
- availability (or lack) of money (attitudes of lenders, interest rates, salary levels and job security).

In short, the **economic model** is affected by the **legislative and social environment,** for within the UK economy an unfettered free market does not exist.

Figure 10.3 provides a representation of the creation of a new building, showing a synthesis of the major influences on the process. These have been discussed above and can be classified as:

- **the creative elements**, comprising those agencies directly involved in the production of a building (contractors, developers, advisers, etc.);
- **the regulatory framework**, comprising legislation (notably planning), fiscal and statutory measures;
- **the market environment**, comprising those factors and influences which determine the attractiveness of (or demand for) the building, from both an occupational and an ownership perspective.

While this model demonstrates why the relationship can not be regarded as one-dimensional or linear, it is still incomplete in its assumptions. Up to now we have

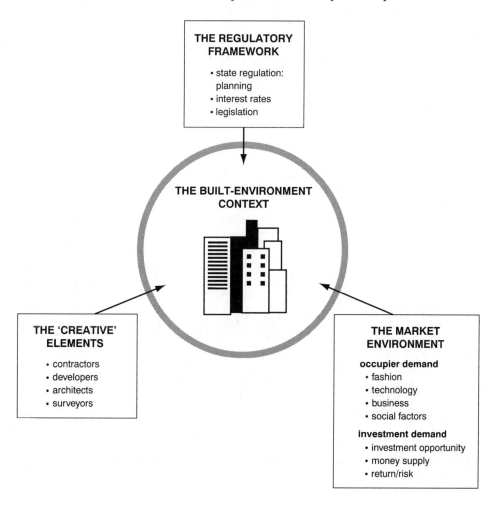

Figure 10.3 An economic model of property development influences

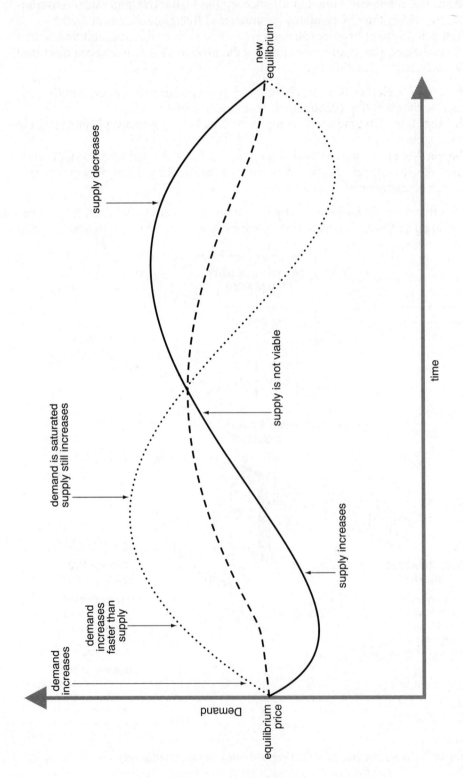

Figure 10.4 The effect of time on the development cycle

not relaxed the assumption that the supply of stock can react instantaneously with changes in demand, whereas in practice one of the major characteristics of the property and construction industries is the notion of time lag. If the model is now adjusted for time lag and for the factors identified above a more complex set of interreactions is presented. The impact of time lag on development and its ability to produce distortion in the balance (as researched by both Parry Lewis (1965) for construction and Key *et al*. (1994) for property). This is demonstrated simply in Figure 10.4.

Even this model, while it now recognizes that the property and construction market is far removed from the neo-classical ideal, is incomplete. This is because Figure 10.4 fails to accommodate the notion that **supply does not automatically follow demand**. Just as we observed earlier (in Chapter 4) that the power of producers can affect demand for consumer items such as toys and luxury goods (the 'keeping up with the Joneses' syndrome), so with real estate it is possible for supply to generate demand. So, in the residential sector, the demand may be stimulated to prompt developers to construct luxury dwellings, while the poor remain homeless: they have need but lack the ability to demand.

A recent example of this could be argued to exist in the commercial leisure sector. Until recently cinemas were perceived to be a thing of the past: consumers demanded television and videos, and home entertainment was seen as the future. Thus old cinemas, following the model of economic best use, have, up and down the country, been converted to other uses–bingo, DIY stores, night clubs,–etc, or redeveloped for retail or residential use. However, in the mid-1980s the bold move of an American operator (AMC) to develop a multiplex cinema in Milton Keynes (the Point), at a time when it was assumed that cinema as a land use was totally uneconomic, resulted in a resurgence of demand from operators as they perceived that the old land use, respecified and packaged, could bring economic regeneration. At the time of writing, the demand by property companies and developers for land on which to develop leisure schemes 'anchored' on cinemas is enormous, although there are some signs that the market is beginning to be saturated. The question here must be asked: did the supply create the new consumer demand or did supply follow demand? As with seemingly all aspects of economics, the situation is not simple.

10.2 CONSTRUCTION, PROPERTY AND THE WIDER ECONOMY

The analysis above addresses the factors which determine the processes governing the development of individual buildings. It does, of course, acknowledge that an individual building comes about only as a result of complex external influences which affect the **aggregate of supply and demand**. Figure 10.5 attempts to represent these complex interactions and present a model which accommodates the wider environment. The economic influences are summarized below.

The market

The action of the market relies on the interaction between the supply and demand of property, which will determine the price in the short term. Price may

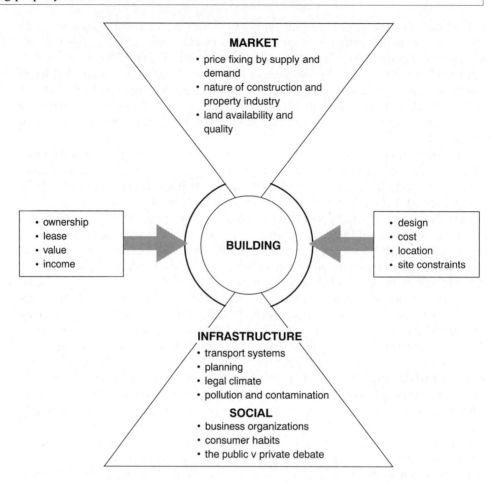

Figure 10.5 Summary and conclusion

be determined by comparison, but where a 'dual market' exists it has two constituents: rent and yield. Rent is a factor, not only of supply and demand, but of the general economic environment and the existence, or otherwise, of substitute buildings of suitable specification and location. The property market is unlike other markets in that few true suitable substitutes exist as property is heterogeneous and many decisions are made on the basis of valuations – estimates of prices – rather than on the basis of prices themselves, as is the case with, for example, the equities market.

The building

Buildings are provided by both the private and public sectors. In some parts of the private sector of the market the transaction base is dominated by investors. Their motivation for ownership is the financial return obtained from rent and potential capital growth. Occupiers of commercial properties are affected by profit levels, normally after tax and depreciation. Property is an asset, used as the environment in which a good/service is produced. For the occupiers of non-commercial property the motivation is based on utility and other non-tangible influences, as well as the ability to pay.

In the public sector, ownership property is viewed not as a financial asset, but as a 'merit good' or asset held for community or public benefit. However, with the introduction of initiatives, such as compulsory competitive tendering 'best value' and the Private Finance Initiative (PFI), both the management and procurement of public-sector buildings are undertaken with decision criteria resembling more closely those of the private sector.

The site

The nature of the site and the legal interest available will influence the economics of construction. The **nature of the interest** (freehold or leasehold) will determine not only what the developer can construct, but the period over which costs must be amortorized. Similarly, the presence of other legal rights or obligations (such as easements or restrictive covenants) may affect the type of design that can be achieved or the use to which the building may be put.

Development is also controlled by the **planning system**, and the need to obtain consent will affect development in several ways: first, whether development can take place at all – and, if so, for what use; second, the design, and thus cost; and, third, the length of 'lead-in' time between site purchase and the commencement of building works.

The **physical nature** of the site, as determined by site survey, will affect economic viability. One reason why developers will often choose to develop so-called 'greenfield' sites is that such sites, not having previously been developed, often present fewer difficulties than sites for redevelopment – so-called 'brownfield' sites. The problems associated with site conditions are:

● the nature of the subsoil, which could increase the cost of laying foundations if unsuitable;
● adverse terrain, requiring excavation or levelling;
● the presence of contaminants, either naturally occurring (such as radon gas) or the result of previous development works (such as industrial waste);
● the unexpected presence of archaeologically important remains, which must be excavated before development can commence, or may mean it cannot take place at all.

Construction

The economics of construction for any building will be influenced by many factors. The **design** of a building will have an impact on the costs, not only initial cost, but recurrent or running costs. Where the building is produced speculatively for onward sale there is little incentive for the developer to incur higher initial costs in order to increase energy efficiency or the longevity of individual building components. However, where a building is designed for owner-occupation initial cost may be a lesser consideration than overall costs, including maintenance and running costs incurred over the anticipated holding period. The prevalence of 'spec' building in the UK, for both residential and commercial buildings, has long been regarded as a barrier to achieving sustainable development as has the use of 'green' or 'environmentally friendly' building materials which are non-economic within the prevailing neo-classical market model.

The **procurement method** is also a factor in determining the economics of building construction. Several different systems are currently used, some of which place a greater incentive on the contractor to keep to budget than others. A commonly adopted form is now 'design and build', in which the contractor is responsible for both designing and building. As such contracts are normally awarded on the basis of competitive quotation, at least for the shortlist, the bidder may well be tempted to design to a low standard in order to reduce costs. The use of PFI within the procurement process of major projects is likely to produce new variants on the standard forms of contract. The intention is that greater competitiveness, and hence lower construction costs, will emerge.

Every building contract must be managed. The quality of the **project and on-site management** will have an impact on the economics of the process. The introduction of the Construction (Design and Management) Regulations 1994 may have an adverse affect on costs as they necessitate closer and more formal control, and hence more managerial labour in the building process. However, good project-management practices will help control costs, by ensuring that development proceeds according to plan, with no materials or operatives left idle waiting for other prerequisite processes to be completed. Sudden shortages in either materials or skilled labour can seriously reduce financial viability.

Conditions on-site, however good the supervision and management, are unpredictable due to weather and other considerations. In particular materials created or designed on-site (such as concrete or customized timbers) can cause difficulty. Thus, it is often more economic to construct standardized-unit materials off-site under controlled conditions as a separate function. Since the late 1960s the development of standard roof trusses, to take but one example, has increased the reliability of the product and decreased costs of production as economies of scale are achieved. However, although standard-unit production of many building materials has led to significant economies of scale, the UK has little tradition of off-site production of major elements of building. The late 1940s and early 1950s saw experimentation with prefabricated buildings for council housing after the Second World War, and there was a resurgence of interest in the 1980s for office building, but the experiments were not successful in terms of aesthetics or maintenance and proved difficult to fund. Hence, off-site production has largely been abandoned in favour of traditional techniques; the economies of scale have not proved worth pursuing.

Infrastructure

A building exists only in its context. Although a valuer preparing a valuation or appraisal will take careful note of all the physical and legal characteristics of the property, of equal importance to the final figure is the perception of the surroundings of the building – its built environment, and its legal and social context. Some of the key factors to be evaluated in assessing the infrastructure are considered below.

Many buildings are provided for the **public good**; others, for financial return. In the case of the former the appraisal may be conducted on terms other than financial. In particular, techniques such as cost–benefit analysis, which measures social costs and benefits in money terms for inclusion within the appraisal, may be adopted in evaluating whether a decision to develop should be taken.

Where financial gain is the sole criterion the appraisal will nonetheless be affected by the quality of the public-good provision nearby. For example, a house situated in an area which is well provided-for in terms of schools, hospitals, leisure centres and other community facilities is likely to have a higher value than one of equivalent design and accommodation situated in a less well-provided-for area. In this case the financial benefit of a non-financially motivated benefit may yield a financial return to the owners and occupiers of private stock. They are, in this case, said to benefit from an **external** benefit.

The notion of **externalities** is important economically. They include not only examples such as that quoted above, but also a whole range of factors outside the control of the owner of the asset being considered. Thus they may comprise physical features which result in changes of economic prospect (a new road for example), as well as intangible features (such as changes in taxation). The difficulty for the economist is in assessing the impact of such externalities and the possibility that they may change in the future.

One of the factors that we have referred to frequently in this book as affecting the provision of new property is the UK **planning system**. Under this system, decisions regarding general allocations of land use are made at local government level, in accordance with the statutory framework and guidance prevailing at the time of plan preparation. Although some notions of economic expediency do affect the plan-making process, essentially the decisions regarding the principles of planned provision are taken on other than purely economic grounds, and issues of sustainability and the community good are paramount. Thus, the 'first-line' decisions regarding how a scarce resource (land) is allocated are made, not in accordance with the economic market model of supply and demand, but in accordance with an admixture of social and economic drivers. Accordingly, any attempt to consider the land and property markets as models of a 'free and unfettered' market are fundamentally misfounded.

The impact of the planning system is to distort the supply of land for development or redevelopment, creating in some cases a restriction which will produce increases in value to the landowner. There is an argument that the rise in land value occasioned by the grant of planning permission should belong, not to the individual landowner, but to the 'community', which pays for the external costs of the development on the surroundings. This argument has resulted in the past in the imposition of land tax on development. However, such attempts have usually failed as they have resulted in landowner reluctance to bring land forward for development in the hope that the tax regime would change – a hope that has always been realized. Currently no such tax exists.

Planning can also affect land markets by increasing supply if planning controls are loosened. Thus, the decision in the mid-1980s to relax the previously stringent controls on office developments in the City of London was followed by oversupply.

One of the major issues facing all those involved in the economics of property and construction is the question of **environmental concerns**. The current operation of the markets means that the full environmental costs of development are not taken into account when decisions are made. The introduction of requirements for environmental-impact studies prior to the granting of consent for some types of major development, such as out-of-town shopping schemes, has gone some way to including environmental costs in site appraisal. However, full environmental costing is not required for the majority of development proposals and the issue remains.

Social

We have alluded throughout the book to the social environment of construction and property. **Social structures** affect the processes in many ways.

The **organizational structure of the building industry** affects the manner in which building contracts are procured and operated. The building industry was traditionally made up of small flexible units. The development of large conglomerates has resulted in organizations, which are still able to operate flexibly. However, the nature of the industry, for social as much as technical and economic reasons, has shown resistance to change.

Property demand is essentially a product of **social organization**. As social patterns change, so the ways in which people use buildings change. The changing age structure of the population and the levels of family break-up directly alter the design of buildings; changes in working and shopping patterns have an impact on the location and specification of commercial property. With the advent of institutional investment in property ownership the financial motivation for property ownership has been underscored, and the need to forecast and interpret trends in terms of their effect on property demand has increased.

Property construction takes place, not only for economic reasons, but also for **public benefit**. As social attitudes towards the provision of goods in the public interest change, so too do the nature, level and funding of property for the public benefit.

10.3 CONCLUSION

The study of economics is both complex and dynamic; this is because the underlying subject matter is similarly complex and ever-changing. Economists claim to offer solutions to a wide range of problems, but they can do so only through the role of models. These models have ultimately failed to deliver universal solutions, being limited to single times and places for their success. Over time, various models have been proffered and used politically in attempts to control either domestic or national economies, but they have been unable to do so. Property and construction, as economic products and as services offered by professionals, are important parts of economies and the study of economics. Whatever theories economists devise and politicians implement, the built environment, including its production, maintenance and financing, will form an important part of them.

The lack of conditions relating to perfect competition, and the unusual characteristics of both the property and construction industries and their sensitivity to manipulation render these industries a separate branch of study in their own right. Within the study of property and construction economics the true nature of 'economics' can be appreciated; namely, that it interlinks with the way in which societies are organized and managed – it is truly to do with the management of the industrial and national 'household'.

10.4 SUMMARY
- Building is an economic process and development mirrors economics.
- The built environment is an important locus within which economics occurs.
- The built environment is both product and image of the economic system.
- Both physically and in financial matters, the decision-making process reflects the wider picture of the way in which buildings are procured and used.

FURTHER READING

Fraser, W. D. (1993) *Principles of Property Investment and Pricing*, 2nd edn, Basingstoke: Macmillan.
Key, T., McGregor, B., Nanthakumaran, N. and Zarkesh, F. (1994) *Economic Cycles and Property Cycles: Understanding the Property Cycle: Main Report*, London: Royal Institution of Chartered Surveyors.
Parry Lewis, J. (1965) *Building Cycles and Britain's Growth*, London: Macmillan.

EXAMPLE QUESTIONS

Below are questions relating to this chapter and a set of revision questions relating to the whole book. Model answers have been prepared for some of the questions set; these are found in the Appendix.

10.1 There are two types of freedom: gathered freedom, the right to live in an agreeable manner in an agreeable environment; and dispersed freedom, the need to travel in an alien world seeking agreeable areas where one can live in an agreeable manner (for a time). Consider the following:

A property developer owns half a street and seeks to redevelop that half in order to raise a greater return on his/her investment. The other half of the street, however, consists of individual households, which object to this development as it will destroy their environment and mean that they will lose their current agreeable community lifestyle.

(a) The property developer has perfect freedom to redevelop his/her own property.
(b) The residents are free to choose the standards of their own lifestyle and environment.

What should happen?

(c) Also consider how your response would change if some members of the community wished to sell their gardens to the developer.

10.2 Describe the UK economy, and the place of construction and property within it.

10.3 Find a recent development close to your university or college. Investigate what economic factors led to the development; which came first, supply or demand?

10.4 Under a standard mortgage a purchaser takes on a long-term debt. However, the concept of a 'job for life' is now outdated. Consider what impact this decline in job security might have on the operation of the housing market.

10.5 Consider the implications for the construction industry if the government was to impose a tax on taking on new employees.

10.6 New technology is said to make the future need for offices redundant. Using a suitable model, seek to explain how technological changes might affect the demand and supply of offices in an area known to you.

REVISION QUESTIONS

R.1 According to the Ancient Greeks, economics is the fair government of the family, where the family may be any group of individuals, such as parents and children or the state. Examine how this statement differs from your view of economics.

R.4 'I will make housing the way we make cars' (Le Corbusier). Analyse this proposition and explain why attempts to do this have failed.

R.5 Examine the following and their views on 'settlements':

(a) Engels;
(b) Wordsworth;
(c) Dickens;
(d) Conan Doyle;
(e) Sartre.

Discover other views on 'settlements'.

R.6 Split into groups and devise a model/sample/hypothetical settlement for one of the following:

● a Greek city state;
● Roman Britain;
● a Norman town of twelfth-century Wales;
● a modern European city;
● a modern Third-World city;
● a model European city;
● London AD 2050;
● a Martian colony

(a) List all necessary and preferable characteristics.
(b) Consider restraints.
(c) Sketch out and create a key for your settlement.
(d) Consider the model from different perspectives.

R.7 How does the state involve itself in the operation of the construction industry and the construction process?

R.8   Examine the assumptions of perfect competition and their relevance to the construction industry. Comment upon how these affect the economic structure of the construction industry.

R.9   (a) Describe the main functions of the Bank of England, explaining in particular how it serves the government.

     (b) Explain the role of the various banks as financial intermediaries within the money market.

R.10   'It is interesting to see how our modern economic institutions slowly evolved from feudal times. The usual textbooks start off cold from the present. We believe it is much more meaningful to witness all of the curious zigzags and the fighting that occurred in the development of our present institutions. How our economic ideas and institutions developed in the past gives us a key to understanding the present and, we hope, the future.

    The history of economic ideas and the history of economic institutions are not totally independent of one another. In reality, they are very closely related, each affecting the other at all times. Thus, we shall see that the specific problems and interests of various groups gave rise to very specific economic ideologies and that these ideologies served as an excuse for the status quo or as a call for drastic change.

(Sherman and Hunt 1990: p:xvii)

Explain this statement with reference to the history of economic thought.

R.11   Compare and contrast economists' views on price, cost and value with those used by construction and property professionals.

R.12   Buchinsky and Polak, in their investigation into capital markets in England 1710–1880, stated that 'Building was not a so-called modern sector and building did not undergo major technical changes' (Buchinsky and Polak 1993). What do they mean by this, and how would you describe the modern British industry?

Appendix: Model answers to selected questions

The book has aimed to encourage an independent and personal view of the subject material, and it is with this in mind – and the need for the student to be able to integrate and apply knowledge – that the questions were set. Therefore the outline answers given below should be seen, not as closed-ended requirements, but as indications to provide guidance. Remember that economics is an idiosyncratic subject.

The general level of knowledge, as represented by correctly used supporting references and a logically presented argument, is very important and marks would always be awarded for those responses showing an understanding of the question environment.

1 PROPERTY ECONOMIC CONCEPTS

1.1   (a) It is a social science, not an exact science.
       (b) Theories are ways of explaining the real world, of building models and advising on future actions.

1.4   (a) Rationality is a major precept of modern life; it is thus a term of approval.
       (b) Means.

1.5   Market societies use the market price mechanism; planned societies use state planning.

1.6   Opportunity cost = (Cost of course + Living expenses + Loss of wages/benefits) − grant.

2 THE PECULIAR NATURE OF THE CONSTRUCTION INDUSTRY

2.1   Property can be defined in terms of its legal, philosophical and physical characteristics.

3 A BRIEF HISTORY OF PROPERTY AND CONSTRUCTION ECONOMIC THOUGHT

3.1   Modern economics began with Adam Smith; economics as an unspecialized body of information existed thousands of years before.

3.3   Marx provides a very detailed analysis of capitalism – probably the best at the time. Thus, all economists should find Marx useful, even if they do not accept his socialist manifesto.

3.6   Property and construction economics were frequently major considerations for early economists, and much of the UK's infrastructure is the result of 200 years of economic and political practice and theory. History is also important to where we are now, and to an understanding of the reasoning behind our current theories and ideology.

4 THE THEORY OF THE MARKET AND ITS APPLICATION TO CONSTRUCTION AND PROPERTY

4.1   A market is where buyers meet sellers. It is no longer necessarily a physical space, but may be a virtual one, created by technology.

4.6   Elasticity is a measure of responsiveness to changes in the supply or demand of a good or service.

5 THE CONSTRUCTION AND PROPERTY FIRM

5.1   A firm can be described in economic, legal and organizational terms: in economics, the firm is the unit of production; in law, it is a sole trader, partnership, private limited company (Ltd) or public limited company (plc); organization theory has many ways of describing management structure.

5.2   (a) Both are eponymous. Price takers must charge the market price; price makers may create their own price. Price takers operate in conditions of perfect competition.

       (b) Contractors are price takers; speculators are price makers.

6 THE NATURE AND FUNCTIONING OF THE REAL PROPERTY MARKET

6.3   In answering this question the student should first explore the literal accuracy of the fixed supply of land and may pick up on issues such as the economic case for land reclamation – which of course is almost always an economic decision – but then go on to examine ways in which supply is not fixed in terms other than physical. In a UK context this relates to land use and planning, which in effect control the supply of land for any particular type of use. Thus, with no physical change to land, supply for any given use can change. However, in addition to planning, supply is dependent on finance to create the development which fulfils demand.

       So having established that supply is not fixed, and may be altered for economic and planning reasons, it is possible to examine the issue of demand determinants. Demand determinants are the result of economic factors (such as the availability of money and general economic conditions); social, political and fiscal factors are also of importance. The time lag in the change in supply means that disequilibrium can occur quickly, and when this happens price will alter. To this extent price is demand-led.

       The student should also mention the fact – a particularity of land and property – that substitution may not be possible in all cases, and this will potentially lead to a relative inelasticity in some parts of the property market. This is more likely for owner-occupied property than investment property, for which demand is price-sensitive as substitution outside the property sector may exist.

6.5 This question is very wide and requires that the student explore beyond the conventional economic modelling. It is best suited to seminar or tutorial discussion as it could lend itself to students undertaking some practical investigation – by discussing property requirements with either agents or occupiers, or both.

There are essentially two parts to the question:

(a) The student(s) should consider the determinants of occupational demand: use, design, costs-in-use, the economic well-being of the potential occupier, location, accessibility, availability of finance, etc. All this should be addressed in terms of principles.

(b) The student(s) should next seek to relate this theory to practical case studies and to compare their economic 'drivers'. The needs of each company chosen are likely to be very different in terms of flexibility, financial standing, 'bespoke costs' (e.g. fit-out, and plant and machinery). Only when this is done can the occupier perspective on the economic case for renting versus owning be explored.

The better students will also pick up on the issue of choice: for a decision to rent to be capable of realization, a decision to invest (without occupation) must be made by another party. Only if the type of property is attractive to investing owners does a tenure choice exist.

7 THE STATE AND PROPERTY ECONOMICS

7.1 Inflation is obviously a problem. It is also psychologically associated with poorly managed economies. However, inflation is also endemic in capitalism and it can prevent firms from becoming inefficient. It also discourages hoarding and encourages investment.

8 THE PRIVATE SECTOR AND THE FINANCIAL MARKETS

8.1 The student should introduce his/her answer by first defining what is meant by investment, and briefly distinguish between direct and indirect property investment. The ideal character of investment could be referred to by way of introduction, e.g. liquidity, ease of divisibility, marketability, security of capital and income, etc. and the student should suggest the qualities the investor most likely desires.

With regards to direct property investment, the student should explain the difference between freehold and leasehold interests, and then describe the various opportunities available, i.e. retail (high-street shops, shopping centres, retail warehouses), industrial (warehouses and factories), offices (business parks, purpose-built offices, converted houses/shops, etc.), leisure, etc. Geographical location also provides diversity within a portfolio. The characteristics of direct property investment should be covered, e.g. illiquidity, high fees/costs of purchase due to the need for a variety of professionals (such as surveyors, lawyers, etc.), cost and need for management, security of income through the lease, capital and rental growth through the provision of rent reviews, high initial capital cost and indivisibility, the life of the investment, and the fact that it is subject to depreciation and obsolescence, etc.

The student should describe the various indirect opportunities to invest in property and their associated characteristics; for example, shares in a property company are very liquid, divisible, homogeneous, require no management, are easily priced, etc. Other indirect investments should include investment in units in a property unit trust, shares in a property trust, property bonds. Insurance policies and a pension are also indirect – but more obscure – ways of investing in property.

8.2 (a) The student should briefly introduce the Bank of England and then describe the three main objectives of the Bank of England. These should include: to maintain the value of the nation's money by maintaining stable price levels through policy and market operations; to ensure the soundness of the financial system by the authorization and supervision of the banks, and the gold and foreign-exchange markets; and to promote the efficiency and competitiveness of the financial system. It should also be noted that the Bank of England prints notes, manages the governments bank account, coordinates the accounts of the commercial banks, merchant banks, overseas banks, International Monetary Fund (IMF), large industrial companies and some official reserves of certain countries.

The student should explain in more detail how the Bank serves the government by (i) managing its account, i.e. tax revenue and expenditure; (ii) advising on and administering the monetary policy by controlling the interest rates and therefore the money supply through the issue or purchase of Treasury bills from the discount houses as lender of last resort; (iii) enabling the repayment of the PSBR by issuing gilts on the stock exchange; and (iv) advising on policy.

(b) The different types of banking institution referred to should include commercial banks such as Lloyds, NatWest, Barclays, discount houses, merchant banks (e.g. Rothschild) and their respective roles should be described. Essentially, a bank seeks to make a profit by lending money at a higher rate of interest than that at which it borrows. Commercial banks act as financial intermediaries by lending money (e.g. loans, credit facilities, hire and leasing, overdraft, mortgages for borrowers) and borrowing money from lenders through current accounts, short- and long-term deposit accounts. They provide investment advice, and executor and trustee services for lenders. Merchant banks tend to lend money to large companies, accept bills of exchange, provide financial advice (e.g. raising finance, prospectus, etc.), and manage pension funds and unit trusts. Discount houses act as financial intermediaries between the government and banks, lending and borrowing money on a short-term basis through Treasury and commercial bills.

9 FINANCIAL INTERMEDIARIES

9.1   (a) The student should explain how pension funds obtain their funds through pension schemes, where the employer and employee contribute, on a regular (e.g. monthly) basis, funds to be invested to provide for future retirement. The better student might explain the different pension schemes that are available and define a mature pension fund. The student should explain that a pension fund can estimate its future liabilities by predicting future salaries and the age of employee, type of industry, etc. and can try to match its liabilities with its investments.

          The student should be able to explain the difference between general insurance companies and long-term insurance companies, and should mention that the latter are the major investors. They obtain their funds by individuals taking out life-assurance policies, where the insured pays a regular premium or lump sum in return for a life policy (e.g. term, endowment, with or without profits) which requires the insurer to pay out money on maturity or death, whichever is earlier. The regular premiums are invested and, using actuarial tables, the insurance company can estimate its future liabilities with its investments.

          The student should then suggest ways in which the funds might invest their monies, i.e. gilts, debentures, equities, overseas equities, property and cash assets. The better student might refer to average percentages in a typical portfolio.

  (b) The student should explain that they both serve industry by investing their funds on the stock market. The purchase of shares helps companies to acquire real assets, pay off debts and expand, and indirectly helps the economy to grow. The purchase of gilts helps the government to fund its PSBR, pay for expenses such as social benefits and for the provision of public services (e.g. police, defence, etc.). They also help the individual by providing pensions for an income on retirement, and insurance for life and health to give peace of mind and future financial security.

9.2   (a) The student should first describe the different types of property companies – property investment companies, property development companies, building contractors and dealers. The better student will also quote names and give details of some well-known property companies. The student should then briefly outline the ways of raising finance through the issue of equity and debentures on the stock market, bank loans and partnership with financial institutions.

  (b) An explanation of high risk in terms of these companies' financial gearing and the financial difficulties they face when interest rates rise at the start of an economic recession, having an adverse effect on their cash flow; or when completed developments come on to the market after demand has fallen, so that they are difficult to let and difficult to sell as yields have risen, resulting in falling capital values of assets, high debts and subsequently falling share prices, which make the company vulnerable to takeovers and collapse.

10 MODELLING PROPERTY AND CONSTRUCTION ECONOMICS

R.1   This is principally a 'what is economics?' type of question, but it provides a basis on which to discuss, and allows contextual understanding, personal researches and beliefs. The student should acknowledge the Greek root of the word that forms the framework for the question, but otherwise expect a wide and varied discussion.

R.4   The student should place basic economic principles (e.g. economies of scale) in a real-world context and show an understanding of how economics works in modern capitalist societies, and why the property market is different. It is feasible to discuss Le Corbusier personally, but general principles are acceptable. Most importantly, the student should apply the ideas to construction, building and property economics, not simply economic theory, excluding all pre-Smith economics. The question leaves scope to exhibit personal choice and show a thorough understanding by ignoring minnows. It includes Ricardo, Malthus, Mill, Marx, Walras, Marshall, Keynes, Friedman, Schumacher, etc.

R.5   Engels wrote extensively on the appalling living conditions of the working classes in Manchester, but was not against urbanization itself.

Charles Dickens' novels similarly describe the squalor of Victorian England.

Conan Doyle's Sherlock Holmes stories, set in London, evoke images of a foggy metropolis, packed with all manner of humanity.

Wordsworth's poetry applauds the countryside and appeals to our atavistic nature with its romantic overtures about the wonders of nature.

Sartre's *La Nausée* (*Nausea*) is set in Bouville ('Mudtown'), and the whole dull place is seen as living proof of existentialism, showing that the world lacks an intrinsic, essential meaning and that as individuals we are completely alienated from everything around us. The question invites the student to discuss how far these images can relate the success or failure of economic models to interpret and influence the built environment.

R.7   The question is set at the 'industry' level, but 'firm' and 'project' levels may be applicable. Major areas include the 'multi-industry'; finance; number/size/type of firms; the contractor/speculative builder divide; the design/construction split; markets; and production.

R.8   The student should discuss the formulation of costs and sources of information, as well as contractors' pricing policy. Mention of economic views (e.g. value/utility, cost curves, labour theory of value) and traditional surveying techniques of costing and valuing should be made.

References

Aristotle (1962) *The Politics*, London: Penguin

Armstrong, P., Glyn, A. and Harrison, J. (1991) *Capitalism Since 1945*, Oxford: Basil Blackwell.

Ball, M. (1988) *Rebuilding Construction*, London: Routledge.

—— (1996) *Housing and Construction: A Troubled Relationship*, London: HMSO.

Bank of England (1997) 'Changes at the Bank', *Bank of England Quarterly Bulletin*, August, 37(3).

Barber, W. J. (1967) *A History of Economic Thought*, London: Pelican.

Barnes, B. and Bloor, D. (1988) 'Relativism, rationalism and the sociology of knowledge', in M. Hollis and S. Lukes (eds) *Rationality and Relativism*, Oxford: Blackwell.

Barrie, D. S. and Paulson, B. C. (1992) *Professional Construction Management*, New Jersey: McGraw-Hill.

Boardman, J., Griffin, J. and Murray, O. (1991) *The Oxford History of the Classical World*, Oxford: Oxford University Press.

Brett, M. (1991) *How to Read the Financial Pages*, 3rd edn, London: Century Business.

Brown, G. (1991) *Property Investment and the Capital Markets*, London: E. & F. N. Spon. Ltd.

Buchinsky, M. and Polak, B. (1993) 'The capital market in England, 1710–1880', *Journal of Economic History*, March, 53(1): 7.

Burke, J. (1985) *The Day the Universe Changed*, London: BBC.

Burnham, J. (1972) *The Managerial Revolution: What is Happening in the World*, Westport, CT: Greenwood Press.

Case, K. E. and Fair, R. C. (1989) *Principles of Economics*, Englewood Cliffs, NJ: Prentice-Hall.

Clarke, W. M. (1991) *How the City of London Works*, 3rd edn, London: Waterlow Publishers.

Clarke, L. (1992) *Building Capitalism*, London: Routledge.

Colander, D. and Coats, A. W. (eds) (1993) *The Spread of Economic Ideas*, Cambridge: Cambridge University Press.

Cole, K., Cameron, J. and Edwards, S. (1983) *Why Economists Disagree*, Harlow: Longman.

Dicken, P. (1992) *Global Shift*, London: Paul Chapman Publishing.

DTZ Debenham Thorpe Research (1994) *Special Report Overseas Investment in UK Property 1993*, London: DTZ Debenham Thorpe.

—— (1995) *Money into Property 1995*, London: DTZ Debenham Thorpe Ltd.

—— (1996) *Money into Property 1996*, London: DTZ Debenham Thorpe Ltd.

—— (1997) *Money into Property 1997*, London: DTZ Debenham Thorpe Ltd.

Dubben, N. and Sayce, S. (1991) *Property Portfolio Management: An Introduction*, London: Routledge.

Farley, J. and Geison, G. (1974) 'Science, politics and spontaneous generation in nineteenth century France: the Pasteur–Pouchet debate', *Bulletin of the History of Medicine*, 48(2), summer: 161–98.

Fellows, R., Langford, D. A. and Newcombe, R. (1991) *Construction Management in Practice*, Harlow: Longman.

Financial Services Authority (1997) *Financial Services Authority: an Outline*, London: Financial Services Authority.

Fisher, D. (1976) *Monetary Policy*, London: Macmillan.

—— (1988) *Monetary and Fiscal Policy*, London: Macmillan.

Fraser, W. D. (1993) *Principles of Property Investment and Pricing*, 2nd edn, Basingstoke: Macmillan.

Friedman, M. and Friedman, R. (1980) *Free to Choose*, New York: Harcourt Brace Jovanovich.

—— (1985) *The Tyranny of the Status Quo*, Harmondsworth: Penguin

Gaffney, M. and Harrison, F. (1994) *The Corruption of Economics*, London: Shepheard-Walwyn.

Galbraith, J. K. (1989) *A History of Economics*, Harmondsworth: Penguin.

Galbraith, J. K. and Salinger, N. (1981) *Almost Everyone's Guide to Economics*, London: Penguin Books.

Gellner, E. (1993) *Nations and Nationalism*, London: Blackwell.

Goff, T. G. (1986) *Theory and Practice of Investment*, 5th edn London: Heinemann.

Gough, L. (1995) *The Investor's Guide to How the Stock Market Really Works,* London: Pitman.

Gray, B. (1993) *Investors' Chronicle Beginners' Guide to Investment*, 2nd edn, London: Century Business.

Hampson, N. (1983) *Will & Circumstance*, London: Duckworth.

Hillebrandt, P. M. (1975) 'The capacity of the construction industry', in D. Turin (ed.) *Aspects of the Economics of Construction*, London: George Godwin.

—— (1988) *Analysis of the British Construction Industry*, London: Macmillan.

Hobbes, T. (1986) *Leviathan*, Harmondsworth: Penguin; originally published in 1651.

Howells, P. G. A. and Bain, K. (1994) *Financial Markets and Institutions*, 2nd edn, London and New York: Longman.

Hunt, E. K. and Sherman, H. J. (1990) *Economics*, 6th edn, New York: Harper & Row.

Investment Property Forum Working Group (1995) *Property Investment For UK Pension Funds*, consultation document, London: Investment Property Forum.

Isaac, D. (1994) *Property Finance*, Basingstoke: Macmillan.

—— (1998) *Property Investment*, London: Macmillan.

Kerridge, D. S. (1988) *Investment: A Practical Approach,* M & E Handbook Series, London: Pitman.

Key, T., McGregor, B., Nanthakumaran, N. and Zarkesh, F. (1994) *Economic Cycles and Property Cycles: Understanding the Property Cycle: Main Report*, London: Royal Institution of Chartered Surveyors.

Latham, Sir M. (1994) *Constructing the Team*, London: HMSO.

Locke, J. (1911) *The Two Treatises of Government*, J. M. Dent.

London Stock Exchange (1993) *Introduction to the London Stock Exchange*, London: International Stock Exchange of the United Kingdom and the Republic of Ireland Ltd.

London Stock Exchange (1997) *Fact File 1997*, London: London Stock Exchange.

Malthus, T. R. (1973) *An Essay on the Principle of Population*, J. M. Dent.

Mannix, D. P. (1973) *Those About to Die*, London: Grafton Books.

Manser, J. E. (1994) *Economics: A Foundation Course for the Built Environment*, London: E. & F. N. Spon Ltd.

Marriott, O. (1967) *The Property Boom*, London: Pan Books.

Marshall, A. (1920) *Principles of Economics*, 8th edn, London: Macmillan.

Marx, K. and Engels, F. (1964) *The Communist Manifesto*, New York: Modern Reader Paperbacks.

Maslow, A. H. (1954) *Motivation and Personality*, New York: Harper & Row.

Millington, A. F. (1995) *An Introduction to Property Valuation*, 4th edn, London: Estates Gazette.

Molyneux, P. (1991) *Banking: An Introductory Text*, London: Macmillan.

Myers, D. (1994) *Economics and Property*, London: Estates Gazette.

NEDO (National Economic Development Office) (1978) *How Flexible is Construction?*, London: HMSO.

Nozick, R. (1974) *Anarchy, State and Utopia*, London: Blackwell.

O'Shea, D. (1991) *Investing for Beginners*, 5th edn, London: Financial Times Business Information.

Parry Lewis, J. (1965) *Building Cycles and Britain's Growth*, London: Macmillan.

Pen, J. (1965) *Modern Economics*, London: Pelican.

Peters, R. (1956) *Hobbes*, Harmondsworth: Penguin.

Plato (1975) *The Laws*, London: Penguin.

—— (1987) *The Republic*, London: Penguin.

Plender, J. (1982) *That's the Way the Money Goes*, London: André Deutsch.

Plutarch (1973) *The Age of Alexander*, London: Penguin.

Reaedon, A. M. (1994) *Pensions Handbook: Allied Dunbar*, London: Longman.

Reekie, W. D. *et al.* (1991) *The Economics of Modern Business*, Oxford: Blackwell.

Ricardo, D. (1971) *Principles of Political Theory and Taxation*, Harmondsworth: Penguin.

RICS (1995) *Valuation and Appraisal Manual*, London: RICS.

Robinson, J. (1964) *Economic Philosophy*, London: Pelican.

Ross Goobey, A. (1992) *Bricks and Mortals*, London: Century Business.

Rostow, W. W. (1959) *The Stages of Economic Growth*, Cambridge: Cambridge University Press.

Rousseau, J.-J. (1986) *The Social Contract and Discourses*, J. M. Dent.

—— (1991) *Emile*, Harmondsworth: Penguin.

Routh, G. (1989) *The Origin of Economic Ideas*, Basingstoke: Macmillan.

Ruddock, L. (1992) *Economics for Construction and Property*, London: Edward Arnold.

Sahlins, M. (1974) *Stone Age Economics*, London: Tavistock.

—— (1988) *Stone Age Economics*, 2nd edn, London: Tavistock.

Schumacher, E. F. (1974) *Small is Beautiful*, London: Abacus.

Schumpeter, J. A. (1994) *Capitalism, Socialism and Democracy*, London: Routledge.

Scott, P. (1996) *The Property Masters*, London: E. & F. N. Spon. Ltd.

Securities and Investment Board (1992) *The Background to Investor Protection*, London: Battley Brothers Ltd.

Sekunda, N. (1994) 'The Roman army and the Samnite wars', *Ancient Warrior* 1, winter: 12–17.

Shutt, R. C. (1988) *Economics for the Construction Industry*, Harlow: Longman.

Smith, A. (1986) *The Wealth of Nations*, London: Penguin; originally published in 1776.

Stewart, M. (1986) *Keynes and After*, Harmondsworth: Penguin.

Tawney, R. H. (1926) *Religion & the Rise of Capitalism*, Harmondsworth: Penguin.

Turin, D. (ed.) (1975) *Aspects of the Economics of Construction*, London: George Godwin.

Vaughan, R. (1969) *The Age of Great Cities*, London: Woburn Press; originally published in 1843.

Warren, M. (1993) *Economics for the Built Environment*, Oxford: Butterworth-Heinnemann.

Williams, G. (1972) *The Economics of Everyday Life*, 3rd edn, London: Pelican.

Index